# Metonymy and Pragmatic Inferencing

# Pragmatics & Beyond New Series




**Volume 113**

Metonymy and Pragmatic Inferencing
Edited by Klaus-Uwe Panther and Linda L. Thornburg

# Metonymy and Pragmatic Inferencing

*Edited by*

Klaus-Uwe Panther
Linda L. Thornburg
University of Hamburg

John Benjamins Publishing Company
Amsterdam / Philadelphia

The paper used in this publication meets the minimum requirements of American National Standard for Information Sciences – Permanence of Paper for Printed Library Materials, ANSI Z39.48-1984.

**Library of Congress Cataloging-in-Publication Data**

Metonymy and pragmatic inferencing / edited by Klaus-Uwe Panther, Linda L. Thornburg.

p. cm. (Pragmatics & Beyond, New Series, ISSN 0922-842X ; v. 113)

Revisions of papers presented in the workshop Metonymy and Pragmatic Inferencing organized for the 7th International Pragmatics Conference held in Budapest, Hungary, July 7-14, 2000.

Includes bibliographical references and indexes.

1. Metonyms--Congresses. 2. Pragmatics--Congresses. 3. Inference--Congresses. 4. Speech acts (Linguistics)--Congresses. 5. Liguistic change--Congresses. I. Panther, Klaus-Uwe, 1942- II. Thornburg, Linda L. III. International Pragmatics Conference (7th: 2000: Budapest, Hungary) IV. Series

P301.5. M49M488 2003

306.44-dc21 2003050290

ISBN 90 272 5355 2 (Eur.) / 1 58811 400 7 (US) (Hb; alk. paper)



John Benjamins Publishing Co. · P.O. Box 36224 · 1020 ME Amsterdam · The Netherlands

John Benjamins North America · P.O. Box 27519 · Philadelphia PA 19118-0519 · USA

*We dedicate this volume to Dr. William M. Thornburg, in his 92nd year, and to the memory of Hermann and Charlotte Panther.*

# Table of contents

# List of contributors

## Editors

Klaus-Uwe Panther
Universität Hamburg
Institut für Anglistik und Amerikanistik
Von-Melle-Park 6
D-20146 Hamburg, Germany
E-mail: panther@uni-hamburg.de

Linda L. Thornburg
Universität Hamburg
Institut für Anglistik und Amerikanistik
Von-Melle-Park 6
D-20146 Hamburg, Germany
E-mail: lthornburg@alumni.usc.edu

## Contributors

Antonio Barcelona Sánchez
Departamento de Filología Inglesa
Universidad de Murcia
30071 Murcia, Spain
E-mail: abs@um.es

Mario Brdar
Department of English Language
and Literature
Josip Juraj Strossmayer University
Lorenza Jägera 9
HR-31000 Osijek, Croatia
E-mail: mario.brdar@os.hinet.hr

Rita Brdar-Szabó
Germanistikai Intézet
Eötvös Loránd University
19-21 Ajtósi Dürer sor
1146 Budapest, Hungary
E-mail: ritamario@somogy.hu

Seana Coulson
University of California, San Diego
Cognitive Science Center 0515
9500 Gilman Drive
La Jolla, CA 92093-0515, USA
E-mail: coulson@cogsci.ucsd.edu

Klaus-M. Köpcke
Universität Hannover
FB Erziehungswissenschaft
Bismarckstr. 2
30173 Hannover, Germany
E-mail: koepcke@erz.uni-hannover.de

Todd Oakley
Department of English
Guilford Hall 106b
Case Western Reserve University
Cleveland, OH 44106-7117, USA
E-mail: tvo2@po.cwru

Shigeko Okamoto
Department of Linguistics
California State University, Fresno
Fresno, CA 93740, USA
E-mail: shigekoo@csufresno.edu

Klaus-Uwe Panther
Universität Hamburg
Institut für Anglistik und Amerikanistik
Von-Melle-Park 6
D-20146 Hamburg, Germany
E-mail: panther@uni-hamburg.de

Lorena Pérez Hernández
Universidad de La Rioja
Departamento de Filologías Modernas
Edificio de Filología

c/San José de Calasanz s/n
Campus Universitario
26004 Logroño, La Rioja, Spain
E-mail: lorena.perez@dfm.unirioja.es

Günter Radden
Universität Hamburg
Institut für Anglistik und Amerikanistik
Von-Melle-Park 6
D-20146 Hamburg, Germany
E-mail: radden@uni-hamburg.de

Francisco J. Ruiz de Mendoza
Universidad de La Rioja
Departamento de Filologías Modernas
Edificio de Filología
c/San José de Calasanz s/n
Campus Universitario
26004 Logroño, La Rioja, Spain
E-mail: franruiz@dfm.unirioja.es

Ken-ichi Seto
Osaka City University
Faculty of Literature
3-3-138 Sugimotocho, Sumiyoshi-ku
Osaka, Japan 558
E-mail: seto@lit.osaka-cu.ac.jp

Anatol Stefanowitsch
Universität Bremen
Fachbereich 10: Sprach-
und Literaturwissenschaften
Bibliothekstraße, GW1
D-28334 Bremen, Germany
E-mail: anatol@alumni.rice.edu

Linda L. Thornburg
Universität Hamburg
Institut für Anglistik und Amerikanistik
Von-Melle-Park 6
D-20146 Hamburg, Germany
E-mail: lthornburg@alumni.usc.edu

Debra Ziegeler
School of English and Linguistics
University of Manchester
Oxford Road
Manchester M13 9PL, UK
E-mail: Debra.P.Ziegeler@man.ac.uk

David A. Zubin
Department of Linguistics
609 Baldy Hall
State University of New York
Buffalo, NY 14260, USA
E-mail: linzubin@acsu.buffalo.edu

# Acknowledgments

This volume is an outgrowth of a workshop entitled "Metonymy and Pragmatic Inferencing" that we organized for the 7th International Pragmatics Conference in Budapest in the summer of 2000. We are grateful to the workshop participants for their strong encouragement to pursue publication of the presentations, for committing their papers to the project, and for their subsequent endeavors in revising and preparing the chapters in their present form. In particular, we thank Antonio Barcelona for his excellent suggestion to invite an additional contribution on conceptual blending and metonymy and Seana Coulson and Todd Oakley for writing a chapter on this topic.

At John Benjamins, we would like to thank Bertie Kaal for her immediate interest and support, which was instrumental in moving the project forward in its initial stages, and Isja Conen, whose continuing assistance was invaluable in the later and final stages of production. We are also grateful to Andreas Jucker, editor of Pragmatics & Beyond New Series, for his very positive response to our book proposal. Finally, we are indebted to two anonymous referees for their constructive criticisms. We hope we have put their ideas to the best use in improving the volume; of course all remaining errors and infelicities accrue to us.

K.U.P.
L.L.T.
*Hamburg, April 2003*

# Introduction

## On the nature of conceptual metonymy

Klaus-Uwe Panther and Linda L. Thornburg

### 1. Background and purpose of the volume

The chapters in the present volume may be roughly characterized as contributions to pragmatics from a cognitive linguistics perspective. Cognitive linguistics and modern pragmatics share a number of objects of inquiry, although their theoretical assumptions are often at odds. Both fields are, among other things, concerned with the investigation of principles of language use, the organization and functions of discourse, the conceptual and inferential nature of rhetorical tropes and figures of thought such as metaphor and metonymy, and the relationship between language function and grammatical structure.

The purpose of this introductory chapter is to point out some commonalities and differences between contemporary pragmatic approaches and cognitive linguistics, focusing on the relation between metonymy and pragmatic inference (for a useful overview of pragmatics and cognitive linguistics, see Marmaridou 2000; for conceptual metonymy see the contributions in Panther & Radden 1999, Barcelona 2000, Dirven & Pörings 2002, and the monograph by Ruiz de Mendoza and Otal Campo 2002). We undertake this task at the risk of somewhat simplifying the issues at stake – given that neither pragmatics nor cognitive linguistics (especially the former) constitutes in itself a unified field of inquiry and theoretical orientation.[1]

### 2. Some properties of conceptual metonymy

In what follows we undertake to define some properties of metonymy, focusing specifically on the problem of how metonymy differs from other semantic relations and how it relates to types of pragmatic implication such as implicature and explicature (for a more detailed discussion, see Panther & Thornburg, forthcoming).

Metonymy as a conceptual phenomenon first caught the attention of cognitive linguists in 1980, the publication date of George Lakoff and Mark Johnson's influential book *Metaphors We Live By*, in which the linguistic function of metonymy is claimed to be mainly one of indirect reference (e.g. *the crown* standing for 'the monarchy'), i.e. as a relationship where one entity "stands for" another. A few years later Lakoff (1987:68ff.) introduced the notion of *idealized cognitive model* (ICM). ICMs are structures that represent speakers' conceptual (including their semantic) knowledge. Lakoff posits four types of such ICMs: image-schematic, propositional, metaphorical and *metonymic* models, the latter being the basis of prototype effects. For example, Lakoff observes that in Western culture many people associate the concept MOTHER with the concept HOUSEWIFE MOTHER, i.e., they regard mothers who stay at home, organize the household, raise the children, etc. as the typical representatives of mothers. There seems to exist a metonymic model in which the superordinate category MOTHER (stereotypically) evokes the subordinate category HOUSEWIFE MOTHER. Lakoff contrasts metaphor as an *isomorphic mapping* between two distinct domains – a source and a target – with metonymy, which is seen as operating only within a single conceptual domain. Lakoff's conception of metonymy is an important step forward – away from the traditional view of metonymy as a relation of "real-world" contiguity/association to an abstract view of metonymy in which 'contiguity' is understood as closeness in a conceptual model.

Metonymy is often regarded as a *referential* phenomenon where the name of a referent is used to stand for another referent. In accordance with the contributors to this volume, we argue below (Section 2.2) that this view is too narrow. Furthermore, the characterization of metonymy as a 'stand for' relation suggests that metonymy is a substitution relation, a reflection of which is that metonymies are usually represented by the schema X FOR Y, where X represents the source (also called 'vehicle') and Y symbolizes the target of the metonymic operation. It should however be borne in mind that the substitution view of metonymy is inadequate because the source of a metonymy is not simply replaced by the metonymic target, except in cases involving historical semantic change. Recent work on metonymy has shown that metonymy is better viewed as a cognitive trigger providing access to a targeted concept (see Section 2.1 below). This is the view, which in some variant or other, is shared by most cognitive linguists working on metonymy, including the contributors to this book. Nevertheless, throughout the book the 'X FOR Y' notation will be maintained because it has become an established convention in cognitive linguistics. The use of small capitals is meant to reflect the assumption that metonymy is a relation between concepts, rather than between real-world denotata or referents.

### 2.1 Metonymy as a contingent relation

On the basis of George Lakoff's (1987) and Ronald Langacker's (1993) work, which emphasizes the conceptual nature of metonymy, Günter Radden and Zoltán Kövecses (1999: 21) have proposed a widely accepted characterization of metonymy: "Metonymy is a cognitive process in which one conceptual entity, the vehicle [also often called the 'source', KUP/LLT], provides mental access to another conceptual entity, the target, within the same cognitive model."

In what follows, we adopt this definition as a convenient starting point for our discussion of metonymy. However, we see a need to constrain the scope of this definition somewhat because it covers some linguistic phenomena that are arguably very different from clear cases of metonymy. Consider, for example, the italicized referential noun phrases in (1) and (2):

(1) *The piano* is in a bad mood.

(2) *The loss of my wallet* put me in a bad mood.

In sentence (1) the subject noun phrase has the standard metonymic interpretation 'the musician playing the piano', with the meaning of *piano* providing mental access to the concept of piano player. In sentence (2), the sense of *the loss of my wallet* provides access to the concept of 'non-possession (of the wallet)'. Are we therefore entitled to conclude that the relation between the concept of loss and that of non-possession is a metonymic relationship, just as the relation between the concept of piano and that of piano player is metonymic? Intuitively, the answer seems 'no'; and in fact, there is an important difference between the two cases. In sentence (2) the relationship between 'loss' and 'non-possession' is *conceptually necessary*, i.e., the proposition presupposed by the referring expression in (1), 'I lost my wallet at time t', *entails* 'I did not have my wallet for some time span beginning at time t'. In sentence (1), the relationship between the piano and the piano player is *contingent*; the presupposition 'There is a piano' does not entail 'There is a piano player'. In other words, there is no metonymy LOSS FOR NON-POSSESSION, but there is an often exploited metonymy MUSICAL INSTRUMENT FOR MUSICIAN.

## 2.2 Metonymy and speech acts

The notion of metonymic model, as developed by Lakoff (1987), suggests that metonymy does not occur only on the referential level as in

(3) General Motors is on strike.

where the company name is used to refer to the automobile workers who walk out of the work place. Pragmatically, metonymies are also found on the predicational, propositional (where referential and predicational metonymies occur in combination), and illocutionary levels, respectively. An example of a predicational metonymy is

(4) General Motors had to stop production.

where the necessity or obligation to stop production stands for the actually occurring event of stopping production (OBLIGATION TO ACT FOR ACTION). The metonymy involved is an instance of a high-level metonymic principle that is very common in English and other languages: A potential event (e.g. the ability, possibility, permission, obligation to undertake an action) is metonymically linked to its actual occurrence. Events are conceptualized here as ICMs that contain as subcomponents the modalities of their realization. Sentence (4) is also a propositional metonymy because *General Motors* metonymically refers (in this case) to the executive officers of the company.

Finally, an example of an illocutionary metonymy is given by the well-known phenomenon of conventionalized indirect speech acts as in (5a), in contrast to (5b):

(5) a. I would like you to close that window.
    b. Close that window.

where the expression of the wish with regard to the action to be carried out by the addressee (signaled by *would like you to*) metonymically evokes the request (5b) itself (see Gibbs 1994, 1999; Thornburg & Panther 1997; Panther & Thornburg 1998). The basic idea is that an attribute of a speech act can stand for the speech act itself in the same way that an attribute of a person can stand for the person (see also Panther & Thornburg's and Radden & Seto's contributions in this volume).

## 2.3 Do referential, predicational, and illocutionary metonymies form a "natural class"?

Our contention that the relation between *the piano* and 'the piano player', on the one hand, and that between *General Motors had to stop production* and 'General Motors stopped production', on the other hand, is of the same kind, viz. metonymic, may look surprising at first sight. One might object that the target meaning of (4) is really an implicature that comes about through pragmatic strengthening of the proposition expressed in (4).[2]

However, note first that a metonymic analysis does not preclude a pragmatic analysis in terms of conversational implicature. On the contrary, we assume that conversational implicatures, or more generally, pragmatic inferences, are often guided by preexisting metonymic principles.[3]

Second, and more importantly, referential, predicational, and illocutionary metonymies share the property of *highlighting* or *foregrounding* their respective target meanings. The source of a metonymy serves as a "reference-point" (see e.g. Langacker 1993) whose sole purpose is to provide access to a target meaning. That metonymy involves highlighting is a common assumption among cognitive linguists (see e.g. Croft 1993). To illustrate, consider the following larger context for sentence (4):

(6) General Motors had to stop production on Monday but they resumed it on Thursday.

The *but*-clause in (6) only makes pragmatic sense if the clause *General Motors had to stop production on Monday* has the foregrounded target meaning 'General Motors stopped production on Monday'. Obviously, the backgrounded source meaning of the first clause in (6) (the 'obligation' sense) is still activatable, but this holds for standard cases of referential metonymy as well, i.e., it is a general property of metonymy that source meanings are "active" to some degree.

Third, the same metonymy can be triggered predicationally and referentially. The OBLIGATION TO ACT FOR ACTION metonymy triggered in (4) and (6) can also be derived from the nominalized (referential) counterpart of (4):

(7) *General Motor's obligation to stop production* had a devastating effect on the economy.

The target meaning of the referring expression in (7) can be paraphrased as 'the fact that General Motors stopped production'. This meaning is very strongly foregrounded given the ensuing predication *had a devastating effect on the economy*.

Finally, what we call illocutionary metonymies can also be triggered in referential positions. For example,

(8) I am willing to lend you my car.

is often understood as an *offer* of the speaker to lend her car to the hearer (for a metonymic treatment of speech acts, see Panther & Thornburg, this volume). In utterance (9) a proposition analogous to the one in (8) is nominalized and used referentially.

(9) *My willingness to lend you my car* surprised everybody.

The referential noun phrase in (9) lends itself quite readily to the (foregrounded) target meaning 'My *offer* to lend you my car'. We see no reason to treat the pragmatic implication of the noun phrase in (9) differently from the target meaning of uncontroversial metonymies as in *Table Four wants another Chardonnay* where *Table Four* stands for 'the customer sitting at Table Four'.

### 2.4 Strength of metonymic link

The link between a metonymic source and its target may vary in strength. The strength of a metonymic link depends on how conceptually close source and target are to each other (cf. Panther & Thornburg 1998). The relevance of the strength factor becomes obvious when an utterance like (5a) – where the conceptual link between the mental attitude literally conveyed by the utterance, i.e. the speaker's wish that the addressee perform the action, and the targeted actual request itself is very strong – is compared to the relatively weak metonymic connection between the contents of (10a) and (5b) (repeated below as (10b)):

(10) a. There's a draft in here.
b. Close that window.

Utterance (10a) is in many contexts understood as a request such as (10b). However, different from the fairly straightforward metonymic connection between (5a) and (5b) where the mental attitude associated with the speech act provides direct access to the speech act itself, the conceptual distance between (10a) and (10b) is much greater. One may assume a metonymic *chain* with at least the following *links*: P → NOT-DESIRABLE (P) → DESIRABLE (NOT-P) → CAUSE (Q, NOT-P) → DO (Q), where P represents the propositional content of the assertion (10a) and Q stands for the propositional content of the request (10b).

### 2.5 The ubiquity of metonymy

Metonymy is found in both what is usually considered to be the domain of linguistic meaning (semantics) and the domain of linguistic use (pragmatics). In fact, the existence of metonymy is evidence that a strict borderline between semantics and pragmatics may be difficult to draw. A metonymy such as SALIENT BODY PART FOR ANIMATE BEING is completely conventionalized in the compound *redbreast* as the designation for a bird; but a person with very little ornithological knowledge may describe birds she has seen in the woods to a friend whose conventional names she does not know by using unconventional "names" like *yellowbeak*, *purplehead*, *bluetail*, etc. The same holds for cases of conventionalized polysemy: Metonymies that *statically* distinguish conventionalized senses of a lexical item such as *potbelly* ('large round stomach' vs. the metonymically derived 'person with large round stomach') may be *dynamically* used to yield pragmatically derived meanings such as *balloonnose*, *fatface*, *skinnylegs*, etc.

### 2.6 Summary

To summarize the above observations, metonymy in our view is minimally characterized by the following properties:

- Conceptual metonymy is a cognitive operation where a source content provides access to a target content within one cognitive domain.
- The relation between source content and target content is contingent (conceptually non-necessary), i.e. in principle defeasible.
- The target meaning of a metonymy is foregrounded (highlighted); the source content is backgrounded.
- Metonymy performs various functions in speech acts: It is operative on the levels of reference, predication, proposition, and illocution.
- The strength of metonymic link between source and target may vary, depending on, among other things, the conceptual distance between source and target.
- Metonymy is a conceptual phenomenon that cuts across the traditional distinction between semantics and pragmatics.

## 3. Metonymy and pragmatic inferencing

The characterization of metonymy given in Section 2.6 reveals a common object of inquiry of pragmatics and cognitive linguistics: inferencing. A thesis that most likely all authors of the present volume share is that the knowledge of metonymic principles such as CAUSE FOR EFFECT, RESULT FOR ACTION, PRODUCER FOR PRODUCT, MANNER FOR ACTION, SALIENT PARTICIPANT OF EVENT FOR EVENT, etc., play an important role in utterance interpretation. Metonymies may be called *natural inference schemas*, i.e. easily activatable associations among concepts that can be used for inferential purposes (see Panther & Thornburg 1998). Metonymic links may become completely conventionalized, i.e. result in lexical polysemy as pointed out in Section 2.5. Diachronically, the source concept may be backgrounded or vanish completely with only the target concept left behind. An example of the latter is the illocutionary verb *implore*, which etymologically contains the sense 'in tears' no longer necessarily present in present-day English.

### 3.1 Metonymy and implicature

If metonymies function as guideposts in pragmatic inferencing, the question immediately arises how they relate to conversational implicature in the Gricean or neo-Gricean sense. On closer inspection, some interesting parallelisms emerge between Lakoff's (1987) metonymic models and Levinson's (2000: 37) *I*-Heuristic (where *I* stands for 'Informativeness'). Levinson argues that lexical items routinely implicate stereotypical pragmatic default readings: "What is expressed simply is stereotypically exemplified." He relates this heuristic to Grice's (1975) second Maxim of Quantity "Do not make your contribution more informative than is required." For example, a defeasible I-Implicature of *drink* in English is 'alcoholic beverage'. An utterance like

(11) I need a drink.

would normally not be understood as expressing the (adult) speaker's desire for a glass of milk. Nevertheless the 'alcoholic beverage' reading is cancelable as becomes evident in (12):

(12) I need a drink, but no alcohol, please.

Defeasibility also holds for the metonymically evoked stereotypical meanings discussed by Lakoff (1987: 77ff.) (see Section 2 above): Although the concept HOUSEWIFE MOTHER is almost automatically activated when the word *mother* is used in linguistic communication, the metonymic link between the two concepts can be explicitly canceled without contradiction: *She is a mother of two daughters but she is not a housewife* is semantically well-formed. A meaning that, in cognitive linguistic terms, is stereotypically evoked via metonymy (see Radden & Kövecses 1999: 27) or, in neo-Gricean parlance, via a generalized conversational implicature, is generally not expressed through a separate lexical item; e.g., there are no simple lexemes for the concepts HOUSEWIFE MOTHER or ALCOHOLIC BEVERAGE in English, and, in fact, it would be redundant to have such lexemes because their senses are easily accessible via metonymically based conversational implicatures.

Regrettably, so far, there has been relatively little dialogue between scholars working in a neo-Gricean framework and cognitive linguists, although the objects of inquiry and even the analyses proposed do not seem incompatible to us but point to possible avenues of convergence.

### 3.2 Metonymy and explicature

The main competitor of neo-Gricean pragmatics, relevance theory, has generally been critical, if not dismissive, of cognitive linguistic approaches to metonymy (and metaphor). Papafragou (1996a, b) and Song (1997) argue that metonymy and other figures of speech can be subsumed under general principles of pragmatic inferencing (in their framework, deductive inferences) and that there is no need to postulate the existence of a separate domain of metonymic reasoning. Papafragou (1996a: 181) criticizes the cognitive 'associationist' approach to metonymy as suffering "from serious drawbacks on both descriptive and explanatory levels" because this approach supposedly cannot handle creative ad hoc uses of "metonymy". Papafragou does not grant any special status to metonymic elaborations but regards them as *explicatures*, i.e. as pragmatic inferences derived from underspecified (decoded) semantic contents to yield the explicit content of an utterance. The opposite view is held by probably most authors of this volume: The retrieval of utterance meaning requires the activation of metonymic relations from long-term memory as interpretive guideposts (see e.g. Ruiz de Mendoza & Pérez Hernández, this volume, who argue that metonymic mappings are activated in explicature derivation). The aim of researchers is to find a reasonably restricted set of metonymic inference schemata that can be quickly accessed and be exploited by language users in utterance interpretation (see e.g. Norrick 1981 for a list of such metonymic principles).

## 4. The contributions to this volume

The contributions to this volume have been organized into four parts. Part I is concerned with defining the role of metonymy in inferential utterance interpretation (Ruiz de Mendoza & Pérez Hernández, Barcelona) and conceptual blends (Coulson & Oakley). Part II focuses on the metonymic motivation of grammatical structure (Stefanowitsch, Panther, & Thornburg, Köpcke & Zubin). Part III explores the role of metonymic inferencing in linguistic change (Ziegeler, Okamoto). Part IV closes the book comparing the exploitation of metonymies from a cross-linguistic perspective (Radden & Seto, Brdar & Brdar-Szabó).

### 4.1 The place of metonymy in cognition and pragmatics

The first three chapters of the volume demonstrate the significance of metonymy as a conceptual tool for guiding inferencing in language and other cognitive domains. Ruiz and Pérez's paper sets the stage relating work on metonymy in cognitive linguistics to relevance theory; Coulson and Oakley's and Barcelona's papers are case studies that show the power of metonymic principles in conceptual integration and the interpretation of humorous discourse, respectively.

In the first chapter "Cognitive Operations and Pragmatic Implications," Francisco Ruiz de Mendoza and Lorena Pérez Hernández link work on conceptual metonymy in cognitive linguistics to Gricean pragmatics and relevance theory. The authors start with the assumption generally accepted in cognitive linguistics that metonymy and metaphor are tools for understanding and reasoning about the world. They reduce metonymy to two basic types: metonymies where the target concept is part of the source concept (target-in-source metonymies) and metonymies where the source is part of the target (source-in-target metonymies). Relying on recent work by Papafragou and Carston, Ruiz and Pérez argue that metaphor and metonymy are part of what is said, rather than what is implicated – in contrast to previous relevance-theoretic and Gricean analyses. However, the authors strongly object to Carston's idea that metonymy and metaphor are "loose" ways of speaking with the principle of relevance as sufficient to account for their interpretation. Rather, Ruiz and Pérez propose that the principle of relevance must be supplemented by metaphoric and metonymic *mappings*, i.e. cognitive operations available to speakers and hearers that are part and parcel of the their semantic and conceptual knowledge. The authors also argue for a view of metaphor and metonymy as a continuum. They present an interesting new analysis of anaphoric relations in discourse that involve referential metonymic shifts as in ***The ham sandwich** is waiting for **his** check and **he** is getting upset* where the grammatical form of the anaphoric pronouns *his* and *he* is determined by the targeted referent of *ham sandwich*. In contrast, in ***Nixon** bombed Hanoi and **he** killed countless civilians*, it is the source expression *Nixon* that determines the grammatical properties of the coreferential pronoun. Ruiz and Pérez account for such examples by means of a principle that they call the *Domain Availability Principle*, according to which the larger domain (matrix domain) – be it the source or the target – determines the domain of coreference.

In Chapter 2, "Metonymy and Conceptual Blending," Seana Coulson and Todd Oakley explicate the role of metonymy in the process of conceptual blending. The theory of conceptual blending has been developed since the 1980s by Gilles Fauconnier and Mark Turner and their collaborators. Blending involves several operations for combining cognitive models in a network of *mental spaces* and is guided by a set of constraints, known as optimality principles. To understand a blend, it is important to identify the mappings between different aspects of the model in the blended space and their counterparts in the input spaces. These mappings can be based on identity, similarity, analogy, and many other sorts of pragmatic functions, including metonymy. Indeed, one advantage that Coulson and Oakley see in the blending framework is that it allows the treatment of complex examples in which many sorts of conceptual mappings operate in parallel. Coulson and Oakley analyze a number of diverse phenomena ranging from ordinary language idioms like *blowing your own horn*, literary blends in the writings of Ernest Hemingway, to metonymic blends in works of sculptural art (Viktor Schreckengost's *Apocalypse '42*). Their study shows that conceptual metonymies are important in conceptual blending by "tightening" metonymic relations thus contributing substantially to integrating "juxtapositions of conceptual structure from distally related domains." Metonymies thus help satisfy one of the *optimality principles* postulated by Fauconnier and Turner (1999) and Turner and Fauconnier (2000), viz. the *integration principle,* which demands that the events in the blended space form an integrated mental scene. Metonymy accomplishes this conceptual integration at the expense of the *topology principle*, which requires that models in each of the mental spaces be structurally as isomorphic as possible. In general, the presence of metonymic connections in the blend performs the crucial function of "holding together" the network of mental spaces that are necessary for reasoning on a particular topic over a period of time.

The contribution in Chapter 3, "The Case for a Metonymic Basis of Pragmatic Inferencing: Evidence from Jokes and Funny Anecdotes" by Antonio

Barcelona, presents four case studies of the humorous mechanisms of jokes and anecdotes. The interpretation of these genres requires – as has been pointed out by a number of humor theorists like Attardo (1990) and Raskin (1985) – complex inferential work on the part of the hearer. Barcelona wonders how it is possible that listeners often arrive at the intended humorous reading of a joke or anecdote at "lightning speed." For him, this feat cannot be explained on the basis of Gricean maxims alone (or their variants in the discourse world of humor). Adopting a conception of metonymy that is inspired by Radden and Kövecses (1999) (cf. Section 2.1 above) Barcelona proposes that in many if not all cases the inferential work is facilitated by pre-existing metonymic connections in a cognitive frame or domain or by pre-existing metaphorical connections across frames. Metonymies thus help achieve the *frame adjustment* (cf. Attardo 1990; Raskin 1985) that is necessary in order to grasp the punch line of a joke or anecdote. Barcelona shows that the value of metonymy for pragmatic inferencing can be appreciated only if one discards the traditional view of conceptual metonymy as a purely referential phenomenon. As to the question whether pragmatic inferencing can be reduced entirely to metonymic reasoning, Barcelona is not willing to commit himself to a wholly affirmative answer, but he certainly thinks that metonymically based inferencing plays an essential role in utterance interpretation.

### 4.2 Metonymic inferencing and grammatical structure

The chapters in Part II of the volume are concerned with the interaction between metonymy and grammatical structure (see also the contributions in Part III and Brdar & Brdar-Szabó in Part IV). In the three studies summarized below metonymic origins of the linguistic phenomena under investigation are still visible, but the metonymic relationship in many cases has become such an integrative part of grammatical meaning that it is no longer defeasible.

In Chapter 4 "A Construction-Based Approach to Indirect Speech Acts" Anatol Stefanowitsch offers an account of conventionalized indirect speech acts (ISAs), specifically, requests such as *Will/can you close the door?* in terms of Construction Grammar (see e.g. Goldberg 1995). Using some of Sadock's (1974) collocational criteria for conventionalized indirect requests (e.g. the possibility to insert politeness markers like *please*, *kindly*, the conditional *would/could*, and preposed reason clauses), Stefanowitsch shows that certain aspects of conventionalized indirect requests are not predictable from their form and meaning components and that they therefore qualify as constructions. Stefanowitsch calls them ISA constructions and contrasts them with utterances such as *Are you able to close the door?*, which can in certain contexts be used as an indirect request, but does not qualify as an ISA construction because the above-mentioned test criteria fail to apply to it. Stefanowitsch argues that ISA constructions are completely conventional, but that, despite their partially unpredictable properties, they are *motivated* metonymically in the sense of Panther and Thornburg (1998). However, there is no need for the speaker/hearer to *process* them metonymically because their pragmatic function is part of their meaning. The metonymic motivation is captured in the construction grammar framework by positing *metonymic inheritance links* between direct questions and conventionally indirect requests. Stefanowitsch's analysis amounts to postulating that there are two constructions of the form *Can you do A?* One of them signifies a question and the other a conventional request. In the last part of his paper Stefanowitsch tests the predictions of the construction grammar analysis against the neurolinguistic literature on indirect requests. Although the psycholinguistic evidence is not conclusive in all respects, there are some interesting indications that individuals with right-hemisphere damage, who generally have trouble recovering nonliteral meaning, have no problems interpreting indirect request *constructions* as requests, but they do have trouble interpreting other non-conventionalized indirect requests as requests.

In Chapter 5 "Metonymies as Natural Inference and Activation Schemas: The Case of Dependent Clauses as Independent Speech Acts" Klaus-Uwe Panther and Linda L. Thornburg investigate some *if*-clauses that look "incomplete," i.e. lack a syntactically realized consequent clause. Many such "truncated" conditional clauses qualify however as constructions in the sense of Goldberg (1995) because they have a non-compositional conventional sense associated with them. Panther and Thornburg identify three kinds of conventionalized pragmatic functions of such *if*-clauses: deontic (involving speaker commitment or hearer obligation) as in *If you would like a cookie* (offer) or *If you will come to order* (request); expressive (e.g. surprise, shock, etc.) as in *Why, if it isn't Susan!* (expression of surprise); and epistemic (reasoning, expression of belief) as in *If it was a warning* (challenge of a prior assumption). Using the concept of *mental space* from conceptual blending theory and an approach to indirect speech acts as conceptual scenarios, Panther and Thornburg make extensive use of the cancelability test known from Grice's work on implicature to determine the degree of conventionalization of the *if*-clause types they investigate. They argue, quite in line with Stefanowitsch's analysis of indirect requests (this volume), that many truncated conditionals do not require any inferential work on the part of the hearer even though the metonymic motivation of their pragmatic meaning is still transparent. Panther and Thornburg claim that, on the one hand, conceptual metonymies constitute natural inference schemas that are exploited by participants in linguistic communication to arrive at utterance meanings; on the other hand, such metonymic inference schemas may become completely entrenched and are then automatically activated in the interpretation process. Whatever the degree of routinization, the availability of metonymic links within conceptual scenarios enables interlocutors to access intended meanings quickly and effortlessly.

In Chapter 6 "Metonymic Pathways to Neuter-Gender Human Nominals in German" Klaus-Michael Köpcke and David Zubin show that metonymic principles interact in complex ways with grammatical gender in German. They observe that certain neuter-marked nominals referring to human females evoke complex affective metonymic models. The assignment of neuter gender to female human referents is somewhat surprising – given the otherwise highly systematic masculine-feminine gender distinction in German between male and female humans. Köpcke and Zubin identify nine subtypes of metonymic grounding that account for about 80% of their exhaustive sample of *neut*-gender human nouns. Many of these often derogatory or dismissive designations for females are found as early as in Middle High German, e.g. *das Luder* ('loose woman', originally 'bait') or *das Reff* ('skinny old woman', originally 'skeleton'). Other neuter nouns designating females trigger negative affect such as disapproval, scorn, and the like, such as *das Weib* 'woman' or *das Aas* 'nasty woman', originally 'carcass'). The female human referent can also be viewed as a mere visual object on display (e.g. *das Mannequin* 'female model' or *Revuegirl* 'show girl'. The class of neuter-gender female referents is still productively enlarged in present-day German with e.g. Anglo-American loanwords such as *das Groupie, das Model, das Bunny*, etc. Especially these latter neuter-gender loanwords from English can be regarded as a strong indicator of a metonymically motivated gender assignment. At the end of their contribution, Köpcke and Zubin explore the role of metonymic scenarios in the selection of anaphoric pronouns in discourse referent tracking in some contemporary journalistic sources and also in an in-depth analysis of a narrative by Karl Heinrich Waggerl.

## 4.3 Metonymic inferencing and linguistic change

The contributions of Part III of the volume are concerned with the role of metonymy and implicature in linguistic change, i.e. with the implicatures and metonymic inferences associated with modals and their periphrastic counterparts in English (Ziegeler), and the role of metonymy in certain grammaticalization processes in Japanese (Okamoto).

Debra Ziegeler's contribution in Chapter 7 on "The Development of Counterfactual Implicature: A Case of Metonymy or M-inference?" discusses the problem that statements of past ability or potentiality sometimes metonymically evoke the actuality but also sometimes the non-occurrence (counterfactuality) of the event expressed in the infinitival complement clause. She challenges Levinson's (1995, 2000) view that an utterance like *John could solve the problem* implicates *John solved the problem* on the basis of the second Gricean quantity maxim (Q2), and that *John had the ability to solve the problem* conveys the complementary implicature that John did not solve the problem. The latter is supposed to be an *M-implicature*, an inference that, according to Levinson, applies to the more marked (periphrastic) member of a manner set <*can, have the ability to*>. M-implicatures are not metonymic inferences in the prototypical sense, since they are not content-to-content relations but associate a comparatively marked *form* with the negation of the content that is assigned to the unmarked member of the set. Ziegeler provides empirical evidence against Levinson's analysis, which seems to be based on made-up examples. She questions the tacit assumption that *could* and *had the ability* are synonymous concepts that contrast in "prolixity" in the same way as pairs like *drink/beverage* or *house/residence.* Among other things, she shows that *could* is hardly ever used in present-day English in connection with single past events and that the more marked "alternative" of *could*, the periphrastic *was/were able to*, does not produce an implicature of non-actuality (via M-implicature) as predicted by Levinson's model – on the contrary, the latter has a strong suggestive force of actuality. Ziegeler arrives at the conclusion that the opposite directionality of the metonymies POTENTIALITY FOR ACTUALITY VS. POTENTIALITY FOR NON-ACTUALITY is due to principles that "appear to be founded in pragmatics and the notion of scalar relationship between items."

In Chapter 8 on "Metonymy and Pragmatic Inference in the Functional Reanalysis of Grammatical Morphemes in Japanese," Shigeko Okamoto focuses on the reanalysis of complementizers of subordinate clauses (COMP) as sentence-final particles (SFP) expressing a certain modality or illocutionary force. In Japanese, both grammatical categories occur in final position in subordinate clauses. She argues that the complementizer *koto* has developed into a marker of either exclamatory or directive speech act force. Okamoto proposes that underlying the shift from COMP to SFP is a part-whole metonymy that is motivated by rhetorical and social concerns of appropriateness of expression. The use of the subordinate clause [S *koto*] suggests that the complement is the most important part of the message, thereby "bring[ing] about a certain expressiveness, that is, to perform a given speech act with particular stylistic nuances [...]." More formally, Okamoto proposes a metonymic inference that the addressee draws "on the basis of his/her knowledge of certain frames and understanding of the specific context." There is thus a metonymic shift from '[S *koto*]' to '[[P *koto*] Modality]' where 'Modality' is supposed to stand for the pragmatic function of the proposition P. For example, the use of [S *koto*] as a directive speech act as in *Mainichi ha o migaku koto* 'You brush your teeth every day-*koto*' is more indirect; and an exclamation such as *Maa oishii koto* 'Oh, it is delicious-*koto*' is "less imposing and 'feminine'." The original subordinate clause construction [S *koto*] develops thus into an independent construction analogous to the *if*-clause constructions analyzed by Panther and Thornburg (this volume). The illocutionary function of *koto*-clauses in these constructions seems comparable to that of the German clauses introduced by the complementizer *dass* in directives such as *Dass du das nicht noch einmal machst!* ('Don't ever do that again') or exclamations such as *Dass ich das noch erleben durfte!* ('That I would live to see this').

### 4.4 Metonymic inferencing across languages

The last two contributions to this volume demonstrate that the use of metonymic principles may vary cross-linguistically and that metonymy interacts with and is constrained by grammatical structure (see also Stefanowitsch, this volume; Panther & Thornburg, this volume). Radden and Seto's paper is more pragmatically oriented comparing commercial events in English-speaking and Japanese-speaking cultural contexts; Brdar and Brdar-Szabó analyze the role of metonymy in coding linguistic action in English, Croatian, and Hungarian from a typological perspective.

In Chapter 9, Günter Radden and Ken-ichi Seto investigate "Metonymic Construals of Shopping Requests in HAVE- and BE-Languages." The classification into HAVE- and BE- languages derives from how the concept of possession is encoded. HAVE languages include English, German, Lithuanian, and Croatian; BE languages are Japanese, Chinese, Korean, Finnish, Hungarian, Polish, and Hausa. The authors focus especially on the wording of shopping requests in English and Japanese. An English sentence such as *John has two children* would have to be rendered in Japanese as 'At/To John are two children'. This structural difference has consequences for how the two languages linguistically code certain stages in the shopping scenario. Radden and Seto distinguish two main phases in the shopping scenario: (i) the *precondition*, i.e. the availability of the requested articles and (ii) the *transaction*, which is further subdivided into (a) the *transfer* of the article from the salesperson to the customer, (b) the *reception* of the article by the customer, and (c) the *result*, i.e. the customer's possession of the article. They then show that the metonymic coding of the speech acts that characteristically occur during these stages is partially dependent on the structural resources of the language in question (see also Brdar & Brdar-Szabó for grammatical constraints on metonymy). For example, stage (i) of the shopping scenario is typically referred to in both languages by means of a metonymy, which, in a HAVE-language like English, is POSSESSION FOR AVAILABILITY (e.g., *Do you have 40-watt light bulbs?*) and, in a BE-language like Japanese, EXISTENCE FOR AVAILABILITY (40 *watto no denkyuu (wa) ari-masu ka* 'Are there 40-watt light bulbs?'). Radden and Seto also point out that in English a question about the possession and thus (metonymically induced) availability of an article can stand for the requested transaction itself, i.e. stage (ii) of the shopping scenario, whereas in Japanese the same pragmatic function is achieved by means of a question about the existence of the article. The authors demonstrate that politeness factors may actually cut across the typological properties of languages. Thus an English speaker would avoid a direct expression of stage (iia) (*#Give me "The Times"!*) whereas in other HAVE-languages, such as Lithuanian and Croatian, this wording would not be considered inappropriate; analogously in a BE-language like Hungarian the literal translation of the above would be infelicitous whereas in Japanese a direct reference to the requested transfer would not sound offensive if it is used in combination with deference markers.

Chapter 10, Mario Bdrar and Rita Brdar-Szabó's contribution "Metonymic Coding of Linguistic Action in English, Croatian and Hungarian," is a detailed study of English sentences like *The President was* **clear** *on the matter* and their equivalents in Croatian and Hungarian. What is peculiar about the verbal locution *to be clear on some matter* is that it is conventionally used to refer to a speech act ('to *speak* clearly on some matter') where the speech act itself is not explicitly coded in the expression but conventionally evoked via a metonymy MANNER (OF LINGUISTIC ACTION) FOR LINGUISTIC ACTION. The degree of conventionalization of this metonymy varies from a strongly implicated but still cancelable target meaning to complete lexicalization that defies defeasibility. Brdar and Brdar-Szabó demonstrate that this predicational metonymy is much more constrained in Croatian and Hungarian than in English. Thus the above sentence would have to be rendered in Hungarian as *Az elnök világosan nyilatkozott ezzel az üggyel kapcsolatban* ('The president *spoke clearly* on that matter'). Both Croatian and Hungarian are more likely to explicitly code the linguistic action itself. The authors see a more general typological tendency for these languages to avoid predicational metonymies, whereas referential metonymies of the type *Beijing's difficulties in Tibet* are also systematically exploitable in Croatian and Hungarian. Bdrar and Brdar-Szabó suggest an implicational relationship between referential and predicational metonymies: Languages that systematically exploit predicational metonymies will also make extensive use of referential metonymies; some languages will be largely restricted to referential metonymies. In fact, Brdar and Brdar-Szabó argue that cases such as *I'll be brief* (without a complement like *about NP*), which actually have literal counterparts in Croatian and Hungarian, are really reducible to referential metonymies of the type SPEAKER FOR UTTERANCE, a subtype of the more general metonymy AGENT FOR ACTION. These cases would thus not constitute counterexamples to the generalization proposed by the authors.

## 5. Prospects for studies in metonymy

The authors of this volume share the belief that the study of conceptual metonymy provides important insights into language use and language structure. Metonymy appears to be on a par with metaphor as far as its conceptual import is concerned. Promising projects for further research on the role of metonymy in natural language would include a more systematic comparison of the exploitation of metonymies from a typological perspective (cf. Radden & Seto, Brdar & Brdar-Szabó, this volume), the role of metonymic thinking in language acquisition, discourse-pragmatic conditions of metonymic uses, constraints on the creation of metonymic links, and, last not least, a hierarchically organized taxonomy of conceptual metonymies found in human language.

## Notes

1. Compare e.g. Verschueren's (1999: 1) definition of pragmatics as the "*study of linguistic phenomena from the point of view of their usage properties and processes*" [italics in original] with Levinson's (2000) neo-Gricean approach and Sperber and Wilson's Relevance Theory (1995).

2. This argument has in fact been made by an anonymous reviewer of the volume.

3. That metonymic principles guide the production and comprehension of pragmatic inferences is argued for by Ruiz de Mendoza and Pérez Hernández (this volume) for explicature derivation and by Barcelona (this volume) for more indirect pragmatic implications.

## References


Attardo, Salvatore (1990). The violation of Grice's maxims in jokes. *Berkeley Linguistics Society, 16*, 355–362.

Barcelona, Antonio (Ed.). (2000). *Metaphor and Metonymy at the Crossroads: A Cognitive Perspective* [Topics in English Linguistics 30]. Berlin and New York: Mouton de Gruyter.

Croft, William (1993). The role of domains in the interpretation of metaphors and metonymies. *Cognitive Linguistics, 4*, 335–370.

Dirven, René & Pörings, Ralf (Eds.). (2002). *Metaphor and Metonymy in Comparison and Contrast* [Cognitive Linguistics Research 20]. Berlin and New York: Mouton de Gruyter.

Fauconnier, Gilles & Turner, Mark (1999). Metonymy and conceptual integration. In K.-U. Panther & G. Radden (Eds.), *Metonymy in Language and Thought* [Human Cognitive Processing 4] (pp. 77–90). Amsterdam and Philadelphia: Benjamins.

Gibbs, Raymond W., Jr. (1994). *The Poetics of Mind: Figurative Thought, Language, and Understanding.* Cambridge: Cambridge University Press.

Gibbs, Raymond W., Jr. (1999). Speaking and thinking with metonymy. In K.-U. Panther & G. Radden (Eds.), *Metonymy in Language and Thought* [Human Cognitive Processing 4] (pp. 61–76). Amsterdam and Philadelphia: Benjamins.

Goldberg, Adele (1995). *Constructions: A Construction Grammar Approach to Argument Structure* [Cognitive Theory of Language and Culture]. Chicago and London: The University of Chicago Press.

Grice, H. Paul (1975). Logic and conversation. In P. Cole & J. L. Morgan (Eds.), *Speech Acts* [Syntax and Semantics 3] (pp. 41–58). New York: Academic Press.

Lakoff, George (1987). *Women, Fire, and Dangerous Things: What Categories Reveal About the Mind.* Chicago and London: The University of Chicago Press.

Lakoff, George & Johnson, Mark (1980). *Metaphors We Live By.* Chicago and London: The University of Chicago Press.

Langacker, Ronald W. (1993). Reference-point constructions. *Cognitive Linguistics, 4*, 1–38.

Levinson, Stephen C. (1995). Three levels of meaning. In F. Palmer (Ed.), *Grammar and Meaning* (pp. 90–115). Cambridge: Cambridge University Press.

Levinson, Stephen C. (2000). *Presumptive Meanings: The Theory of Generalized Conversational Implicature.* Cambridge, MA, and London: The MIT Press.

Marmaridou, Sophia S. A. (2000). *Pragmatic Meaning and Cognition* [Pragmatics and Beyond New Series 72]. Amsterdam and Philadelphia: Benjamins.

Norrick, Neal R. (1981). *Semiotic Principles in Semantic Theory.* Amsterdam and Philadelphia: Benjamins.

Panther, Klaus-Uwe & Radden, Günter (Eds.). (1999). *Metonymy in Language and Thought* [Human Cognitive Processing 4]. Amsterdam and Philadelphia: Benjamins.

Panther, Klaus-Uwe & Thornburg, Linda L. (1998). A cognitive approach to inferencing in conversation. *Journal of Pragmatics, 30*, 755–769.

Panther, Klaus-Uwe & Thornburg, Linda L. (forthcoming). Metonymy. In D. Geeraerts & H. Cuyckens (Eds.), *Handbook of Cognitive Linguistics*. Oxford: Oxford University Press.

Papafragou, Anna (1996a). Figurative language and the semantics-pragmatics distinction. *Language and Literature, 5*(1), 179–193.

Papafragou, Anna (1996b). On metonymy. *Lingua, 99*, 169–195.

Radden, Günter & Kövecses, Zoltán (1999). Towards a theory of metonymy. In K.-U. Panther & G. Radden (Eds.), *Metonymy in Language and Thought* [Human Cognitive Processing 4] (pp. 17–59). Amsterdam and Philadelphia: Benjamins.

Raskin, Victor (1985). *Semantic Mechanisms of Humor*. Dordrecht: Reidel.

Ruiz de Mendoza, Francisco J., & Otal Campo, José L. (2002). *Metonymy, Grammar, and Communication*. Albolote, Granada: Editorial Comares.

Sadock, Jerrold M. (1974). *Toward a Linguistic Theory of Speech Acts*. New York: Academic Press.

Song, Nam Sun (1997). Metaphor and metonymy. In R. Carston & S. Uchida (Eds.), *Relevance Theory: Applications and Implications* (pp. 87–104). Amsterdam and Philadelphia: Benjamins.

Sperber, Dan & Wilson, Deirdre (1995). *Relevance: Communication and Cognition* (2nd ed.). Oxford: Basil Blackwell.

Thornburg, Linda & Panther, Klaus (1997). Speech act metonymies. In W.-A. Liebert, G. Redeker, & L. Waugh (Eds.), *Discourse and Perspectives in Cognitive Linguistics* [Current Issues in Linguistic Theory 151] (pp. 205–219). Amsterdam and Philadelphia: Benjamins.

Turner, Mark & Fauconnier, Gilles (2000). Metaphor, metonymy, and binding. In A. Barcelona (Ed.), *Metaphor and Metonymy at the Crossroads: A Cognitive Perspective* [Topics in English Linguistics 30] (pp. 133–145). Berlin and New York: Mouton de Gruyter.

Verschueren, Jef (1999). *Understanding Pragmatics*. London: Arnold.

Part I

# The place of metonymy in cognition and pragmatics

# Cognitive operations and pragmatic implication

Francisco José Ruiz de Mendoza Ibáñez
and Lorena Pérez Hernández

## 1. Introduction

In this chapter we explore some possible connections between the relevance-theoretic view of pragmatic implication and the Cognitive Linguistics approach to metaphor and metonymy. A major theoretical objective of both Cognitive Linguistics and modern pragmatics (e.g. Neo-Gricean Pragmatics and Relevance Theory) is to model human understanding and reasoning and how they are reflected in language (cf. Lakoff & Johnson 1980, 1999; Lakoff & Turner 1989; Lakoff 1987, 1993; Panther & Radden 1999; Barcelona 2000; Levinson 2000; Sperber & Wilson 1995). Modern pragmaticists generally assume that understanding an utterance crucially involves the ability of an addressee to draw inferences, i.e. to detect what a speaker pragmatically implies on the basis of what is literally said. In Gricean and Neo-Gricean Pragmatics such implications are known as *implicatures*, meanings that are derivable from, but are not part of, what is said. In Relevance Theory (cf. Sperber & Wilson 1995) implicature derivation is contrasted with explicature derivation, another form of pragmatic operation involving some inferential activity. In the relevance-theoretic framework, explicatures are assumptions that are derived in part by inference and in part by decoding. Some of the inferential operations that play a role in explicature-derivation have already been identified, e.g. disambiguation, fixation of reference, and enrichment. Other operations have been proposed – saturation (Recanati 1989) and loosening (Carston 1997) – and still others remain unidentified in the standard relevance-theoretic literature and require inclusion into this framework. However, in Relevance Theory (and in Gricean and Neo-Gricean Pragmatics) metaphoric and metonymic meanings are not regarded as being part of what is said or explicated, but as being derived via implicature.

In Cognitive Linguistics, metaphor and metonymy are not considered as tropes of figurative language, but as cognitive mechanisms used for drawing inferences, and to reason about and understand the world. These cognitive operations are accomplished by means of conceptual mappings of knowledge from a source domain into a target domain and are crucial for concept formation and concept understanding. We shall propose in this chapter that metaphoric and metonymic mappings are to be rightfully included in the relevance-theoretic list of mechanisms that are used to obtain explicated meaning. In so doing, we argue in support of Sperber and Wilson (and against Levinson 2000: 193–198) that the distinction between explicature and implicature is a valid one, but that metaphoric and metonymic interpretations – rather than being implicated meanings – should be viewed as part of the explicit meaning of utterances, i.e. as enrichments that come about by explicature.

## 2. Implicatures and explicatures

Sperber and Wilson (1995) have criticized those pragmaticists who, following Gricean postulates, have adopted as a working principle the view that any aspect of utterance interpretation that falls outside the domain of disambiguation and reference assignment is an implicature. Instead, Sperber and Wilson have made the interesting claim that some of the cases that have been regularly treated as implicatures are in fact cases of explicit meaning, which they call *explicatures*. For them, an assumption is explicit if it is a development of the logical form encoded by an utterance (Sperber & Wilson 1995: 182). A logical form, in turn, is "a well-formed formula, a structured set of constituents, which undergoes formal logical operations determined by its structure" (*ibid.* p. 72). When a logical form is semantically complete – and therefore capable of being true or false – it becomes a *proposition*. Incomplete logical forms are stored in conceptual memory as *assumption schemas* that may be completed on the basis of contextual information. Since, for Sperber and Wilson, completing an assumption schema – which has a logical form – in order to obtain a proposition – which also has a (more developed) logical form – is an inferential activity (i.e., it exceeds mere decoding), it follows that, for them, studying the way the logical form of an utterance is developed into its explicature is a matter of pragmatics.[1]

Sperber and Wilson, together with other relevance theorists (e.g. Carston 1988; Blakemore 1992), have defended the view that there are three processes involved in getting from an assumption schema to a full proposition: disambiguation, fixation of reference, and enrichment. While disambiguation and reference assignment are familiar linguistic phenomena, the notion of enrichment is entirely new. Consider the following example by Carston (1988; in Davies 1991: 39):

(1) The park is some distance from where I live.

By mere linguistic decoding and fixation of reference we obtain the information that the park is at some distance from where the speaker lives. However, this remark is but a truism in the sense that it is obvious that there must be some distance between the park and the speaker's home. In order for the utterance to be relevant, the expression *some distance*, which is manifestly vague, has to be enriched to mean 'further away (from where I live) than you think.' As Carston (1988) has observed, when we deal with enrichment, the richer explicated proposition entails what is literally said.

In order to work out an implicature, on the other hand, the hearer needs to supply some implicit information that allows him or her to construct a reasoning formula of the condition-consequence type. Consider the following example, from Blakemore (1992: 58):

(2) A: Did you enjoy your holiday?
B: The beaches were crowded and the hotel was full of bugs.

For B's response to be relevant, A needs to have access to the (implicit) assumption that one's comfort while on holiday may typically be affected by insects (rather than hidden microphones) and an excess of people. As a consequence, we reason that the speaker did not enjoy his holiday. This information is an implicature since it has its own distinct propositional form that functions independently of the explicated information as the conclusion of an argument.

Both Sperber and Wilson (1995) and Blakemore (1992) interpret the lack of literalness of metaphor and other 'tropes' as a matter of producing implicatures. For example, according to Blakemore (1992: 163), the metaphor

(3) My neighbor is a dragon.

will yield implicatures such as those in (4):

(4) a. The speaker's neighbor is fierce.
b. The speaker's neighbor is unfriendly.

These are the more central implicatures. Other weaker ones would have to do with the nature of the neighbor's unfriendliness, together with her behavior and appearance. It is these weaker implicatures that justify the speaker's not using a non-metaphorical utterance like *My neighbor is fierce and unfriendly*. Metaphor is thus seen as a way of optimizing relevance, which Sperber and Wilson understand as achieving the adequate balance between processing cost and meaning effects.

The implicature-explicature distinction, as it stands in the traditional relevance-theoretic literature, has been the subject of considerable revision and criticism. Among its weaknesses stands the problem of finding solid criteria to distinguish what is implicated from what is explicated. Carston (1988) and Recanati (1989) are classic attempts to remedy this shortcoming. Carston (1988) puts forward what she calls the 'functional independence' criterion, according to which there is no functional independence between what is said and the enriched version of what is said, since the latter entails the former. This means that the enriched interpretation cannot be an implicature. For example, as we have seen above, in the sentence *The park is some distance from where I live* the expression *some distance* is usually interpreted as a 'long distance' or 'further away than you think.' This interpretation is a development of the blueprint provided by what is said and entails it. In genuine implicated meaning, what is said and what is implicated do not stand in the same kind of relationship. For example, the same sentence could be used to convey a warning that the addressee may not be able to walk such a long distance and should, therefore, take a bus. The functional independence criterion has been criticized by Recanati (1989), who argues that Carston makes the mistake of using a formal property of propositions (i.e. entailment) to distinguish explicatures from implicatures. Recanati's insight is essentially correct since what is involved in explicature derivation is not necessarily a logical development of what is said, but an adaptation of what is said to contextual requirements. Thus, Carston's functional independence test does not fare well in cases of what Recanati has called 'saturation' as a form of deriving explicatures. For example, the sentence *John is not good enough* is to be interpreted as John is not good enough for a certain activity or purpose (e.g. *John is not good enough for that job/for Mary*, etc.). This development of the initial expression does not entail what is said (cf. Ruiz de Mendoza 1999). Additionally, as we shall see below, Carston's criterion is unable to handle other forms of deriving explicatures such as the 'loose use' of concepts ('loosening') (cf. Carston 1997: 106).

Levinson (2000: 195–196) points out a number of problems in the analysis provided by both Sperber and Wilson (1995) and Carston (1988). Thus, he notes that, contrary to what Sperber and Wilson assume, the representations of explicatures do not necessarily contain the semantic representation associated with what is said. For example, as he aptly observes, any implicature can be added as a conjunct to what is said. In *John's three children came to the party*, it is possible to phrase the corresponding scalar inference in terms of either explicated meaning ('the totality of John's children, of cardinality three, came to the party') or as an implicated separate proposition ('John has no more than three children'). This same observation affects the theoretical status of Carston's functional independence criterion, since adding an implicature to what is said yields a complex proposition that may entail what is said. For example, the sentence *The beach was crowded* may be used to implicate 'I couldn't rest.' The sentence *The beach was crowded and I couldn't rest* makes explicit such an implicature, which thus becomes functionally dependent on what is said.

More recently, Carston (1997, 2000) has attempted to refine the explicature-implicature division by looking in greater depth into the concept of enrichment and by specifying further mechanisms of explicature generation. As a result, some cases of what was previously considered a matter of implicated meaning have been transferred to the domain of explicature derivation. Initially, Carston (1988), following Sperber and Wilson (1995), accepted the proposal of three mechanisms to derive explicatures: fixation of reference, disambiguation and enrichment. Later, it was realized that, just like enrichment, cases of what Sperber and Wilson (1985–1986) had called 'loose use' of language, which included all tropes, also involved a departure from literalness, although in an opposite direction. Thus, while the non-literal expression *some time* required strengthening into 'a long time,' the interpretation of non-literal *raw* in an utterance like *This steak is raw* involves a loosening of the lexical concept 'raw' from 'not cooked' to 'underdone' (and, therefore, 'difficult to eat'). Consequently, Carston proposed loosening as a mechanism to derive explicatures. This mechanism typically applies to metaphor, which, thus far, had been dealt with in relevance theory as a matter of implicature derivation.

In Carston (2000) both strengthening and loosening of concepts are treated as forms of what in Relevance Theory circles has come to be known as *ad hoc* concept construction, a term that goes back to earlier work by Barsalou (1983). This involves the creation of a concept – as an adjustment to contextual requirements – on the basis of a linguistic cue. In *This steak is raw* the loosening process of *raw* is only possible in a context in which it is evident that the steak is not literally raw (e.g. a customer is complaining about his steak being too underdone for his taste). Interestingly enough, the strengthening of scalar concepts also requires some sort of contextual adjustment. The expression *some time* requires strengthening in *It will take some time to repair your watch*, but not in *He returned some time later* (meaning 'just a little bit later').

The construction of an *ad hoc* concept is regulated by the principle of relevance, according to which the hearer is entitled to assume that the intended interpretation of an utterance creates the intended contextual effects with no unjustifiable processing effort. Of course, this principle is sufficient to constrain the number of possible meaning implications of an expression that needs this kind of adjustment. However, consistency with the principle of relevance is insufficient to explain how the implications come about or what conceptual mechanisms are involved in their derivation. Thus, the principle of relevance does not account for what regulates the connection between 'raw' and 'underdone,' or between 'raw' and any other target of the explicature derivation task. For example, the sentence *My steak is raw* is not a complaint in a context in which the customer likes 'rare' meat. The cognitive mechanisms underlying the derivation of a whole range of different explicatures for the lexical concept 'raw' have to do with the conventionalized scalar nature of the various targeted values and their connotations. Deriving explicatures on the basis of a scale is tantamount to going up or down the scale (this is the cognitive operation) until the hearer finds a point on the scale that will yield the relevant meaning effects in terms of the context.

The example above is a case of what Carston (1997, 2000) categorizes as loosening. We face similar problems when confronted with examples of strengthening. Consider again the expression *some time* meaning 'a long time'. Interpreting this expression requires going up a scale of time measurement until a point is reached where adjustment to contextual parameters is possible. The principle of relevance regulates the extent of the strengthening task, but it does not control how the task itself is achieved. The foregoing discussion suggests that loosening and strengthening are cognitive mechanisms operating on scalar concepts. But, there are also other cognitive mechanisms that play a role in explicature derivation.

In Carston's (1997, 2000) more recent work, metaphor and metonymy are treated as other forms of constructing *ad hoc* concepts, which involve loosening and strengthening respectively.[2] We believe this approach evinces the same kind of weakness that we have already identified when dealing with scalar concepts. For example, let us consider the metaphor *Bill is a bulldozer* (Carston 1997: 113), meaning that Bill is self-confident and determined. For Carston, this expression makes a loose use of 'bulldozer' thereby creating an *ad hoc* concept. However, by itself this is not enough to explain how we obtain the relevant interpretation. In Cognitive Linguistics (cf. Lakoff & Johnson 1980,

1999; Lakoff 1987, 1993; Lakoff & Turner 1989), it would be postulated that what guarantees the interpretation is the existence of an underlying conceptual mapping from 'bulldozer' to 'human being' whereby we understand Bill's behavior in terms of the figurative behavior (i.e. the way the machine functions) that we attribute to a bulldozer. In other words, as with scalar concepts, we have an underlying mental operation (i.e. a conceptual mapping) at work to provide the range of meaning implications that are adequate to the context.

As the example above illustrates, a metaphor involves a conceptual mapping across two domains. Metonymy also involves a conceptual mapping, but within one domain. In the sentence *The sax has the flu* there is a metonymic shift from 'sax' to 'saxophone player,' where the player and his instrument stand in a domain-subdomain relationship. As with 'bulldozer' above, 'sax' is constructed *ad hoc* for the purpose of identifying another concept with which it has some sort of connection. However, the *kind* of metaphoric or metonymic connection is not a matter of the principle of relevance as such. What this principle does is merely draw our attention as interpreters to the necessity of making a connection. Understanding how this connection is made and finding out its communicative consequences depends on our ability to determine the cognitive operation to be carried out for the sentence to be relevant in context.

What our discussion above suggests is that the task of deriving explicated meaning involves performing any of a number of cognitive operations on the basis of the blueprint provided by the linguistic expression and in connection with – or as constrained by – the principle of relevance. To the mechanisms of fixation of reference, disambiguation, saturation or completion, strengthening, and loosening, we need to add conceptual mappings as discussed in the cognitive linguistics literature. It must be noted that we have restricted the scope of application of the notion of loosening, which, in our view, only holds for some scalar concepts (those that do not require strengthening). So-called tropes like metaphor and metonymy need separate treatment. This decision is in keeping with what language itself reveals about the nature of these mechanisms:

(5) Loosely speaking, this steak is raw.

(6) *Loosely speaking, Bill is a bulldozer.

(7) *Loosely speaking, the sax has the flu.

As is evident from the examples above, the hedge *loosely speaking* is only compatible with the hyperbole in (5), but not with the metaphor and metonymy in (6) and (7) respectively. This suggests that these latter tropes are not cases of loosening. In what follows we shall study in more detail how conceptual mappings are used to produce explicatures of different kinds. It will be shown that both the nature of the domains involved and the nature of the mapping place constraints on the kind of explicatures that can be obtained through this mechanism.

## 3. Metaphoric mappings and pragmatic implication

As we have already mentioned, in Cognitive Linguistics metaphor has been studied as a conventional conceptual mapping from a source to a target domain. The source usually allows us to understand and reason about the target in terms of some of the relevant aspects of its conceptual structure (for details see Lakoff 1993). Thus, when faced with an expression like the one in (3) we reject the literal interpretation and find some (culturally attributed) characteristics of dragons that apply to the speaker's neighbor's behavior. Since the literal interpretation is never entertained, it can be neither an explicature nor a source for explicatures. This is in keeping with how we interpret utterances like (1), where the expression *some distance* needs to be developed into the explicature 'a longer distance than you expected' by means of enrichment; likewise, in (3) the expression *a dragon* needs to be converted into 'someone fierce and unfriendly' by means of a conceptual mapping.

It is possible to classify metaphor from two points of view, taking into account the conceptual nature of the domains involved. Lakoff and Johnson (1980) have distinguished ontological, orientational, and structural metaphors. Ontological metaphors, like PEOPLE ARE ANIMALS, highlight a quintessential feature of the source domain that is then attributed to the target. For example, in the metaphoric utterance *Achilles is a lion* we take a culturally attributed quintessential feature of lions (their courage) and ascribe this feature to Achilles (Lakoff & Turner 1989: 195–196). Orientational metaphors have to do with spatial orientations like up-down, in-out, front-back, on-off, central-peripheral, etc., and are grounded in our physical and cultural experience. Thus, the fact that humans and many animals sleep lying down and stand up when they awaken provides the experiential grounding for the metaphors CONSCIOUS IS UP, UNCONSCIOUS IS DOWN (e.g., *Get up!*, *He fell asleep*). In fact, orientational metaphors, in being spatial constructs, are a subcase of metaphors based on image-schemas. Image-schemas, as defined by Johnson (1987), are abstract topological constructs that have their origin in our bodily experience. Among the most basic schemas, besides orientations, we have such notions as CONTAINER, PATH, and PART-WHOLE. Finally, structural metaphors allow us to understand an abstract concept in terms of a concrete one. For example, in the metaphor ARGUMENT IS WAR (e.g., *He shot down all my arguments, He attacked my views,* etc.), there is a correspondence between different aspects of both conceptual domains; thus people arguing, like contenders, figuratively deploy their resources for war, work on their tactics, attack the enemy, defend their positions, counterattack, gain or lose ground, and ultimately they win or lose.[3]

With regard to the formal nature of metaphoric mapping, Ruiz de Mendoza (1998) has made a division between two kinds of metaphor: one-correspondence and many-correspondence metaphors. In the former, only one correspondence between the source and target domains is exploited, while in the latter, there is a fully-fledged system of correspondences that is available in the interpretation process. One-correspondence metaphors closely correlate with ontological and orientational metaphors. This is due to the fact that, in both cases, the conceptual structure of the domains involved is very simple. Thus, in PEOPLE ARE ANIMALS, attributed animal behavior is mapped onto human behavior; in HAPPY IS UP, SAD IS DOWN, as in the utterances *I am feeling up* or *I am really down,* a certain emotional state is understood in terms of verticality. The rest of the conceptual structure of the source and target domains is irrelevant for the purpose of metaphor interpretation. Many-correspondence metaphors exploit a richer conceptual structure and thus correlate with structural and non-orientational image-schematic metaphors. By way of illustration, consider the following sentences:

(8) He was in a horrible predicament, but eventually he managed to get out of it.

(9) We have to keep searching for a solution to this problem.

Sentence (8) depicts a figurative situation in which a negative state is seen as a container with a person in its interior. The fact that the person is affected by the negative conditions inside the container is felt to be the reason why he does everything in his power to get out of it. This sentence exploits the structural elements and logic associated with the CONTAINER schema (cf. Lakoff 1989; Peña 1997): there is an interior and an exterior separated by boundaries, the boundaries are impediments to getting out of the container, the entities inside the container are affected by the conditions prevailing inside it, etc. As is evident from these observations, a metaphor based on the CONTAINER schema will develop more than simply one central correspondence for full understanding. A similar situation holds for example (9) in which a problem is seen as a region in space (e.g. a landscape), the solution to the problem is an object hidden somewhere in that region, and searching the region is searching for a solution. For a complete understanding of the full range of meaning implications of the sentence, it is necessary to activate all the relevant correspondences.

The pragmatic notion of explicature as used by relevance theorists can be improved from a cognitive linguistic perspective, if we regard explicature-derivation as the result of cognitive operations. Moreover, a classification of these operations may elucidate the nature of the explicatures that are obtained through metaphoric mappings. In principle, in the case of many-correspondence mappings, we expect a larger number of potential explicatures than in the case of one-correspondence metaphors. Compare the following sentences:

(10) John is a lion.

(11) You're going nowhere that way.

From sentence (10) we obtain the explicature that John is courageous in the same way as a lion is thought to be courageous (i.e. in a fierce instinctual way). Remember that in the one-correspondence metaphor PEOPLE ARE ANIMALS, behavior usually maps onto behavior. Sentence (11), on the other hand, may generate a greater number of explicatures based on the hearer exploring different aspects of the structure and logic of the many-correspondence journey metaphor that is based on the path schema. One of the explicatures will be more central than the others. However, in our view, this does not take away from the explicit nature of all the inferences that are developed on the basis of the conceptual material associated with the expression. Thus, in a situation in which sentence (11) is uttered by an angry father to a rebellious teenage son, it is possible to derive at least the following potential explicatures, of which the first one is more central:

(12) a. The addressee is not going to achieve his expected goals (if he persists in his behavior).
b. The addressee is not making any progress in life.
c. The addressee may make progress if he changes his way of doing things.
d. The addressee is acting in an erroneous way.
e. The addressee may not have clear goals.
f. The addressee has erroneous goals.

As Lakoff and Johnson (1999) have noted, the central correspondence in journey metaphors is GOALS ARE DESTINATIONS. This correspondence allows us to derive the central explicature, i.e. (12a), which focuses on reaching the goal. The other explicatures are exploitations of remaining correspondences together with their structural and logical relationships. Thus, (12b) focuses on the action; (12c) and (12d) on the manner of action; (12e) and (12f) on the kind of goal.

Note that (12c–f) would not be considered explicatures, but rather implicatures, in canonical views of Relevance Theory. However, in our view, the inferences in (12) are explicatures for two reasons: (i) they are developments of what is said by the expression, and (ii) they are calculated independently of supplementary contextual information. There are neither implicated premises, nor implicated conclusions involved in their derivation. However, consider a context in which the addressee knows that his father is angry at his lack of achievement in life. The implicated conclusion, which hinges upon the central explicature (12a), would be that the speaker wants the addressee to be successful by changing his course of action. Utterance (11) would thus be interpreted as a warning. Or consider a different context in which the father is not really worried about what his son does, but knows that his wife will be extremely upset, which distresses him. In this situation, the implicated conclusion is that the speaker wants the addressee to act in a different way for his mother's sake. It would be roughly equivalent to saying 'You are hurting your mother's feelings by acting in such a way.' Such an implicature would be based on explicatures (12c) and (12d), which focus on the manner of action.

In our view, the nature of the metaphoric mapping and of the domains involved constrain the kind and number of explicatures that may be derived from an expression. Simultaneously, the principle of relevance determines which of all the potential explicatures is to be activated in a particular context. This proposal departs from the canonical understanding of explicature-derivation in Relevance Theory, according to which explicatures are constructed on-line as a combination of decoding and inference and not activated out of a potential set of options. However, it is evident that metaphorical and metonymic systems do provide us with such sets of options and that these naturally constrain what we can do in the interpretation process. In this view, linguistic expressions act as cues to the activation of the relevant mapping system.

## 4. Metonymic mappings and pragmatic implication

As defined above, metaphor involves a mapping across discrete conceptual domains, whereas metonymy involves a mapping within a single domain. Consider:

(13) Napoleon lost at Waterloo.

(14) You know, Superman fell off his horse and broke his back.

In (13) it was not Napoleon but the army under his command that was defeated. In (14) it is not the fictional character Superman, but the actor Christopher Reeve, who broke his back. The metonymy in (13) is a way of avoiding the use of a longer and perhaps rather vague definite description that would be more difficult to process; it is also a means of emphasizing Napoleon's more prominent role in the defeat. All this information is part of the explicature derived with the aid of the metonymic mapping. This is so because it is part of our knowledge that Napoleon organized an army with which he invaded Belgium, but was later defeated at Waterloo by the English.

The metonymy in (14) would normally be used to avoid a long paraphrase such as *Christopher Reeve, the actor who played Superman,* in order to achieve successful reference. Despite the similarities of metonymic reference in (13) and (14), the two metonymies are different in two respects. First, (13) instantiates a metonymy in which the target domain (the army) is a subdomain of the source domain (Napoleon), while (14) instantiates a metonymy in which the source (Superman) is a subdomain of the target (Christopher Reeve, the actor). Examples like (13) are cases of what we may call target-in-source metonymy; (14), on the other hand, illustrates a case of source-in-target metonymy (see discussion of examples (16) and (17) below for details on the relevance of this distinction). Note additionally that, since the source in (13) and the target in (14) provide frameworks of reference for their corresponding subdomains, it is appropriate to refer to them as *matrix domains*.[4] Second, the difference between the two types of domain-subdomain relationship we have identified has communicative consequences that have a bearing on the kind of explicatures to be derived. Thus, metonymies like the one in (13) allow the speaker to focus on the source domain as the most relevant one while avoiding an uneconomical description like *the army commanded by Napoleon*. This mechanism is often used when the speaker is unable to find the expression that actually designates the intended referent, as in:

(15) The White House is trying to avoid another scandal.

whereby using the expression *the White House* the speaker avoids the problem of having to name the accurate White House official in question.

On the other hand, metonymies like the one in (14) allow a speaker to bring to the fore a cognitively salient subdomain of the matrix domain, with its accompanying inferential effects. Thus, part of our conventional knowledge about Superman (i.e. his supernatural strength) makes (14) a rather shocking sentence from the point of view of the information it conveys. It is not only sad but also ironic that the "man of steel" has seriously damaged his back.

It must be noted that metonymies are cases of one-correspondence mapping. This is a necessary consequence of the fact that in metonymies there is a domain-subdomain relationship. This relationship only allows for two kinds of conceptual operation: one involves highlighting a subdomain of the source, as in (13) and (15) above; the other requires the expansion of the source into a wider conceptual structure, as the case of (14). In having just one correspondence, metonymies allow us to derive only one explicature, as will be illustrated below.

In this connection, Ruiz de Mendoza (1997, 2000) argues for the existence of a metaphor-metonymy continuum based on the distinction between one-correspondence and many-correspondence metaphors. Here we want to suggest that understanding the nature of this continuum is crucial to determining the communicative effects of the explicatures derived by means of metaphoric and metonymic mappings. Ruiz de Mendoza notes that while metaphors are typically non-referential, one-correspondence metaphors may occasionally be referential in nature, as in *My tender rose abandoned me* (cf. *She is a tender rose*). Many-correspondence metaphors, on the other hand, can only be predicative, and metonymies – which are by definition one-correspondence mappings – are usually referential. It is true that it is possible to find instances of non-referential metonymies, as in *She is a real brain* or *She's just a pretty face*, or as in expressions containing verb-based metonymies (cf. Goossens 1990) such as *giggle* in *'Oh dear,' she giggled*, where this verb stands for 'to say something while giggling.' However, verb-based metonymies are necessarily predicative and could not possibly function referentially, while predicative uses of noun-based metonymies, which are very rare, need some sort of parameterization (adjectival or otherwise) of the source domain in order to single out a feature that will subsequently map onto the target, just like in one-correspondence metaphors (cf. Section 3). Because of this, it is possible to regard them as borderline cases of metonymy: on the one hand, they share with all metonymies the fact that there is an evident domain-subdomain relationship between source and target; on the other hand, the operation of singling out a feature of the source, rather than using its whole conceptual structure, makes them resemble metaphors. If these observations are correct, the metaphor-metonymy continuum would have cases of many-correspondence mappings (which are predicative) at one end and clear cases of referential metonymy at the other end. Referential uses of metaphor, verb-based metonymies (which are necessarily predicative), and noun-based metonymies used predicatively would be in the middle. From the point of view of explicature derivation, predicative uses of metonymy would yield explicatures similar to those provided by one-correspondence metaphoric mappings, while purely referential uses of metonymy would involve domain expansion or domain highlighting, as shown in relation to examples (13)–(15).

Our discussion has provided indirect evidence for the division between source-in-target and target-in-source metonymies in terms of the different kinds of explicatures that are derived on the basis of the activity of each metonymy type. Ruiz de Mendoza (2000) provides a number of additional reasons substantiating the usefulness of the division. One such reason will prove relevant for the purpose of our discussion. Consider the following examples:

(16) The ham sandwich is waiting for his check and *he* is getting upset.

(17) Nixon bombed Hanoi and *he* killed countless civilians.

Ruiz de Mendoza (2000) and Ruiz de Mendoza and Pérez (2001) have postulated the existence of what they call the *Domain Availability Principle* (or DAP). According to this principle, only the matrix domain of a metonymic mapping is available for anaphoric reference. In (16), the matrix domain is the target of the metonymic shift (i.e. the customer who has ordered the ham sandwich), while in (17), the matrix domain is the source of the metonymy mapping Nixon onto the air force that carries out the orders he has sanctioned. The selection of the matrix domain for anaphoric reference, rather than a subdomain, is perhaps due to the fact that the matrix domain is conceptually more salient, since it provides a larger amount of easily retrievable conceptual structure. This last observation particularly holds for target-in-source metonymies, since it is often the case that their targets are not clean-cut specifications. Thus, in (17) it is not known what specific section of the air force is involved in the bombing, but we do know that Nixon is ultimately responsible for that action. In both kinds of metonymic mapping, the explicature includes the information provided by the linguistic expression, although each in a different way. In source-in-target metonymies, what is said is conceptually expanded to include as much conceptual material as is necessary for the target concept to be compatible with the rest of the predication. How much conceptual material is called up is regulated by consistency with the principle of relevance, that is, we do not want to activate more material than needed, but enough for the interpretive demands of the moment. In target-in-source metonymies, whatever subdomain is highlighted is determined by its degree of compatibility with the information provided by the non-metonymic part of the utterance. Such a degree of compatibility is constrained by the principle of relevance. In a target-in-source metonymy the explicature is constructed on the basis of a reduction of the conceptual material provided by the source of the mapping. It must be observed that in both kinds of metonymy the source is still active to provide subsidiary meaning effects. Thus, (16) is more than a quick way of identifying a customer by his order. The customer could have been identified by other salient features. For example, imagine a situation in which a well-dressed customer leaves without paying and one of the waitresses remarks *The gold cuff links has not paid his bill.* In this sentence there is irony in selecting *gold cuff-links* as the source of the mapping. Similarly, the choice of the source domain in (17) is significant in that it is not the air force but Nixon that is felt to be responsible for the actual bombing.

Finally, it may be interesting to note that one-correspondence metaphoric mappings used referentially also select – as do metonymic mappings – the best-developed conceptual domain for anaphoric reference. Consider:

(18) My tender rose abandoned me, but I still love *her*.

In (18), *my tender rose* roughly means 'the girl or woman that arouses in me the same feelings as a tender rose.' This explicature provides enough conceptual material for successful anaphoric reference. So, it is preferred – for this purpose – to what is literally said by the expression.

The fact that anaphoric reference can be made to one of the conceptual domains involved in metaphor and metonymy further supports our view that these cognitive mechanisms generate only explicatures, since implicated meanings seem to be poor candidates for anaphoric reference. In this connection, consider again the short exchange in (2), expanded here as (19):

(19) A: Did you enjoy your holiday?
B: The beaches were crowded and the hotel was full of bugs.
A: I am sorry about *that*.

As remarked in Section 2, the implicated conclusion is that B did not enjoy his holiday. However, this proposition is not the best candidate as antecedent for anaphoric *that*, but rather the explicated information given by B's response.

## 5. Explicature derivation through double metonymic mapping

So far, we have looked into the communicative import of what we can call *single metonymies*. However, sometimes metonymic mappings evince a rather more complex structure. Consider the following examples:

(20) I love Picasso.

(21) I have a Picasso in the living room.

(22) Can you imagine? He is using Picasso as a bookend.

At first sight, *Picasso* in (20) stands for 'Picasso's pictorial work,' but as in the Napoleon example in (13), the conceptual structure of the matrix domain 'Picasso' is somehow present in the explicature generated by the metonymic mapping. Thus, (20) communicates not only that the speaker likes Picasso's work a lot, but also that there is some reason for this, which is to be found in our knowledge about Picasso (e.g. the speaker may be impressed by Picasso's style, by his mastery of color, and so on). Whatever additional knowledge is imported from the matrix domain to construct the relevant explicature must be in harmony with the context and regulated by the principle of relevance. The situation is slightly different in (21). Here *Picasso* stands for 'a specific sample of his work.' So, *I have a Picasso* can be paraphrased as 'I have a specific painting by Picasso.' In order to arrive at this meaning, we need a double metonymic operation from *Picasso* to 'Picasso's work' to 'a (unique) sample of his work.' This situation is represented in Figure 1 below.

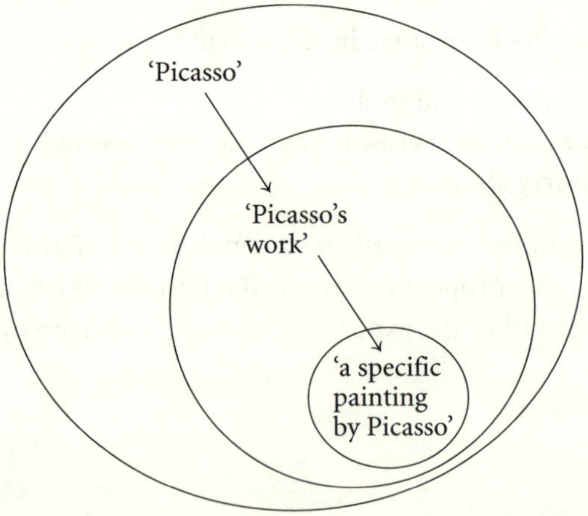


**Figure 1.** Double metonymy: AUTHOR FOR WORK FOR UNIQUE SAMPLE

Example (21) instantiates two operations of highlighting and two matrix domains. Thus something about Picasso as well as something about our knowledge of his work is brought into the interpretation process, blocking out a sense of *Picasso* as any other thing than his artistic production. Example (21) contrasts with (22), where *Picasso* may refer, for example, to 'a (probably) small bust' or to 'a statuette' of Picasso as a result of a single metonymic mapping. We note also that these contrasting interpretations are reflected in grammatical structure by the presence of the indefinite article in (21) and its absence in (22).

A different form of double metonymic mapping is illustrated by one interpretation of example (23) below:

(23) Shakespeare is on the top shelf.

In this sentence, *Shakespeare* typically stands for 'a book or books containing Shakespeare's writings.' On another interpretation, *Shakespeare* might refer to 'a (probably) small bust' or to 'a statuette' of Shakespeare. While the latter reading requires only one metonymic shift, the former reading calls for a double metonymic mapping of the form AUTHOR FOR WORK FOR (NON-UNIQUE) SAMPLE, as shown in Figure 2 below.

This mapping instantiates one highlighting operation and two matrix domains, one of which involves an operation of conceptual expansion. In the first mapping, from *Shakespeare* to 'Shakespeare's work,' relevant structure from our knowledge about Shakespeare (e.g. his writing style, selection of topics, etc.) is imported. However, the fact that there is a second mapping involving a shift of matrix domain somehow neutralizes the communicative import of the previ-

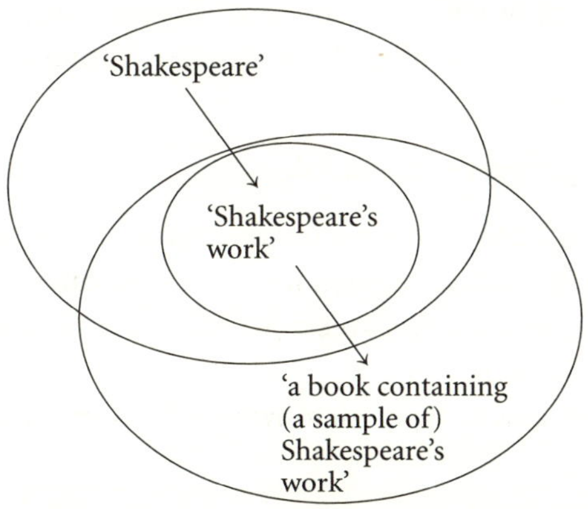


**Figure 2.** Double metonymy: AUTHOR FOR WORK FOR (NON-UNIQUE) SAMPLE

ous operation. This second mapping, from 'Shakespeare's work' to the format in which it is presented (typically a book or a number of books), allows us to identify the referent in an economical way, while at the same time preserving the conceptual relevance of its source domain in such a way that not only the format in which Shakespeare's work is presented, but also its content is important. Observe in this connection that the metonymic expression in (23) highlights the content of Shakespeare's writing rather than its material form, in contrast to a non-metonymic paraphrase such as *The book by Shakespeare is on the top shelf*, where it is the material form (e.g. a book rather than a CD-ROM, microfiches, etc.) that is more central.

## 6. Conceptual interaction between metaphor and metonymy as a form of deriving explicatures

The division between explicature and implicature has obviously benefited from our explanation of metaphor and metonymy as not only communicative phenomena, but also as conceptual mappings whose particular natures predetermine their communicative potential. In this section, we shall explore how various possibilities of interaction between metaphor and metonymy generate explicatures that become available to specific situations together with the subsequent production of implicatures.

The notion of conceptual interaction between metaphor and metonymy has been elaborated by Goossens (1990). In broad outline, he distinguishes three types of interaction: metaphor from metonymy, metonymy within metaphor, and metaphor within metonymy.[5] Exemplifying the first type of interaction is the figurative use of *applaud* meaning 'express a strong agreement with a person, idea, etc.,' as in:

(24) These changes will be applauded.

The interpretation of (24) involves a metonymic mapping from *applaud* onto 'express agreement by (actual) applauding.' This metonymic expansion of the meaning of *applaud* to indicate agreement may then be used in cases lacking an actual act of applauding.

The second interaction type, metonymy within metaphor, is exemplified in (25):

(25) I could bite my tongue.

This example incorporates a metonymic mapping from *tongue* to the speech faculty as a whole. The figurative action of biting one's tongue maps onto the actual linguistic action of depriving oneself of one's ability to speak.

The third pattern of interaction can be exemplified by the expression

(26) Get up on one's hind legs.

In the context of Goossens' (1990: 172) analysis of expressions having a target domain of linguistic action, he argues that this expression evokes a scene in which a person stands up and speaks publicly; the addition of the term *hind* forces a reinterpretation of the scene in terms of an animal standing up, thereby suggesting a greater effort.

In our interpretation, the first two interactional patterns distinguished by Goossens exploit the same kind of conceptual operation since both involve a metonymic development of the underspecified source domain of a metaphor. Thus (24) *These changes will be applauded* evokes a metaphoric source domain in which people express agreement by applauding. This metaphoric source is an expansion of what is literally given in the expression. The target characterizes a related situation where applauding corresponds to expressing agreement by means of some other kind of action. Similarly, in (25) the utterance *I could bite my tongue* involves a metonymic expansion of the metaphoric source from the action of tongue biting to a situation in which a person bites his tongue to refrain from speaking. However, there is a difference – captured by Goossens' labeling – between the two expressions in that applauding to express agreement is not necessarily a figurative action, while biting one's tongue to refrain from speaking has a stronger figurative component (it is unlikely that a person literally bites his tongue in order not to speak). In any case, the difference is just a matter of degree of figurativeness and does not affect the nature of the underlying cognitive operation. Figures 3 and 4 below attempt to capture the essentials of the operation we have just described.

The status of the third interactional pattern distinguished by Goossens – metaphor within metonymy – may require different treatment. While it is true that deleting the metaphorically interpreted element *hind* leaves a meaningful expression (e.g. *He got up on his legs to defend his views*), it may also be argued that *get up on one's hind legs* as a whole seems to invoke the scene of a quadruped, e.g. a horse (energetically) rearing up (perhaps out of fear) as if to attack. This scene is mapped onto the target-domain situation in which a person rises to his feet with determination to speak in public. Since the linguistic expression underspecifies the conceptual material necessary to construct the source domain of this metaphor, it is not unreasonable to regard the cognitive

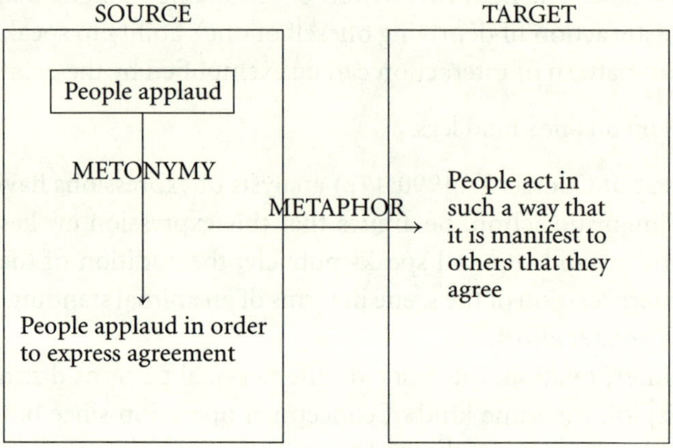


**Figure 3.** Metonymic development of the metaphoric source in *These changes will be applauded*

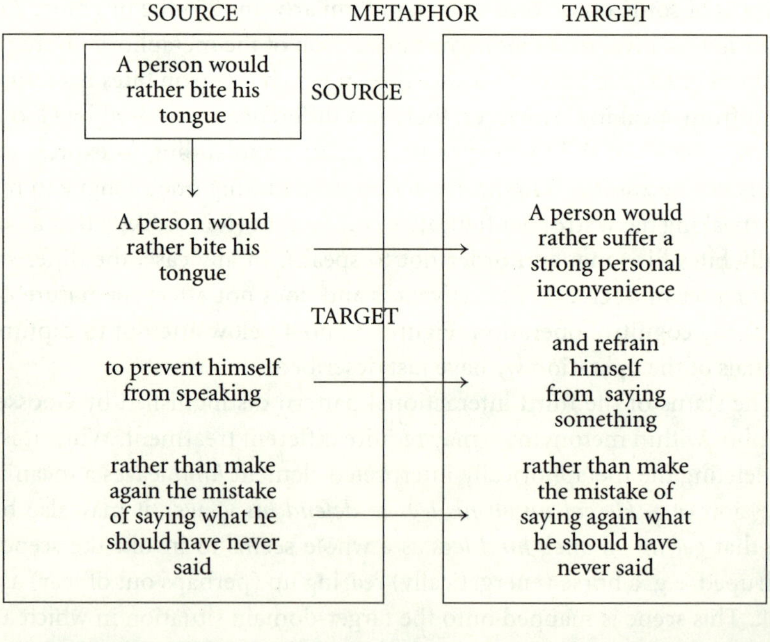


**Figure 4.** Metonymic development of the metaphoric source in *I could bite my tongue*

operation at issue as one of metonymic development of the metaphoric source, as was the case with the two previous examples. This situation is diagrammed in Figure 5 below.

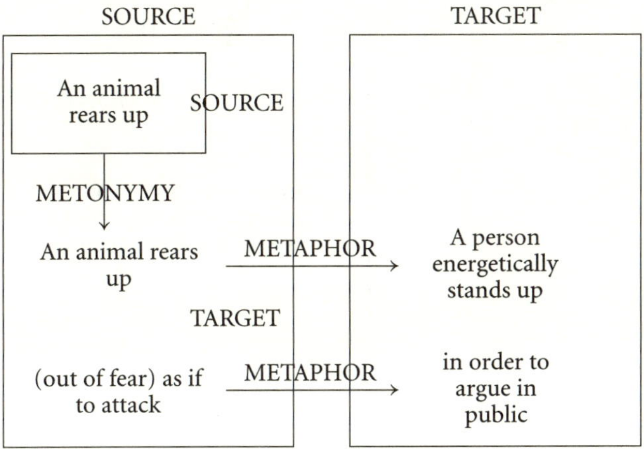


**Figure 5.** Metonymic development of the metaphoric source in *get up on one's hind legs*

The examples we have discussed so far illustrate but one kind of interactional pattern in our analysis, namely, metonymic development of a metaphoric source. However, we propose others. Consider first the metaphoric expression in (27):

(27) My lips are sealed.

This utterance may be used by a speaker to make a binding promise that he will not reveal a secret. The act of sealing his lips is a figurative indication that he will in no way open his mouth to disclose any information. But this indication is part of a more general situation in which the speaker voluntarily decides to keep certain information confidential.

Consider now the expression in (28):

(28) to win someone's heart

The source domain of this metaphor contains a winner and a prize. The target domain contains a lover who has succeeded in figuratively obtaining someone's heart. The heart, as a container of feelings, is chosen to stand for the feeling of love. Since 'heart' and 'love' stand in a domain-subdomain relationship, we have a case of metonymic highlighting of (a relevant part of) the metaphoric target. Winning requires effort and tactics, an implication that is carried over to

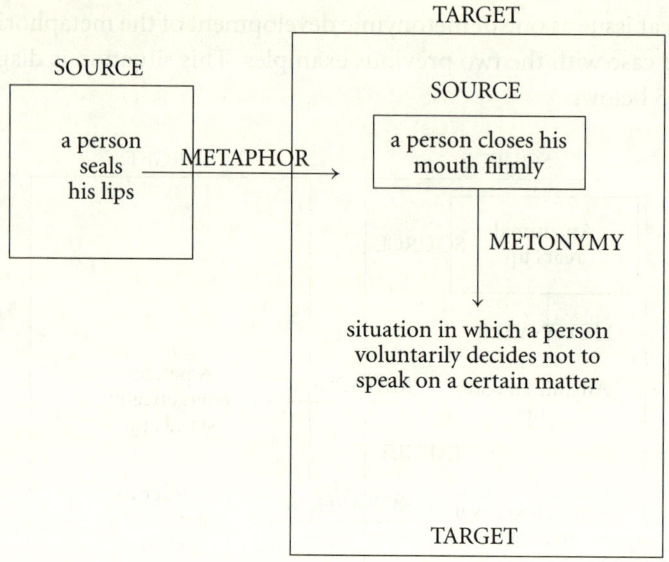


**Figure 6.** Metonymic development of a metaphoric target in *My lips are sealed*

the target domain of the metaphor, thus suggesting that the action of obtaining someone's love has been a difficult one. Figure 7 illustrates this process.

One final pattern of metaphor-metonymy interaction is illustrated in (29):

(29) She is the life and soul of the party.

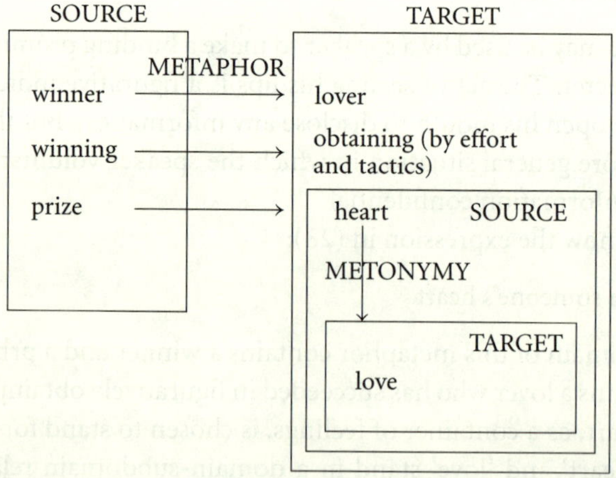


**Figure 7.** Metonymic highlighting of a metaphoric target in *to win someone's heart*

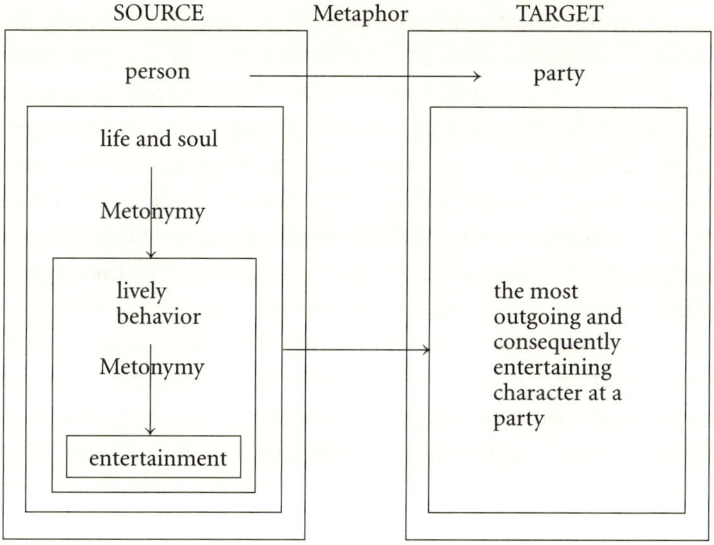


**Figure 8.** Metonymic highlighting of a metaphoric source in *She is the life and soul of the party.*

in which *party* is understood metaphorically as a person whose life and soul stand for her lively behavior, which in turn stands for the person's ability to be entertaining. In these two metonymic mappings, which are of the target-in-source kind, there is highlighting of a relevant part of the domain to which they belong. In the first metonymy, the person's lively behavior is seen as a consequence (and therefore, as a subdomain) of the person's having *life and soul*; in the second metonymy, the resultant entertainment of others is seen as a consequence (then, a subdomain) of the person's lively behavior.

To conclude this section, we observe that in all the patterns of interaction between metaphor and metonymy that we have described, metonymy plays a subsidiary role to the extent that the interactional process has a metaphoric base. As a result, the explicated meaning of each of the expressions corresponding to a given pattern is to be found in the metaphoric target.

## 7. Summary and conclusion

In this chapter we have discussed the standard relevance-theoretic proposal that there are two kinds of communicated assumptions involving inferential activity: explicatures and implicatures. By examining more closely the means by which different mechanisms of explicature function, we have been able to refine this distinction. Our major claim is that explicatures include the cognitive operations of metaphoric and metonymic mapping – though regulated by the principle of relevance – that work on the basis of the (usually underspecified) information directly provided by what is said. Implicatures, on the other hand, are the result of deriving conclusions with the help of relevant implicated premises obtained from the context. We have also restricted the scope of application of the notion of loosening, which from our perspective does not apply to so-called tropes like metaphor and metonymy, but only to scalar concepts as in examples of hyperbole. Furthermore, we have analyzed the different ways that metaphoric and metonymic mappings are used to obtain explicated meaning and we have established correlations between these different kinds of mapping and the explicatures they produce. In this connection, we have proposed a distinction between one-correspondence and many-correspondence metaphors and have argued that the existence of one-correspondence metaphors provides the basis for a metaphor-metonymy continuum. We have been able to see that predicative uses of metonymy yield explicatures similar to those derived from one-correspondence metaphoric mappings (by singling out a feature that applies to the target), while referential uses of metonymy involve either domain expansion or domain highlighting. Finally, we have studied more complex cases of explicature derivation by means of double metonymic mappings and conceptual interaction between metaphor and metonymy. We have observed that in double metonymies that exploit domain highlighting, the relevance of the conceptual structure of the two metonymic sources is kept intact, whereas in those double metonymic mappings involving both highlighting and expansion only the structure of the source domain of the second mapping is preserved. A different situation can be seen in cases of metaphor-metonymy interaction. Here we have noted that metonymy may function either to develop or highlight the source or the target of a metaphor. These cognitive operations are necessary for the derivation of the intended explicated meaning, which, whatever the interaction pattern, is to be found always in the metaphoric target.

## Notes

1. The relevance of the explicatures-implicature distinction for linguistics is probably evidenced from the fact that the linguistic devices that impose constraints on implicatures (e.g.

discourse connectives) are different from those that impose constraints on explicatures (e.g. pronouns) (see Wilson & Sperber 1993: 19–23).

2. In canonical accounts of Relevance Theory (e.g. Sperber & Wilson 1995; Blakemore 1992), metaphor and metonymy are treated as cases of interpretive (as opposed to descriptive) use of language bringing about the production of strong and weak implicatures. In this respect, Carston's proposal, where – as we shall see below – loosening and strengthening are forms of deriving explicatures, involves a relatively important readjustment in the theory. The idea that metonymic shifts generate explicatures is also found in Papafragou (1995).

3. To Lakoff and Johnson's (1980) classification, it is possible to add situational metaphors like *He left the room with his tail between his legs*. This metaphor invokes a situation in which a person who has been defeated and humiliated decides to forego the pursuit of a certain goal. This is based on the stereotypical representation of a dog leaving with its tail between its legs after being defeated or otherwise punished. Situational metaphors are a type of structural metaphor. It must additionally be noted that metaphors based on image-schemas are also a type of structural metaphor, since they allow us to understand abstract concepts in terms of others grounded in bodily experience. For example, in the metaphor LOVE IS A JOURNEY (Lakoff 1993), different aspects of a love relationship are understood in terms of different elements of a journey: lovers are travelers, the vehicle is a love relationship, difficulties in the relationship are impediments to travel, and goals are destinations (e.g., *This relationship is going nowhere, We are spinning our wheels*, etc.).

4. Ruiz de Mendoza and Díez (forthcoming) discuss a number of criteria that may be used to determine which of the two domains of a metonymy qualifies as a matrix domain. Generally, the matrix domain of a metonymy is the most encompassing and/or most clearly delineated (and therefore more readily accessible) of the two domains involved in a mapping. When two domains are equally accessible, the matrix domain is a matter of the application of a number of principles of cognitive saliency, like those identified by Langacker (1993) and Kövecses and Radden (1998): human over non-human; container over content; controlling entity over controlled entity; whole over part, among others. In the Napoleon-army relationship it is the controlling over controlled principle that holds.

5. According to Goossens (1990: 171) there is an additional possibility of interaction type, namely demetonymization within a metaphorical context, as illustrated in the expression *pay lip service to* meaning 'support in words, but not in fact.' Goossens argues that at first sight this expression seems to be an example of metonymy within metaphor, where *lip(s)* stands for 'speaking,' but that the figurative expression will work only if, in a second stage, *lip service* is interpreted as 'service as if with the lips only,' where 'lips' is somehow dissociated from 'speaking,' However, the status of such a process of demetonymization is questionable. Contrasted with 'actual (or genuine) service,' *lip service* suggests that the person who offers the service has no intention of keeping his word. Thus, *lip service* means 'a promise or an offer of service,' and this linguistic action is carried out by means of speech.

## References

Barcelona, Antonio (Ed.). (2000). *Metaphor and Metonymy at the Crossroads: A Cognitive Perspective* [Topics in English Linguistics 30]. Berlin and New York: Mouton de Gruyter.

Barsalou, Lawrence (1983). Ad hoc categories. *Memory & Cognition, 11*, 211–227.

Blakemore, Diane (1992). *Understanding Utterances.* Oxford: Basil Blackwell.

Carston, Robyn (1988). Implicature, explicature, and truth-theoretic semantics. In R. M. Kempson (Ed.), *Mental Representations: The Interface Between Language and Reality* (pp. 155–181). Cambridge: Cambridge University Press. [Reprinted 1991 in S. Davis (Ed.), *Pragmatics: A Reader* (pp. 33–51). New York, Oxford: Oxford University Press.]

Carston, Robyn (1997). Enrichment and loosening: complementary processes in deriving the proposition expressed? *Linguistische Berichte, 8*, 103–127.

Carston, Robyn (2000). Explicature and semantics. *UCL Working Papers in Linguistics, 12*, 1–44. [To appear in S. Davis & B. Gillon (Eds.), *Semantics: A Reader*. Oxford: Oxford University Press.]

Goossens, Louis (1990). Metaphtonymy: the interaction of metaphor and metonymy in expressions for linguistic action. *Cognitive Linguistics, 1*, 323–340.

Johnson, Mark (1987) *The Body in the Mind: The Bodily Basis of Meaning, Reason and Imagination*. Chicago and London: The University of Chicago Press.

Kövecses, Zoltán & Radden, Günter (1998). Metonymy: developing a cognitive linguistic view. *Cognitive Linguistics, 9–1*, 37–77.

Lakoff, George (1987). *Women, Fire, and Dangerous Things: What Categories Reveal About the Mind*. Chicago and London: The University of Chicago Press.

Lakoff, George (1993). The contemporary theory of metaphor. In A. Ortony (Ed.), *Metaphor and Thought* (pp. 202–251). Cambridge: Cambridge University Press.

Lakoff, George & Johnson, Mark (1980). *Metaphors We Live By*. Chicago and London: The University of Chicago Press.

Lakoff, George & Johnson, Mark (1999). *Philosophy in the Flesh: The Embodied Mind and its Challenge to Western Thought*. New York: Basic Books.

Lakoff, George & Turner, Mark (1989). *More Than Cool Reason: A Field Guide to Poetic Metaphor*. Chicago and London: The University of Chicago Press.

Langacker, Ronald W. (1993). Reference-point constructions. *Cognitive Linguistics, 4–1*, 1–38.

Levinson, Stephen C. (2000). *Presumptive Meanings: The Theory of Generalized Conversational Implicature*. Cambridge, MA, and London: MIT Press.

Panther, Klaus-Uwe & Radden, Günter (Eds.). (1999). *Metonymy in Language and Thought* [Human Cognitive Processing 4]. Amsterdam and Philadelphia: Benjamins.

Papafragou, Anna (1995). Metonymy and relevance. *UCL Working Papers in Linguistics* 7. Department of Phonetics and Linguistics, University College London.

Peña, Sandra (1997). The role of the event structure metaphor and of image-schematic structure in metaphors for happiness and sadness. *Miscelanea. A Journal of English and American Studies, 18*, 253–266. Zaragoza: University of Zaragoza Press.

Recanati, François (1989). The pragmatics of what is said. *Mind and Language, 4*, 294–328. [Reprinted 1991 in S. Davis (Ed.), *Pragmatics: A Reader* (pp. 97–120). Oxford: Oxford University Press.]

Ruiz de Mendoza, Francisco J. (1997). Cognitive and pragmatic aspects of metonymy. *Cuadernos de Filología, 6*(2), 161–178.

Ruiz de Mendoza, Francisco J. (1998). On the nature of blending as a cognitive phenomenon. *Journal of Pragmatics, 30*, 259–374.

Ruiz de Mendoza, Francisco J. (1999). From semantic underdetermination via metaphor and metonymy to conceptual interaction. *LAUD*: Paper No 492.

Ruiz de Mendoza, Francisco J. (2000). The role of mappings and domains in understanding metonymy. In A. Barcelona (Ed.), *Metaphor and Metonymy at the Crossroads* [Topics in English Linguistics 30] (pp. 109–132). Berlin and New York: Mouton de Gruyter.

Ruiz de Mendoza, Francisco J. & Díez, Olga (forthcoming). Metonymic motivation in anaphoric reference. In K.-U. Panther & G. Radden (Eds.), *Motivation in Grammar.*

Ruiz de Mendoza, Francisco J. & Pérez Hernández, Lorena (2001). Metonymy and the grammar: motivation, constraints, and interaction. *Language & Communication, 21*, 321–357.

Sperber, Dan & Wilson, Deirdre (1985–1986). Loose talk. *Proceedings of the Aristotelian Society, LXXXVI*, 153–171.

Sperber, Dan & Wilson, Deirdre (1995). *Relevance: Communication and Cognition* (2nd ed.). Oxford: Basil Blackwell.

Wilson, Dan & Sperber, Deirdre (1993). Linguistic form and relevance. *Lingua, 90*, 1–25.

# Metonymy and conceptual blending

Seana Coulson and Todd Oakley

## 1. Introduction

Metonymic language involves the use of a trigger or source term to refer to an associated target concept. Panther and Thornburg (this volume), for instance, use "*The piano* is in a bad mood," as a paradigmatic example of metonymy, as the trigger *piano* is used to evoke the target concept of the person who plays the piano. Though typically considered a referential phenomenon (e.g. Nunberg 1995), recent advances in cognitive linguistics suggest metonymic language use is but the tip of a deep conceptual iceberg. Radden and Kövecses (1999), for example, define metonymy as a process in which one element in a cognitive model is evoked by another element in the same cognitive model. Similarly, Langacker (2000) argues that metonymic language is a reference point phenomenon, a linguistic construction in which a cognitively salient discourse element (the reference point) is used to set up a context within which the conceptualizer can enter into contact with other less prominent entities in the discourse. Thus the trigger – or source – term in a metonymic utterance serves as a reference point that enables the listener to access the target concept.

The cognitive import of metonymy has been less widely acknowledged than that of metaphor, a closely related linguistic and conceptual phenomenon. However, Lakoff and Turner (1989) point out that metaphor and metonymy both involve conceptual mappings, both can be conventionalized, and both are means of extending the linguistic resources of a language. Indeed, more recently, metonymic links have been shown to help motivate conceptual metaphors (Barcelona 2000), and to mediate diachronic language change (Goossens 2000; Pelyvás 2000). The cognitive import of metonymy has also been addressed by Fauconnier and Turner (2000a, b) in the context of conceptual blending theory, a general theory of information integration discussed below.

Fauconnier and Turner (2000a, b) describe the interaction of metaphor, metonymy, and conceptual blending, noting how complex blends often allow non-counterparts to be combined in virtue of metonymic connections in their inputs. We extend this analysis here by discussing the role of metonymy in a range of conceptual blends that span a continuum from instances of ordinary language use to examples of human creativity and artistry operating at its highest pitch. Our examples include uses of the idiom *blowing your own horn*, literary blends in the writings of the American author Ernest Hemingway, and metonymic blends in the sculpture of Viktor Schreckengost. We show how metonymic mappings often play a crucial role in conceptual blends, and suggest that metonymic language results from more general cognitive pressures.

## 2. General definitions of conceptual blending

Conceptual blending theory offers a general model of meaning construction in which a small set of partially compositional processes operates in analogy, metaphor, counterfactuals, and many other semantic and pragmatic phenomena. In this theory, understanding meaning involves the construction of blended cognitive models that include some structure from multiple *input* models, as well as emergent structure that arises through the processes of blending. Discussed at length in Fauconnier and Turner (1998), Coulson (2000), and Oakley (in preparation), blending theory describes a set of operations for combining dynamic cognitive models in a network of *mental spaces* (Fauconnier 1994), or partitions of speakers' referential representations.

### 2.1 Mental space theory

Mental spaces contain partial representations of the entities and relationships in any given scenario as perceived, imagined, remembered, or otherwise understood by a speaker. Elements represent each of the discourse entities, and simple frames represent the relationships that exist between them. Because the same scenario can be construed in multiple ways, mental spaces are frequently used to partition incoming information about elements in speakers' referential representations. For example, the sentence in (1)

(1) Seana thinks the statue is hideous, but Todd thinks it's just wonderful.

prompts the reader to construct two mental spaces, one to represent Seana's opinion of the statue, and one to represent Todd's:

| | |
|---|---|
| Seana | Todd |
| Thinks | Thinks |
| ====== | ====== |
| s | s' |
| hideous(s) | wonderful(s') |

One virtue of mental space theory is that it explains how the addressee might encode information at the referential level by dividing it into concepts relevant to different aspects of the scenario. However, by partitioning the information, this method also creates a need to keep track of the relationships that exist between counterpart elements and relations represented in different mental spaces.

Consequently, the notion of *mappings* between mental spaces is a central component of both mental space theory and the theory of conceptual blending. A *mapping*, or *mental space connection*, is the understanding that an object or element in one mental space corresponds to an object or element in another. For example in (1), the sentence about Seana's and Todd's respective opinions about the statue, there is an identity mapping between the element *s* that represents the statue in Seana's opinion space, and element *s'* that represents the statue in Todd's opinion space. The mental spaces framework thus allows one to represent the fact that the very same statue is referred to in *the statue is hideous* and *it's just wonderful*, in spite of its disparate properties in the two opinion spaces.

Besides identity, such mappings can be based on a number of relationships, such as similarity, analogy, and other pragmatic functions. Once linked, the *access principle* allows speakers to refer to an element in one space by naming, describing, or referring to its counterpart in another space. Interestingly, part of Fauconnier's (1994) justification for the access principle allowing reference across different spaces was the existence of similar connectors operating within a single mental space. For example, Fauconnier suggests that a pragmatic function linking hospital patients to their medical conditions licenses the metonymic reference to the patient in (2):

(2) The gastric ulcer in room 12 would like some coffee.

Just as pragmatic functions connecting (say) patients and their illnesses can allow speakers to access and refer to an associated element in the same mental space (see Nunberg 1978 for extensive review of pragmatic functions), cross-space mappings based on identity and analogy can allow speakers to access and refer to one element by naming or describing its counterpart in a completely different space.

## 2.2 Conceptual blending theory

A development of mental space theory, the theory of conceptual blending was set up to account for cases such as (3) in which some of the content of two or more mental spaces is combined to yield emergent structure.

(3) Coke Flows Past Forecasts: Soft drink company posts gains

This deceptively simple headline involves a combination of a conventionalized metonymy between a corporation (Coca Cola, Inc.) and the signature product of that corporation, as well as a metaphoric construal of Coca Cola, Inc.'s profits in the first quarter of 2001. Although metonymic reference occurs in both (2) and (3), the meaning construction in (3) is slightly more complicated. Example (2) relies on a metonymic link between a patient and his condition to access the patient, and the phrase *wants some coffee* is a perfectly appropriate predication for the patient (albeit not a healthy one given his condition). In (3), by contrast, *flows past forecasts* is an appropriate metaphoric predication for the Coca Cola corporation's profit, and an appropriate literal predication for the Coca Cola corporation's best known product. So, while the *Coke* in (3) is mainly construed as a corporation, it would appear to have some of the properties of the soft drink that corporation produces. Unlike instances of metonymy discussed by Fauconnier and Turner (2000), *Coke* in (3) does not involve a metonymic mapping *within* a blended space, but rather to a blended concept. Similarly, Ruiz and Pérez (this volume) insightfully discuss an example whose irony derives from blended construal of actor Christopher Reeves as being both mortal and a superhuman: *You know, Superman fell off his horse and broke his back.* Examples such as these emphasize the inadequacy of viewing metonymy as strictly referential, as its mechanisms allow us to do more than simply substitute one element for another (Panther & Radden 1999; Barcelona 2000).

## 2.3 Conceptual integration networks

In conceptual blending theory, the way in which the meaning of *Coke* in (3) appeals simultaneously to conceptual structure from multiple domains is captured in a *conceptual integration network* (CIN). A CIN is an array of mental spaces in which the processes of conceptual blending unfold (Fauconnier &

Turner 1998). These networks consist of two or more *input* spaces structured by information from discrete cognitive domains, an optional *generic* space that contains structure common to all spaces in the network, and a *blended* space that contains selected aspects of structure from each input space, and frequently, emergent structure of its own. Blending involves the establishment of partial mappings between cognitive models in different spaces in the network, and the projection of conceptual structure from space to space.

The CIN representing (3) involves two input spaces, a soft drink space and a corporation space. In the soft drink space, an element *d* is set up to represent *Coke*, and is structured by a frame for soft drinks (viz. the element *d* is construed as having the properties of the sugary, carbonated beverage drunk by millions of people every day). In the corporation space, *c’* represents the Coca Cola corporation that manufactures Coke. Though the beverage and the company that makes the beverage have very different properties, the elements *d’* and *c’* are linked by a conventional metonymy that allows corporations to be identified by their products. The corporation space also includes an element *p’* that represents the profit generated by Coca Cola, Inc. during the first quarter of 2001, and *f’* to represent the predicted profit for the same quarter (viz. the economic forecast). Conceptual structure in the corporation space involves a frame for corporate profit, and for evaluating corporate profits. Moreover, a conventional metonymy between corporations and their profits links elements *c’* and *p’*.

| Soft Drink Input | Corporation Input |
|---|---|
| d | d’ |
| | c’ |
| | p’ |
| | f’ |

The blended space in this network contains element *c** linked by identity to *d* in the soft drink space, and by metonymy to *p’* (in the corporation space). While conceptual structure in the input spaces comes from the domains of soft drinks and corporations, the blended space includes partial structure from each of the inputs as well as emergent structure of its own. Consequently, element *c** has some of the properties of Coke (in that it is a liquid), and some of the properties of Coca Cola, Inc.’s first quarter 2001 profit (in that it was greater than the forecasted profit).

Besides the hybrid soft-drink/profit element, the blend in (3) is notable in the way that it recruits $c^*$'s amalgam of properties to construe the relationship between Coca Cola's actual and predicted profit. Objectively considered, the relationship between actual and predicted profit is a static mathematical one. However, the use of the verb *flowed* suggests that (3) is a description of motion. This phenomenon, known as fictive (or abstract, or subjective) motion has been well studied by Langacker (1987) and Talmy (2000). In addition, Fauconnier (1997) has noted that fictive motion constructions involve a blend between an abstract motion scenario and a static representation of the relationship between two or more objects referred to in the particular construction at hand.

(4) The blackboard goes all the way to the wall.

For example, (4) involves a blend of a static construal of the spatial extent of the blackboard (spatial input) with an abstract, image schematic understanding of a trajector that moves relative to a reference point, or landmark. There is a mapping between the blackboard and the trajector and these two elements are fused in the blended space. Similarly, there is a mapping between the wall and the landmark, and these two elements are fused in the blended space. In the motion input, the trajector's motion ends at the landmark. Similarly, in the blended space, the motion of the blackboard/trajector ends at the wall/landmark. The path of motion can then be mapped onto the spatial input to be construed as the spatial extent of the blackboard.

| Spatial Input | Blended Space | Motion Input |
|---|---|---|
| ====== | ====== | ====== |
| blackboard | blackboard/trajector | trajector |
| wall | wall/landmark | landmark |
| (static) | (motion) | (motion) |

The fictive motion in (3) can be analyzed similarly by including a third input space to the CIN (see Figure 1). The third input is structured by a schematic characterization of the fictive motion schema in which a trajector moves along an abstract path with a reference point (as in Fauconnier 1997).

| Soft Drink Input | Corporation Input | Motion Input |
|---|---|---|
| ========= | ========== | ====== |
| d | d’ | |
| | c’ | |
| | p’ | t” (trajector) |
| | f’ | l” (landmark) |

For the fictive motion construal, the most important mappings are between *p’*, the profit in the corporate input, and *t”*, the trajector in the motion input, and between *f’*, the forecast in the corporate input, and *l”*, the landmark in the motion input. Elements *p’* and *t”* are mapped onto *c** in the blend. Similarly, *f’* and *l”* are mapped onto *f**. A static relationship between the actual and the predicted profit is thus construed as the abstract motion of the blended soft-drink/profit/trajector *c** element *past* the blended forecast/landmark *f** element.

The implications that the spatial relationships between elements in the blended space have for their counterparts in the economic space are rooted in conventional metaphoric mappings between progress and movement along a path (see Lakoff 1993 for review). Consequently, the motion of *c** past *f** (viz. the movement of the Coke past the forecast/reference point) can be construed as Coke’s actual profits exceeding their predicted profits. The expression of a static mathematical relationship in terms of motion results from conceptual blending, a process ultimately aimed at allowing conceptual structure from connected mental spaces to be integrated in a single cognitive model. Moreover, the particular verbiage of (3) – the expression of fictive motion in the domain of liquids – is possible only because of a chain of metonymies from products to the corporations that make them, and from corporations to the profits they earn. As in the *Superman* example discussed by Ruiz and Pérez (this volume), metonymy allows the speaker to emphasize a salient aspect of the metonymic source or trigger domain for added inferential effects. Similarly, Barcelona (this volume) argues that pragmatic inferences in jokes are often facilitated by metonymic connections.

Analysis of (3) suggests that natural language constructions (in this case a headline from the business page of *USA Today*, a widely read American newspaper) can combine metonymic and metaphoric mappings not only to exploit inferential structure available in the trigger spaces (in the sense of Fauconnier 1994; Nunberg 1978), but to combine structure from multiple triggers in novel ways. Similarly, Coulson and Oakley (2000) show that conceptual blend-

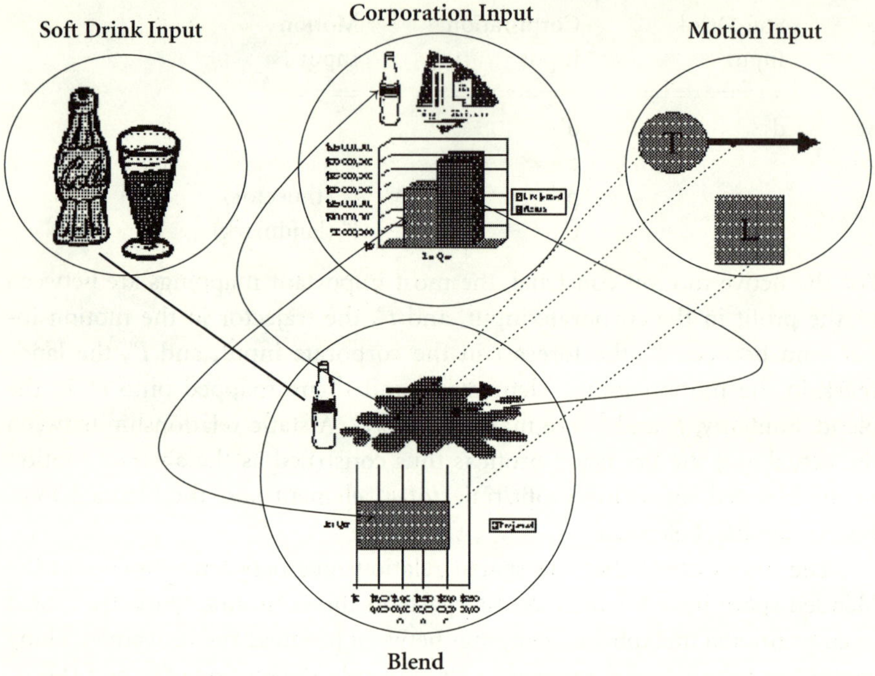


**Figure 1.** Conceptual integration network for (3) *Coke flows past forecasts: Soft drink company posts gains*

ing in the headlines *Tennessee Tramples Kentucky* and *Overseas Ballots Boost Bush* involve conventional metonymies between states and universities, universities and their football teams, politicians and their votes, in combination with metaphoric mappings between combat and sports, and between greater quantities and greater heights. One advantage of the blending framework is that it allows the treatment of examples like (3) that require many sorts of conceptual mappings to be set up in parallel in the course of meaning construction.

## 3. Optimality principles

Conceptual blending theory is an extremely powerful framework for describing the operations of meaning construction at the referential level. Indeed, some have argued the theory is too powerful, as in principle it can explain any example (e.g. Gibbs 2000). In response to such criticisms, Fauconnier and Turner have proposed a set of *optimality principles*, or constraints under which blends are more effective. Fauconnier and Turner (1998) argue for six such optimality principles: (i) the *integration principle*, that representations in the blended space can be manipulated as a single unit; (ii) the *topology principle*, that relations in the blend should match the relations of their counterparts in other spaces; (iii) the *web principle*, that the representation in the blended space should maintain mappings to the input spaces; (iv) the *unpacking principle*, that given a blended model, the interpreter should be able to infer the structure in other spaces in the network; (v) the *good reason principle*, that creates pressure to attribute significance to elements in the blend; and (vi) *metonymic tightening*, that when metonymically related elements are projected into the blended space, there is pressure to compress the "distance" between them. By reducing the space of possible blending analyses, these constraints make blending more principled.

Despite their poetic names, most of these principles invoke standard pressures that obtain in all mapping problems (see Hofstadter 1995 for review). The topology principle, for example, exerts normative pressure to construct and maintain mappings in such a way as to preserve relational structure. In research on analogical reasoning, this pressure is referred to as the structure mapping principle (see Gentner & Markman 1997 for review). In research on metaphorical mapping, this pressure is referred to as the invariance hypothesis, the observation that the underlying mappings in metaphoric expressions are almost always based on shared image schematic structure (see Brugman 1990; Lakoff 1990; and Turner 1990). The web principle, that the representation in the blended space should maintain its mappings to the input spaces, amounts to the extension of the access principle to conceptual content in blended mental spaces. Satisfaction of the web principle is what allows one to access elements in the blend with names and descriptions from the input spaces, as well as what allows the projection of structure from the blended space to other spaces in the network. Finally, the unpacking principle, the dictate that given a blended model, the listener should be able to construct structure in the other spaces in the network, can be thought of as pressure to use conventional mapping schemas that facilitate comprehension. Thus construed, the unpacking principle applies pressure to use conceptual metaphors, such as KNOWING IS SEEING, and conventional metonymic mappings, such as PART FOR WHOLE, PRODUCER FOR PRODUCT, or CONTAINER FOR CONTENTS.

The integration principle, the good reason principle, and the metonymic tightening principle all specifically refer to the blended space, and consequently, are unique to Fauconnier and Turner's theoretical framework. However, we note that the integration principle, pressure to conceptualize the event with an easily manipulable representation, is reminiscent of Miller's (1957) concept of chunking, as well as its more formal incarnation in Anderson's (1983) ACT-* model. Chunking is a process by which one can assimilate a great deal of new information by relating it to knowledge representations in long-term memory. Fauconnier and Turner's insight in blending theory is that comprehenders can "chunk" information by relating it to various juxtapositions of partial structure from multiple domains.

Fauconnier and Turner (2002) further develop these principles and relate them to general cognitive pressures that promote blending. The most significant change to the framework is that the metonymic tightening constraint has been replaced by a far more general notion of *compression*, a process by which relationships between input spaces in the network are represented by a single element in the blend. For example, Fauconnier and Turner (2002) describe an anti-smoking ad that depicts a cowboy smoking a drooping cigarette with the caption, *Smoking causes impotence.* Here the causal relationship between the smoking input and the impotence input has been "compressed" in the representation of the drooping cigarette. Rather than being considered an optimality principle, compression is a major factor in conceptual blending which warrants its own set of governing principles (see Fauconnier & Turner 2002 for details).

In addition, Fauconnier and Turner (2002) have renamed the *good reason principle* the *relevance principle*, in part to highlight its compatibility with a popular approach in pragmatics known as Relevance Theory (Sperber & Wilson 1995). Like its predecessor the good reason constraint, the relevance principle creates pressure to attribute relevance to elements in the blended space. This relevance can consist in establishing links to other spaces and for "running" the blend. Moreover, important relationships between elements in the blend's inputs can be expected to be manifested by a compression in the blend.

Fauconnier and Turner (2002) list a dozen or so *vital relations* that are used repeatedly by speakers to link the contents of two or more mental spaces. Besides identity, analogy, and representation, mentioned above, vital relations include such things as disanalogy, change, part-whole, and cause-effect. It is vital relations that tend to be subject to compression in the blended space. For example, in the smoking cowboy blend discussed above, the cause-effect relationship between smoking and impotence is compressed into the drooping cigarette in the blended space. Moreover, Fauconnier and Turner describe canonical patterns of compression that occur in example after example. Cause-effect relationships, for instance, are often compressed into part-whole relationships in the blend.

In addition, a number of vital relations tend to be compressed into uniqueness in the blend, including representation, part-whole, cause-effect, category, and role. Compression to uniqueness simply means that a single element in the blended space maps to two or more elements in distinct input spaces. For example, one might point to a photograph of a loved one and say *This is my daughter*, thus compressing the representation and its real-world counterpart into a single element in the blended space. In generic statements such as *The lion is a carnivore* the categorical relationship that relates different exemplars of lions to one another is compressed into a single representative lion in the blended space. Metonymic language can thus be construed as referring to compressed elements in blended spaces, while conventional metonymies help speakers to unpack mappings from the compressed element in a blended space to its various counterparts in the input spaces in the integration network.

The optimality principles get their name from a paradigm in phonology that explains phonological regularities by recourse to a set of interacting constraints. Like their namesake, satisfaction of Fauconnier and Turner's optimality principles is selective, and satisfaction of one constraint is often inconsistent with the satisfaction of another. For example, the blend in (3) fulfills the integration principle because the cognitive model set up in the blend concerns a single scene (of Coke literally flowing past the forecast). However, it violates the topology principle because element $c^*$ in the blended space maps onto both *c'* and *p'* in the corporation space.

The characterization of such trade-offs in the operation of such optimality constraints is a critical aspect of conceptual blending theory. As a general framework for meaning construction, conceptual blending has been argued to play a role in a large range of cognitive and linguistic phenomena. As such, it runs the risk of becoming essentially vacuous: the more general the scope of these processes, the greater the need to address the details of the differences in the operation of blending in particular examples. Below we pursue this agenda by exploring the interplay of the optimality principles in a range of examples.

We suggest that metonymic expressions often embody a trade-off between the topology principle, that is, the dictate that models in each of the mental spaces in the network share as much relational structure as possible, and the integration principle, that is, the dictate that the events in the blended space form an integrated mental scene. In general, the presence of metonymic connections in the blend performs the crucial function of holding together the network of mental spaces that are necessary for reasoning on a particular topic to be sustained over time.

## 4. Metonymic shifts

In their book *Mental Leaps*, Holyoak and Thagard (1995) claim that the difference between metaphor and analogy is that metaphors, especially literary ones, are subject to "loose" and "shifting" mappings, which are the side effects of metonymy. Treating it as a somewhat suspect technique, Holyoak and Thagard argue that metonymy's intrusion into metaphoric language places metaphor outside the explanatory bounds of a theory of analogy. An unbridled force at large in the literary universe, metonymy leads at best to analogical inconsistency, at worst to incoherence. In support of their position, Holyoak and Thagard point to the following excerpt from the writings of Ernest Hemingway:

> His talent was as natural as the pattern that was made by the dust on a butterfly's wings. At one time he understood it no more than the butterfly did and he did not know when it was brushed or marred. Later he became conscious of his damaged wings and of their construction and he learned to think and could not fly anymore because the love of flight was gone and he could only remember when it had been effortless.
>
> (Quoted in Holyoak & Thagard 1995: 224)

Analyzing the passage, Holyoak and Thagard point to the fact that the writer's talent is initially mapped to the pattern of dust on the butterfly's wings, and later to the wings themselves. Further, they point out that there is no causal relationship between patterns on a butterfly's wings and its ability to fly, and no reason why consciousness of wings should affect the butterfly's ability to fly. In blending theory, analogical mismatches like this are frequently used to motivate the need for a blended space analysis. Indeed, in their discussion of this example, Holyoak and Thagard resort to the use of slashes to represent the conceptual fusion of ideas: "A butterfly's pattern is not causally related to its flight, so if talent is mapped to the pattern, then there is no reason why consciousness of the talent/pattern should interfere with the ability to exercise it" (Holyoak & Thagard 1995: 224).

In fact, one might also note that real butterflies cannot properly be said to be *conscious* of anything, let alone be the sort of intentional creature whose consciousness of a particular ability impairs the exercise of that ability. There is indeed an analogical mismatch between the domain of the man's consciousness of his own talent and the realistic domain of butterflies. But where Holyoak and Thagard suggest the passage involves metaphor "extended by the associative aura created by metonymy," we suggest it prompts a blended conceptualization of the writer and the butterfly that exploits both metaphoric and metonymic mappings. The first sentence, an explicit comparison between the man's talent and the dust on a butterfly's wings serves to set up the two input spaces for the ensuing blend: a "human" space with the man and his talent, and a "butterfly" space with the butterfly and the dust. The blend between the two spaces is prompted by the second sentence, "At one time he understood it no more than the butterfly did and he did not know when it was brushed or marred."

Although the sentence begins by referring to elements in the human space, the focus gradually shifts to a blended space that concerns a hybrid man/butterfly, exploiting partial structure from each of the input spaces. For example, the initial use of the pronoun "he" ("he understood") refers to the man, while the second refers to the hybrid man/butterfly ("he did not know when it was brushed or marred.") The transition to reference to the blended space is mediated by an ambiguity in the elided phrase "the butterfly did" in "he understood it no more than the butterfly did." This phrase could be interpreted as a comparison between the man's understanding of his artistic talent and the butterfly's understanding of the dust pattern on its wings; or between the man's understanding of his talent and the butterfly's understanding of the man's talent; or even between the man's understanding of his talent and the butterfly's understanding of its own talent. Similarly, the first use of the pronoun "it" (in "he understood it") refers to the man's talent, while the second (in "he did not know when it was brushed or marred") can be understood as referring alternately to the pattern of dust on the butterfly's wing, the man's talent, or an element in the blended space with the attributes of both the dust pattern and the man's talent.

The multiple interpretations for this sentence can be captured in the conceptual integration network in Figure 2. In the human space, the man does not understand his artistic talent; in the butterfly space, the butterfly does not understand the pattern of dust on its wings. In the blended space, the "he" is a butterfly with the intentional powers of a human, and the dust pattern is a feature of its wings that it *could* potentially understand, but doesn't. The initial blend conforms well to the first three optimality principles: integration, topology, and web. A cognitive model of a butterfly that is not conscious of the dust pattern on his wings is an integrated representation that is easy to manipulate. It conforms to the topology principle because the relational structure in the blended space corresponds to relational structure in the inputs. Moreover, it conforms to the web principle because the mappings between elements in the blended space and their counterparts in the input spaces are consistent.

However, the third sentence ("Later he became conscious of his damaged wings and of their construction and he learned to think and he could not fly

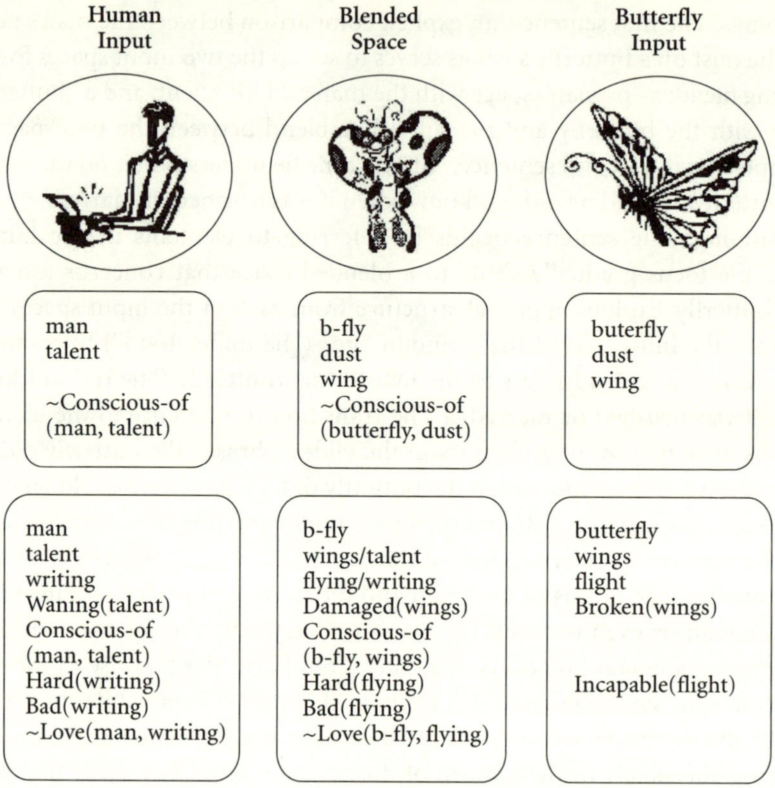


**Figure 2.** Conceptual integration network for Hemingway's description of the artist's talent

anymore because the love of flight was gone and he could only remember when it had been effortless") employs slightly different mappings between the elements in the blend and the inputs, thereby violating the web principle. As Holyoak and Thagard point out, the man's talent is initially mapped to the dust pattern on the butterfly's wings, but shifts to the wings themselves. This violation of the web principle is offset by metonymic tightening, the pressure to compress metonymically related elements in a blended space. In this case, the metonymic relationship of adjacency between the butterfly's wings and the dust pattern licenses a mapping between the man's talent – formerly mapped to the dust on the wings – and the wings themselves.

The need for a blended analysis of the third sentence is readily apparent as it makes little sense to talk about a man "conscious of his damaged wings," nor of a butterfly that, having lost the love of flight, "could only remember when it had been effortless." Though the mapping of the man's talent has shifted from the dust pattern on the wings to the butterfly's wings themselves, the mapping between the man and the butterfly remains intact, and the blended space again features a hybrid creature with the body of a butterfly and the cognitive and emotional capacity of the man represented in the human space. With the new mapping scheme established, the blend in the third sentence satisfies both the web and the topology constraints as the butterfly's wings continue to map to the man's talent in a systematic way. For example, damaged wings correspond to fading talent, inability to fly (an action that requires intact wings) corresponds to the man's inability to employ his talent (viz. writer's block), and the love of flight (enjoyment in the ability to use the wings for their intended purpose) corresponds to the man's love of writing (enjoyment in the ability to exercise his talent).

Though Hemingway's passage does indeed employ a series of *analogical mappings* between conceptual structure taken variously from the domains of butterflies and humans, it does not set up an *analogy* between the two domains. That is, Hemingway does not exploit the reader's knowledge of butterflies to explicate notions pertaining to artistic talent. Rather, he exploits the reader's ability to integrate conceptual structure from disparate domains that enable her to understand and empathize with the aging artist. While the reader may not understand the artist's joy in practicing his art, she can imagine the thrill of flight. Moreover, having imagined the thrill of flight, the reader is in a better position to empathize with the loss of this ability, and consequently its counterpart in the human space, the man's ability to write. If anything, the analogy is from the blended conceptualization of the human butterfly to the experience of the aging artist.

Metonymy is used here to shift the mapping schema in a way that violates the topology constraint, but optimizes integration. The metonymically licensed slip is rhetorically motivated because the first blend serves the original motivation of explicating the utter mindlessness of the artist's talent, and the second best serves the rhetorical motivation of explicating the emotive significance of a whole series of events as the artist's ability changes over the course of time. This includes the euphoric nature of the artist exercising his talent, the loss of this ability and the associated regret, as well as the causal sequence of events that produced the loss of talent. In subsequent examples we explore other ways that metonymy licenses different sorts of blends, and the way in which metonymic mappings affect the interplay of the optimality principles. In particular, metonymic language frequently involves conflict of the integration principle with the web and topology principles.

## 5. Idioms: X your own Y

### 5.1 Digging your own grave

As Coulson (2000) has argued, the idiom *digging your own grave* entails much more than a straightforward mapping from the source domain of grave digging and the target domain of trouble, primarily because default interpretations of this idiom lead to the inference that the deeper one digs the closer one gets to dying, thus positing a direct causal relationship between grave digging and death where none typically exists. The idiom is also fantastic in that the grave digger and the corpse in a typical grave digging scenario both map onto the same element in the blend. This idiom can be applied to any representation of an individual's actions interpreted as having untoward consequences that the speaker thinks the individual does not foresee. Applicable target situations can include anything from romantic disaster to academic failure to financial ruin, as in *You're digging your own financial grave by investing all your money in start-up Internet stocks.*

Interestingly, part of the reason this example has been discussed so frequently with respect to blending theory (e.g. Fauconnier & Turner 1998) is that it cannot be accounted for by approaches to figurative language that involve a strong commitment to the existence of shared conceptual structure in the source and target domains. Indeed, analysis of the "digging" example in terms of conceptual blending is motivated by the violation of the topology principle in the disanalogous mappings that are set up between the grave digger to the wrongheaded agent in the trouble space, and between the act of digging and the wrongheaded act (e.g. investing in Internet stocks).

In accordance with our observations here, though, this stock example is yet another illustration of the tradeoff between the topology principle and the integration and unpacking principles. Although the *digging your own grave* example violates topology, it does fulfill the integration constraint, allowing the hearer to conceptualize the scenario in an integrated scene. Moreover, it fulfills the unpacking principle by utilizing conventional metaphoric mappings between death and failure (Lakoff & Turner 1989), holes and situations (Lakoff 1993), and a conventional metonymic mapping between graves and death (Turner 1987). The digger causes the grave's existence, which maps metonymically onto death, which in turn maps metaphorically onto the wrongheaded agent's failure.

Metaphoric interpretation of the representation in the blended space thus rests crucially on the metonymic identification of the grave with death. Ruiz and Pérez (this volume) provide a number of examples that show the import of metonymic inference for highlighting and expanding an under-specified source domain in a metaphor. The proposal here is that this expansion often occurs in the blended space in the network, rather than in the source input, thus accounting for the inferential influence of the target domain in these processes.

## 5.2 Blowing your own horn

A close relative to *digging your own grave* is *blowing your own horn*, both of which exploit the X-your-own-Y pattern found in non-metaphoric examples, such as *get your own drink*, and *play your own instrument*. In contrast to these conventional examples, and indeed to the *digging your own grave* idiom, the own-Y in *blowing your own horn* is not used in contradistinction to someone *else's* horn, but rather playing a horn *for oneself* rather than for another. The horn in this case refers metonymically to the object of the trumpeting. The puzzling thing about *blowing your own horn*, of course, is how and why blowing your own horn maps onto praising yourself.

The verb *blow* and the noun *horn* provide the verbal cues for opening a mental space representing the act of playing a musical instrument. In this musician space, the focal element 'horn' provides the reference point for accessing and filling other slots in the frame such as 'musician'. The event represented in this space is the effect associated with producing a certain kind of sound. The musician blows into the horn, which produces a distinctive (and loud) sound, which captures the attention of others (possibly an audience). In fact, in western ceremonies, horn playing is often a scripted part of a procession, admonishing the crowd to pay attention. Blowing a horn, in effect, announces the arrival of a very important person such that the attention of the crowd becomes fixated on that person. Horn-playing can evoke this scenario via metonymic inference (Ruiz & Pérez, this volume).

Further, just as there is a close part-whole relation between a musician and her instrument, there is an even closer part-whole relation between a speaker and her voice. This common part-whole topology establishes a close relationship between the horn blowing input and the praising input we call the Encomium space, reminiscent of the formal genre of speech in which the writer enumerates the achievements and deeds of a living person. Since native speakers of English know that this idiom is about acts of praising, the mental space activates the focal element 'speaker' and 'voice'. Once activated, the speaker role and her most relevant feature map onto the focal elements in the musician space, namely musician and horn.

The two spaces are analogically linked by the generic causal and temporal relation obtaining between distinctive sound produced by a human being and the subsequent effect it has on other minds. In the musician space, the musician blows his horn to draw the audience's attention to some notable occurrence. In the Encomium space, the same relation holds between the vocalized act and the subsequent effect it has in getting others to pay attention to the accomplishments, deeds, and character attributed to the individual. This mapping has been lexicalized in the verb *trumpet* meaning 'to praise'. By employing a conventional mapping between encomium and trumpeting, the blend in *blowing your own horn* conforms to the unpacking principle.

Conformity to this entrenched mapping is also evident in the following attested use of the *blowing your own horn* blend from a story in the Metropolitan section of the *New York Times*, September 22, 1998:

> I firmly believe that if you're doing something interesting, you ought to tell people about it," Dr. Olivia said. "And if you're blowing your own horn, do it loudly. There's no sense giving it a little toot."

In this example, Dr. Olivia elaborates the *blowing your own horn* blend with a self-conscious distinction between "blowing" your own horn, and "giving it a little toot." Focusing on the loudness-softness gradient, Dr. Olivia suggests a mapping between the manner of articulation in the blend and the efficacy of the bragging. Soft horn blowing in the blend maps onto less, and less noticeable praise. This elaboration suggests a mapping between the degree of praise and the volume of the trumpet sound – the same mapping that underlies the meaning of the metaphoric expression *muted praise*. This in turn implies a mapping between the praise and the sound, the speaker and the trumpeter. The mappings between elements of a typical Encomium space and a ritualized space we call Trumpeting Royals are listed below.

| Typical Encomium | Trumpeting Royals |
|---|---|
| ======== | ========= |
| speaker | trumpeter |
| hero | royal |
| praise | sound |
| voice | trumpet |

But, as noted above, the idiom refers to an atypical Encomium space in which the speaker is the object of his own praise.

| Typical Encomium | Trumpeting Royals | Atypical Encomium |
|---|---|---|
| speaker | trumpeter | speaker |
| hero | royal | speaker |
| praise | sound | praise |
| voice | trumpet | voice |

A topology-preserving mapping would proceed as in the following:

| Typical Encomium | Trumpeting Royals | Atypical Encomium | Atypical Trumpeting |
|---|---|---|---|
| speaker | trumpeter | speaker | trumpeter |
| hero | royal | speaker | trumpeter |
| praise | sound | praise | sound |
| voice | horn | voice | horn |

In contrast, the idiom employs a mapping scheme like this:

| Typical Encomium | Trumpeting Royals | Atypical Encomium | Blended Space |
|---|---|---|---|
| speaker | trumpeter | speaker | trumpeter |
| hero | royal | speaker | horn |
| praise | sound | praise | sound |
| voice | horn | voice | horn |

The violation of the topology principle inherent in the mapping between the horn in the blended space and the object of the praise (viz. the speaker) in the atypical Encomium space is supported by a conventional metonymic mapping between musicians and their instruments, as in *The trombone is at his AA meeting tonight.* Or, an agent talking to a record producer *Well, I can get you a drummer, two guitars, and a bass, but you'll have to find your own horn.* As in the examples discussed in previous sections, the metonymic mapping between horn and trumpeter in *blowing your own horn* makes it possible to sustain a metaphoric interpretation of the model in the blended space despite the violation of the topology constraint.

## 6. Sculpture

One feature of conceptual blending theory, and indeed of pragmatics more generally, is that in relating certain regularities of utterance interpretation to aspects of cognitive function, it affords the opportunity to highlight commonalities between the conceptual aspects of language comprehension and a broader understanding of human thought and activity. Just as conceptual metaphors are used in the interpretation of art and literature alike (Gibbs 1994; Lakoff & Turner 1989), conceptual blending processes are crucially important for the creation and appreciation of visual art (Fauconnier & Turner 2002). For example, consider Viktor Schreckengost's clay sculpture *Apocalypse '42*, which features the figure of Death, clothed in a German uniform, riding a horse with Hitler, Hirohito, and Mussolini as passengers (see Figure 3). Produced in 1942 at the apogee of Axis domination of Europe and Asia, this sculpture represents the Second World War as an instantiation of the Apocalypse. A highly complex blend involving the allegory of the "Four Horsemen of the Apocalypse" from the Book of Revelations, personification metaphors of death (i.e., The Grim Reaper in Judeo-Christian lore), and geopolitical reference, Schreckengost's clay statue exemplifies pictorially our main point: conceptual integration relies on metonymic and metaphoric mappings that involve trade-offs between satisfaction of the integration and topology principles.

**Figure 3.** *Apocalypse '42* by Viktor Schreckengost's (1942). Printed with permission from the Smithsonian American Art Museum, Gift of the Artist

Our analysis begins by considering the two input spaces that prompt the construction of a third blended space.

| Presentation Input | Apocalypse Input | Blended Space |
|---|---|---|
| ============= | ============== | =========== |
| 4 anthropomorphic figures | 4 horsemen | 4 anthropomorphic figures |
| 1 equine figure | 4 horses | 1 equine figure |

The first space is a Presentation space contributing knowledge of artistic medium: clay and glaze. Specifically, this space includes four anthropomorphic figures astride a single equine figure. The Apocalypse space contributes minimal information about the Four Horsemen from the Book of Revelations, namely that there are four horses and four horsemen, and that their ride heralds the end of the world. Viewers more familiar with the biblical account will open a version of this space that includes knowledge that the four horsemen are, themselves, personifications of Conquest, War, Plague, and Famine, each of which mounts a horse of a different color: Conquest rides a white horse; War rides a red horse; Famine rides a black horse; Plague rides a pale horse. The two input spaces map counterparts onto each other via a similarity connector, since accessing each space depends on a relation of resemblance between elements in each space. The established similarity mapping, in turn, allows referential structure in one space to trigger referential structure in the other. For instance, Todd can now remark to Seana, "That hideous mass of clay predicted the end of the world in 1942," since referring to the medium of representation can provide indirect mental access to the entity represented.

More interesting metonymic issues come to light as we consider features of the composed blended space. In the blend, four anthropomorphic clay figures sit astride a single equine figure, pictorially representing the Four Horsemen of the Apocalypse quite differently from the way they are represented in the Apocalypse space. This is due, in part, to material constraints imposed by the Presentation space, a mental space that determines final material shape of the statue. That is to say, conceptual integration in this blend works optimally only if the representations can be compressed into one tightly integrated form. Presenting four figures astride one horse satisfies this integration constraint because it makes efficient use of the Presentation space to present an integrated scene. Moreover, the viewer's attempt to satisfy the good reason (relevance) constraint might result in the construction of a mapping between the integrated horse-and-riders scene as a snapshot of a singular, coordinated activity.

Satisfying the integration constraint entails considerable metonymic tightening, such that the Four Horsemen of the Apocalypse can only afford to ride one horse. As in many of the examples discussed above, conformity to the integration principle comes at the expense of a violation of the topology principle. In the blend, the precise allegorical interpretation of the four horsemen is not important, and the metonymic relationship between color and symbolized evil (i.e. the coupling of "red" with "war") obtaining in the Apocalypse space is incidental in the blended space. In Schreckengost's sculpture, the color correspondences occur only incidentally. 'Whiteness', for instance, is not a property of the horse but of three riders: Death's face, Hitler's and Mussolini's head and arms) and their accoutrements (i.e. the Japanese flag). Similarly, 'paleness' is not a property of the horse but of Mussolini. In the composed blend, the color-horse-rider topology from the Apocalypse space gets metonymically "loosened," suggesting that such color metonymy functions in this CIN as incidental topology (see Fauconnier & Turner 1998).

Above, we focused on the material conditions governing the composition of a conceptual blend made manifest in a medium requiring great economy of space. Below we complete our analysis by considering the referential import of the figures themselves. In our analysis, three input spaces feed the completed blend.

Apocalypse Space
===========
Conquest
White Horse
War
Red Horse
Plague
Pale Horse
Famine
Black Horse
Time: End of Time
Goal: End of Humanity

Axis Space
====
Germany
Hitler
Italy
Mussolini

Japan
Hirohito
Time: 1942
Goal: World Domination

Death Space
====
Figure of Death
(i.e. Grim Reaper)
Goal: Cause Death

Blended Space
====
Hitler
Mussolini
Hirohito
Japanese Flag
Figure of Death
Missile
Horse
Time: 1942
Goal: World Domination and End of Humanity

The Axis Powers space is structured gradually as the viewer identifies the figures in the statue as Adolf Hitler, Benito Mussolini, and Emperor Hirohito. In mental spaces nomenclature, each clay figure from the Presentation space maps onto each referent in the Axis Powers space by a similarity connector. Once this iconic relationship is established, viewers produce a value-role mapping as each is construed as the leader of his respective country: *Hitler* is *Leader of Germany*, *Mussolini* is *Leader of Italy*, and *Hirohito* is *Emperor of Japan*. The Axis Powers space represents the figures as intentional agents acting in coordination with one another. In this space, each leader stands metonymically for each nation, which, in turn, is understood as part of a corporate entity: a political alliance. Interpreters familiar with modern European history will access relevant background knowledge about the Axis nations, such as the fact that the first 1936 alliance between Germany and Italy (known as the Rome-Berlin Axis) was followed by a second 1940 alliance with Japan and, tangentially with Hungary, Finland, Bulgaria, and Romania. In the Axis Powers space, the individual nations act as one group.

With the blended construal, the formal features of the sculpture take on new significance. For example, the interpreter may understand the referent scene as an alliance wherein the single horse stands for the Axis Powers, and the singular, coordinated event stands for the intentions and actions of each nation under the alliance. In the blend, but in none of the input spaces, riding the horse stands for the sustained, coordinated effort of the three principal nations to conquer the world, an inference licensed by the LEADER FOR NATION metonymy. Consequently, the interpreter does not only see Hitler, Mussolini, and Hirohito riding the horse, she sees Germany, Italy, and Japan acting together in a military alliance.

Although the statue involves integration of conceptual structure from the Apocalypse space with that in the Axis Powers space, three of the four horses from the Apocalypse Input are omitted from the blended space. This occurs because of positive pressure to accommodate structure from the Axis Powers space, as well as an absence of pressure to preserve the precise topology of the Apocalypse space. In the blend, as in the Axis space it projects to, the corporate actions of the Axis powers manifest all the evils of the apocalypse in one political alliance. The image of the three axis leaders riding a single horse in the blend can be mapped onto their coordinated actions in the military alliance. Moreover, while the knowledge that the four horsemen of the apocalypse herald the end of the world is important for producing the inferential implications of the blend, the establishment of a precise mapping between particular leaders and particular horsemen of the apocalypse is not. Consequently, there is no need to preserve the metonymic mapping between horse color and personified evil, noted above in our discussion of conformity to the good reason (relevance) constraint.

The blend represents world conquest in terms of horseback riding, thus compressing the complex chain of events involving millions of people to a much more human scale activity involving four people and a horse. Moreover, the completed blend presents a dynamic event whereby the Axis powers ride the horse of the apocalypse. The completed blend also takes on a distinct temporal dimension, wherein the activities of the horse and the horsemen are playing out in 1942. At this point, the meaning of the sculpture's base takes on new significance. With respect to the Presentation space the base is purely functional, allowing the sculptor to display his figures with proper perspective. But once the interpreter recognizes that the base is the entire Northern hemisphere, she completes the blend in which the leaders of the Axis nations are currently conquering the entire Northern hemisphere, which, in effect, stands for Western civilization itself.

We have chosen to deal lastly with the most salient figure in the sculpture: Death. In the sculpture, Death wears a German uniform, and appears to be the figure actually riding the horse (the others appear as passengers). The interpreter recognizes the figure as Death because its face appears as a skull, thus prompting the well-established metonymic compression of cause and effect, where the effect of corporal decomposition comes to stand for its own cause, death. As Turner (1987, 1991) has noted, the figure of the Grim Reaper is an example of the GENERIC IS SPECIFIC mapping (i.e., Death heralds the death of an individual). The mere presence of death among these figures heralds the death of the West as we know it, a very salient and plausible scenario in 1942. The introduction of Death as the fourth horsemen comes about by virtue of metonymic attribution to Death of elements from other mental spaces in the blend. In our account, the presence of Death in the Apocalypse space automatically opens a mental space for representations of Death as the Grim Reaper, the common representation of death in Judeo-Christian lore.

It would be odd, however, to represent Death with his traditional priestly cowl, robe, and scythe. Instead, Schreckengost represents him in a German uniform, carrying a missile in his right hand. It seems that to bring in wholesale the figure of Death means violating the unpacking constraint, insofar as typical personifications of Death space come "packaged" with the features just described. In this instance, violating the unpacking constraint satisfies the good reason constraint. A priestly cowl and scythe do not have the same degree of geopolitical relevance in 1942 as a German uniform and bomb do. The fact that Death has to be wearing something means that clothing and accessories can be projected from any mental space in the network.

Further, Death's appearance exploits metonymic relations established in the Axis Powers space, such that *military uniform* and *bomb* evoke both *instruments of war* and *effects of the war*. Considered alone, each of these elements has the potential to metonymically evoke various aspects of war. The military uniform, for example, is a salient part of the soldier's appearance; the destructive effects of a bomb are a salient aspect of its intentional construction; and death is a salient side effect of war. Moreover, when presented together in an integrated scene, each potential metonymic interpretation serves to reinforce the others so that Death, the German soldier, serves as a cause-effect compression of the instruments of war with the fatal effects of war. In fact, besides satisfying the relevance constraint, the depiction of Death, the German soldier, helps to optimize the integration principle.

How? We already know that Schreckengost has to choose a fourth horseman to complete his allegorical allusion, but unless he is going to introduce, for instance, the leader of Hungary or Romania or Bulgaria or Finland (none of whom are particularly notorious), he must choose a figure that does not violate the topology of the Axis Powers space. Stalin, for instance, would have been an appropriately menacing choice (even in 1942), but would have disintegrated the corporate image, since Stalin and Russia were enemies to the Axis nations. Choosing the personification of Death as the fourth horseman (i) is appropriately menacing, (ii) preserves specific topology of the Apocalypse space, and (iii) does not violate the topological relations recruited from the Axis Powers space.

This brings us to the central ambiguity of the piece. Who is responsible for the apocalypse? Like Death, the four horsemen are carrying out a divine plan for the end of the world. In the Judeo-Christian tradition, especially, Death is personified as a herald of death, and its heralding is understood to be the proximate cause of an individual's death. In other words, Death is not acting of his own volition (in fact, it is not clear that Death has any volition at all), it is merely acting out a divine mandate. But, is the interpreter to suppose that Hitler, Hirohito, and Mussolini, as agents of the apocalypse, are also executing a divine plan? Schreckengost's own commentary suggests as much, when he writes, "In the Four Horsemen of the Apocalypse … I saw a strange resemblance to the four beasts let loose on the world today" (Adams 2000: 61).

References to the four beasts, then, refer to the leaders, with Death representing the results of their actions; however, Schreckengost's use of the quasi-modal verb phrase "let loose" suggests a more powerful entity permitting them to act, lifting the barrier that holds them from the rest of the world. That an external and more powerful entity is being referred to is not in question. What is in question is what or who is the ultimate instigator of these events? Is it God? Or, is it the sum total of human actions – including World War I, the Treaty of Versailles, the collapse of the Weimar Republic in 1933, the United States territorial control over Hawaii, Chamberlain's policy of appeasement, and so on – that brought forth these beasts? Or, is it some combination of human folly and divine retribution? All of these are plausible interpretations for metaphoric and metonymic mappings.

As complexity increases, trade-offs between optimality principles become inevitable. Comprehending Schreckengost's sculpture involves maintaining certain topological relations from the Apocalypse and Axis Powers spaces such that a total of four horsemen appear and that three of them represent the leaders of the Axis Powers nations. The final blend integrates the biblical and the historical by preserving these topological relations. However, other topological relations, such as the precise analogical mappings between horses color, personified evil as rider, and political figure, are not preserved in the blend. The overriding constraints in this example are integration and relevance as the artist strives to present an integrated scenario whose connections to the other input spaces in the network are easily apprehended.

## 7. Conclusion

As a general model of meaning construction, blending theory posits a small set of partially compositional processes that operate on and constrain a diverse range of semantic and pragmatic phenomena from many different sign systems. Our purpose in this essay was to show how metonymy operates over diverse instances of conceptual blending, and to explore its role in the satisfaction of competing optimality principles during comprehension. We suggested that metonymic language refers to compressed elements in blended spaces and that conventional metonymies help speakers to unpack mappings from the compressed element in a blended space to its various counterparts in other spaces in the network. For example, conventional metonymies help us to understand that the *horn* in *blowing your own horn* maps onto both the speaker and the object of praise. We also suggested that metonymic mappings might help sustain a metaphoric blend even when, as in Hemingway's sympathetic portrait of the aging artist, the mapping schema shifts in violation of the web constraint. Similarly, some of the other optimality principles, such as the relevance constraint, exploit metonymic inference to facilitate integration, but do so by concomitantly preserving topology at higher levels of abstraction, as when the figure of Death trades its usual robe and cowl for a German uniform in Schreckengost's apocalyptic fantasy.

These analyses suggest that meaningful acts are not always supported by orderly structures with neat analogical mappings between domains, but, rather, unruly, ad hoc, conglomerations that, nonetheless, adhere to a few basic principles which Fauconnier and Turner have labeled optimality constraints. By focusing on expressions that employ both metaphor and metonymy, we have attempted to show how the two sorts of mappings can be used to combine structure in novel ways. Though such examples often violate the topology principle, that is, the pressure to preserve shared relational structure, they do so in order to promote the construction of an integrated mental scene that minimizes working memory demands and is useful for the projection of inferences. While the details of these analyses are rather far afield from other approaches to pragmatics, the core observation is remarkably consistent with the fundamental tenet of relevance theory in that speakers pursue the maximum cognitive effects that can be derived from the least cognitive effort. In general, the presence of metonymic connections allows us to maintain connections between networks of mental spaces comprised of opportunistic juxtapositions of conceptual structure from distally related domains that, nonetheless, appear to be important for reasoning. Understanding the role metonymy plays in this process is thus crucial for understanding how human beings make meaningful things.

## References

Adams, H. (2000). *Viktor Schreckengost and 20th-Century Design*. Seattle: University of Washington Press.

Anderson, John R. (1983). *The Architecture of Cognition*. Hillsdale, NJ: Lawrence Erlbaum.

Barcelona, Antonio (2000). On the plausibility of claiming a metonymic motivation for conceptual metaphor. In *Metaphor and Metonymy at the Crossroads: A Cognitive Perspective* [Topics in English Linguistics 30], A. Barcelona (Ed.), 31–58. Berlin and New York: Mouton de Gruyter.

Brugman, Claudia (1990). What is the invariance hypothesis? *Cognitive Linguistics, 1*, 257–266.

Coulson, Seana (2000). *Semantic Leaps*. Cambridge: Cambridge University Press.

Coulson, Seana & Oakley, Todd (2000). Blending basics. *Cognitive Linguistics, 11*(3/4), 1–22.

Fauconnier, Gilles (1994). *Mental Spaces: Aspects of Meaning Construction in Natural Language*. Cambridge: Cambridge University Press.

Fauconnier, Gilles (1997). *Mappings in Thought and Language*. Cambridge: Cambridge University Press.

Fauconnier, Gilles & Turner, Mark (1998). Conceptual integration networks. *Cognitive Science, 22*(2), 133–187.

Fauconnier, Gilles & Turner, Mark (2000a). Compression and global insight. *Cognitive Linguistics, 11*(3/4), 283–304.

Fauconnier, Gilles & Turner, Mark (2000b). Metaphor, metonymy, and binding. In A. Barcelona (Ed.), *Metaphor and Metonymy at the Crossroads: A Cognitive Perspective* [Topics in English Linguistics 30] (pp. 133–145). Berlin and New York: Mouton de Gruyter.

Fauconnier, Gilles & Turner, Mark (2002). *The Way We Think*. New York: Basic Books.

Gentner, Dedre & Markman, A. B. (1997). Structure mapping in analogy and similarity. *American Psychologist, 52*, 45–56.

Goossens, Louis (2000). Patterns of meaning extension, parallel chaining, subjectification, and modal shifts. In A. Barcelona (Ed.), *Metaphor and Metonymy at the Crossroads: A Cognitive Perspective* [Topics in English Linguistics 30] (pp. 149–169). Berlin and New York: Mouton de Gruyter.

Gibbs, Raymond W., Jr. (1994). *The Poetics of Mind: Figurative Thought, Language, and Understanding*. Cambridge: Cambridge University Press.

Gibbs, Raymond W., Jr. (2000). Making good psychology out of blending theory. *Cognitive Linguistics, 11*, 347–358.

Hofstadter, Douglas (1995). *Fluid Concepts and Creative Analogies: Computer Models of the Fundamental Mechanisms of Thought*. New York: Basic Books.

Holyoak, Keith & Thagard, Paul (1995). *Mental Leaps: Analogy in Creative Thought*. Cambridge, MA, and London: The MIT Press

Lakoff, George (1990). The invariance hypothesis: Is abstract reason based on image schemas? *Cognitive Linguistics, 1*, 39–74.

Lakoff, George (1993). The contemporary theory of metaphor. In A. Ortony (Ed.), *Metaphor and Thought* (pp. 202–251). Cambridge: Cambridge University Press.

Lakoff, George & Turner, Mark (1989). *More Than Cool Reason: A Field Guide to Poetic Metaphor*. Chicago and London: The University of Chicago Press.

Langacker, Ronald W. (1987). *Foundations of Cognitive Grammar, Vol. 1: Theoretical Prerequisites*. Stanford, CA: Stanford University Press.

Langacker, Ronald W. (2000). *Grammar and Conceptualization* [Cognitive Linguistics Research 14]. Berlin and New York: Mouton de Gruyter.

Miller, George (1957). The magical number seven, plus or minus two. *The Psychological Review, 63*, 81–97.

Nunberg, Geoffrey (1978). *The pragmatics of reference*. Bloomington: Indiana University Linguistics Club.

Nunberg, Geoffrey (1995). Transfer of meaning. *Journal of Semantics, 12*, 109–132.

Oakley, Todd (in preparation). *A Grammar of Attention*.

Panther, Klaus-Uwe & Radden, Günter (Eds.). (1999). *Metonymy in Language and Thought* [Human Cognitive Processing 4]. Amsterdam and Philadelphia: Benjamins.

Pelyvás, Péter (2000). Metaphorical extension of *may* and *must* into the epistemic domain. In A. Barcelona (Ed.), *Metaphor and Metonymy at the Crossroads: A Cognitive Perspective* [Topics in English Linguistics 30] (pp. 233–250). Berlin and New York: Mouton de Gruyter.

Radden, Günter & Kövecses, Zoltán (1999). Towards a theory of metonymy. In K.-U. Panther & G. Radden (Eds.), *Metonymy in Language and Thought* (pp. 17–59). Amsterdam and Philadelphia: Benjamins.

Sperber, Dan & Wilson, Deirdre (1995). *Relevance: Communication and Cognition*. Oxford: Blackwell.

Talmy, Leonard (2000). *Toward a Cognitive Semantics, Vols. 1 and 2*. Cambridge, MA, and London: The MIT Press.

Turner, Mark (1987). *Death is the Mother of Beauty: Mind, Metaphor, Criticism*. Chicago and London: The University of Chicago Press.

Turner, Mark (1990). Aspects of the invariance hypothesis. *Cognitive Linguistics, 1*, 247–255.

Turner, Mark (1991). *Reading Minds: The Study of English in the Age of Cognitive Science*. Princeton: Princeton University Press.

# The case for a metonymic basis of pragmatic inferencing

## Evidence from jokes and funny anecdotes*

Antonio Barcelona

### 1. Introduction

The study of pragmatic inference has attracted linguists and language philosophers for a long time, as a way of overcoming the limitations of a strictly "logical" approach to the investigation of linguistic meaning. Speech act theory and the theory of cooperative maxims (Grice 1975) greatly advanced our understanding of the way in which linguistic communication operates. Relevance Theory (Sperber & Wilson 1986/1995), which privileges – as a sort of "supermaxim" – the principle of *relevance*, has taken this understanding to a very high degree of sophistication.

Jokes and funny anecdotes, especially those that place heavy demands on the listener's inferencing work, are particularly interesting, both for the pragmaticist and for the cognitive linguist. Indeed, the study of humor has attracted the attention of pragmaticists. Victor Raskin (1985: 103) has applied semantic script theory and Gricean maxims to the study of humor, proposing a specific set of "humor maxims":

| | | |
|---|---|---|
| (1) | Quantity: | Give exactly as much information as is necessary for the joke. |
| | Quality: | Say only what is compatible with the world of the joke. |
| | Relation: | Say only what is relevant to the joke. |
| | Manner: | Tell the joke efficiently. |

Attardo (1990) says that what a speaker does by telling a joke is to violate, not just flout or exploit, a normal conversational maxim. But, Attardo claims, when he does so, he is also being cooperative, because he expects his listeners to switch to a "humor mode" once the punch-line of the joke has been reached.

Grice noted that by violating one of his "standard" maxims the speaker "will be liable to mislead" (1975: 49). And, in Attardo's view, this is exactly what happens in a straightforward interpretation of the text of a joke right before the punch-line; the punch-line defeats this interpretation and the hearer then has to seek an alternative interpretation. To accomplish this, the speaker replaces the normal version of the maxims by Raskin's special set of humor maxims. In this process, he is normally helped by the speaker's cooperative attitude – a faint smile at the right moment, a wink, etc. So joke production and understanding is a kind of cooperative behavior, although it necessarily violates standard conversational maxims. The jokes and anecdotes analyzed below constitute good examples of this cooperative behavior. In one of the anecdotes ("The ironic doctor"), the real punch line, however, consists in the fact that one of the characters fails to get the ironic intent of the doctor's reply.

Attardo claims that the fact that the Gricean maxims of relevance and quantity are necessarily violated in every joke seems to be evidence of the correctness of Relevance Theory (the other three maxims, quality, quantity, and manner being subsumed under relevance); this necessary violation of quantity and relevance also seems to support Horn's (1984) proposal to reduce the maxims to two super-maxims 'Q' and 'R'.

Marín Arrese (1998) locates the main factor motivating a joke in the incongruity of scripts, the "clash of worlds," that, once it is clear to the listener that a "joke-frame" has been created, leads to the operation of a new cooperative principle.

My position will be neutral as regards the number or the status of these communicative principles in humor understanding in the analyses that I will be presenting below, since the goal of this paper is *not* to discuss the correctness of the positions maintained by pragmaticists on these issues. I will simply list *some* of the inferences that appear to become available to the listener of a joke or a funny anecdote. However, I agree with relevance theorists that the list of inferences to be drawn from an utterance is often open-ended (Wilson 1997). I also agree with both Raskin's and Attardo's insightful claim that humor comprehension involves some kind of adjustment or change from the cognitive script or frame (in Fillmore's (1985) sense) that supports the initial, straightforward interpretation of the text of a joke right before the punch-line, to a new script or frame. Therefore, I will also indicate for each joke which type of frame adjustment takes place in it.

The goal of this paper is to study the role of metonymy in pragmatic inferencing. The comprehension of a joke and of similar types of discourse often involves complex inferential chains. The wonderful fact is that people often activate such chains at lightning speed. How is this possible? Communicative principles like those put forward by pragmaticists, doubtless reduce the cognitive effort required to arrive at the intended interpretation. But in many if not all cases, these inferential processes are facilitated by pre-existing metonymic connections in a cognitive frame (Panther 1994; Panther & Thornburg 1998; Thornburg & Panther 1997), or by pre-existing metaphorical connections across frames. Metonymic connections, in particular, seem to lie at the very heart of pragmatic inferencing, as I hope to show by means of the present paper.

## 2. Metonymy

The standard cognitive linguistic notion of metonymy presents a number of problems (referentiality as a necessary requirement for metonymy, "stand-for" relationship, mapping, distinction from metaphor, degrees of metonymicity, etc.), whose discussion is beyond the scope of this paper. In the rest of this section I briefly present a Cognitive Linguistic view of metonymy that avoids most of these problems and lists its fundamental properties.[1]

The value of metonymy for pragmatic inferencing can only be appreciated if one accepts a view of conceptual metonymy that frees it from necessarily being referential (Kövecses & Radden 1998; Barcelona, in press), and which stresses its nature as a fundamental cognitive model. I will offer below a few examples of non-referential metonymies.

The term 'metonymy' is used in cognitive linguistics to cover very different phenomena, including "classical" or "prototypical" examples of linguistic referential metonymies for individuals, "clear" or "typical" instances of referential metonymies with non-individuals as targets or of "clear" or "typical" non-referential metonymies, and relatively "peripheral" instances of metonymy. I will follow in this article a broad definition of metonymy capable of capturing what all of these different phenomena have in common. I call this the *schematic* definition of metonymy, which contains the necessary and sufficient conditions for metonymicity:

(2) A metonymy is a mapping of a cognitive domain, the source, onto another domain, the target. Source and target are in the same functional domain and are linked by a pragmatic function, so that the target is mentally activated. (Barcelona 2002:246)

Metonymies are "mappings" in the sense that the source domain is connected to the target domain by imposing a perspective on it. That is, the target domain is understood "from" the perspective imposed by the source. This is one of the reasons why, e.g. personal pronouns are not necessarily metonymies, even though their abstract meaning (e.g. 'third person, singular') might anaphorically "activate" their antecedents: they are not mapped onto them in this sense. Saying that metonymy is a type of mapping is more adequate than saying that it is a "stand-for" relationship, since the source does not necessarily substitute unambiguously for the target: it merely activates it from a given perspective.[2]

To illustrate the above points, let us examine the sentence *Picasso is not easy to appreciate*. In this sentence, PICASSO'S ARTISTIC WORK is a metonymic target, and the activation of this target is carried out *from* the source *Picasso*, in his role as ARTIST, with the result that the hearer/reader is invited to conceptualize this artistic work primarily as the outcome of Picasso's artistic genius – as an extension of his personality –, other aspects of this work being backgrounded.

Another fundamental property of metonymy is that the source maps onto and activates the target in virtue of the experiential (hence pragmatic) link between the roles each of them performs in the same "functional domain" (i.e. a frame in Fillmore's terms, or an ICM in Lakoff's terms).[3] Fauconnier (1997: 11) regards metonymy as a "pragmatic function mapping"; and Lakoff (personal communication) claims that in metonymy the activation of source role X brings about the activation of target role Y, both in the same conceptual frame or ICM. In the previous example, the role ARTIST (which is a domain in the ARTISTIC ACTIVITY frame) is pragmatically linked to the role ART WORK (another domain in the same frame), so that activation of the former normally leads to activation of the latter.

The schematic definition of conceptual metonymy in (2) is based on Kövecses and Radden's (1998: 39) general definition of conceptual metonymy, but it is more constrained than theirs. In Barcelona (in press), a set of additional specific definitions is proposed for the other general kinds of metonymy represented by each of the various different phenomena ("purely schematic," "typical," "prototypical"), which are covered by the schematic definition. Some examples of the range of phenomena covered by the definition in (2) are (3), (4), (5), (6) and (7).

(3) *This book* weighs two kilograms.

(4) *This book* is highly instructive.

(5) *Belgrade* did not sign the Paris agreement.

(6) She's just a pretty *face*.

(7) He walked *with drooping shoulders*. He had lost his wife.

In example (3), the verb form *weighs* acts as a trigger to activate the PHYSICAL OBJECT sub-domain within the source domain BOOK. That is, the whole domain BOOK is mapped onto its sub-domain PHYSICAL OBJECT, which is thus mentally activated. In (4), the whole domain BOOK is mapped onto its sub-domain SEMANTIC CONTENT, which is thus mentally activated. Example (3) would be a "peripheral" or "purely schematic" instance of metonymy, and (4) would be closer to typical metonymies.[4] As we can see from these examples, metonymy is, under the definition in (2), a very common, in fact omnipresent, phenomenon in most linguistic expressions. This broad conception of metonymy is, in fact, not exceptional in Cognitive Linguistics. A similar conception underlies, for instance, Langacker's notion of "active zone" metonymies (Langacker 1993, 1999).[5]

Example (5) is a "prototypical" instance of metonymy, as it is referential and as it has an individual (the Yugoslavian government is a collective individual) as target. Examples (6) and (7) are simply "typical" metonymies as they are not referential; furthermore, the target in (7) is not an individual, but a property (an emotional state). What is conventionally believed to be a possible behavioral effect of sadness (walking with drooping shoulders) activates its cause (the emotion itself), so that an automatic inference is that the person exhibiting this bodily behavior is sad.

## 3. Analysis of a sample of jokes and anecdotes

I will start with relatively simple examples and then I will present a case that requires extensive inferential work on the part of the reader/listener.

### 3.1 The pediatrician and the innocent young mother

This anecdote is from a best-selling book on medical anecdotes (Arana 2000: 19). I have adapted it from its Spanish original. I hope it will also have an impact on speakers coming from other cultures.

Context

As part of what is known in medicine as *anamnesis* (recalling medically relevant facts), a pediatrician asks a young mother a number of routine questions about her two-month-old baby: pregnancy, birth, weight at birth, and vitality and vigor of the baby. With regard to the last point (vitality and vigor), the doctor asks a very simple question and gets a delightfully naive answer.

Text

Doctor: *And does your baby normally hold on tight to your breasts?*
Mother: *Oh, yes, doctor, just as if he were an adult!*

Some possible inferences:[6]

a. Meant and conveyed by the doctor:

   1. A baby's tight hold on its mother's breasts is a sign of vigor and vitality.

b. Meant and conveyed by the mother:

   2. A baby's holding on tight to its mother's breasts as tightly as an adult would (if breast-feeding) is a sign of extraordinary vigor and vitality.

c. Not meant but conveyed by the mother:

   3. *The mother frequently engages in sexual activity with adults.* (comic inference)

Frame adjustment

*Frame overlap, frame blend* and *frame shift.* The NURTURANCE frame unexpectedly overlaps with, and shifts to, the SEXUALITY frame via a blend of the NURTURANCE frame with the ADULTHOOD frame.

As Raskin (1979: 332) claims, "much of verbal humor depends on a partial or complete overlap of two or more scripts all of which are compatible with the joke-carrying text." I thus will distinguish in the ensuing analyses between "frame overlap" (partial overlap) and "frame blend" (complete overlap). Frame overlap takes place when in the conceptual world created by (part of) an utterance or a text two cognitive frames remain clearly distinct but are linked by means of a shared conceptual substructure; in the case at hand, NURTURANCE and SEXUALITY share a minor sub-frame or sub-domain: THE GRASPING BY A MALE OF A WOMAN'S BREASTS. Frame blend occurs when two mutually independent frames are fused into an imaginary mental scene, or mental space. Under the most likely interpretation of the above anecdote, the mother, in order to highlight her baby's vigor and vitality, merely intends to set up a counterfactual mental scene in which, when breast-feeding, her baby is simultaneously a baby and an adult.[7] In fact, both types of frame interaction can be handled as types of "blending" processes by Fauconnier and Turner's theory of conceptual integration.[8]

The result of frame overlap, of frame blend, or of their combination is normally a shift to the frame that provides the basis for the main inference of the joke or the funny story.

Metonymies guiding these inferences:

*Inference 1* arises on the basis of the metonymy BABY'S TIGHT HOLD ON MOTHER'S BREAST FOR BABY'S VITALITY (SYMPTOM FOR PHYSICAL STATE). This is an automatic metonymy within the NURTURANCE frame, which is the default frame for the doctor-mother dialogue: it is common knowledge that holding on firmly to their mother's breast is typical of healthy newborns. The doctor knows that his question will be interpreted as a question about the baby's health, and the mother correctly interprets it as such. The doctor assumes, and the mother follows, the inferential pathway suggested by this automatic metonymy.

*Inference 2* is an inference possibly meant and certainly conveyed by the mother. The ADULTHOOD frame is of course invoked by the mere mention of the term *adult*.[9] The blend between ADULTHOOD and NURTURANCE is jointly triggered by the grammatical construction *as if* + *NP* + *were* and the coreference between *your baby* and *he* in the dialogue. The main part of the inference, namely, the fact that the baby is *extraordinarily* vigorous, is facilitated by the metonymy linking ADULTHOOD (WHOLE) as a source, to (FULL) VIGOR (PART) as a target within the ADULTHOOD frame. (Full vigor is a defining property of adulthood, a part of it). This part of the inference to exceptional vigor is carried out in the blend in which the baby is at the same time an adult holding tightly to the mother's breast to feed.

*In inference 3,* the sub-inference that the woman engages in sexual activity with (male) adults arises on the basis of a metonymy that links the action consisting of (A [MALE] ADULT) TOUCHING A WOMAN'S BREAST (as CATEGORY MEMBER) to SEXUAL ACTIVITY (as CATEGORY). And the sub-inference "the mother knows how tightly male adults in general hold on to a woman's breast because she has (repeatedly) experienced it" (note the term *frequently* in the wording of inference 3 above) arises on the basis of a metonymy that maps KNOWLEDGE OF AN ACTION (as an EFFECT) onto A (REPEATED) EXPERIENCE OF IT (as a CAUSE).

Figure 1 represents synoptically the frame adjustments and the metonymic connections guiding the various inferences in the anecdote. The details of the blending process are not included, for the sake of brevity.[10]

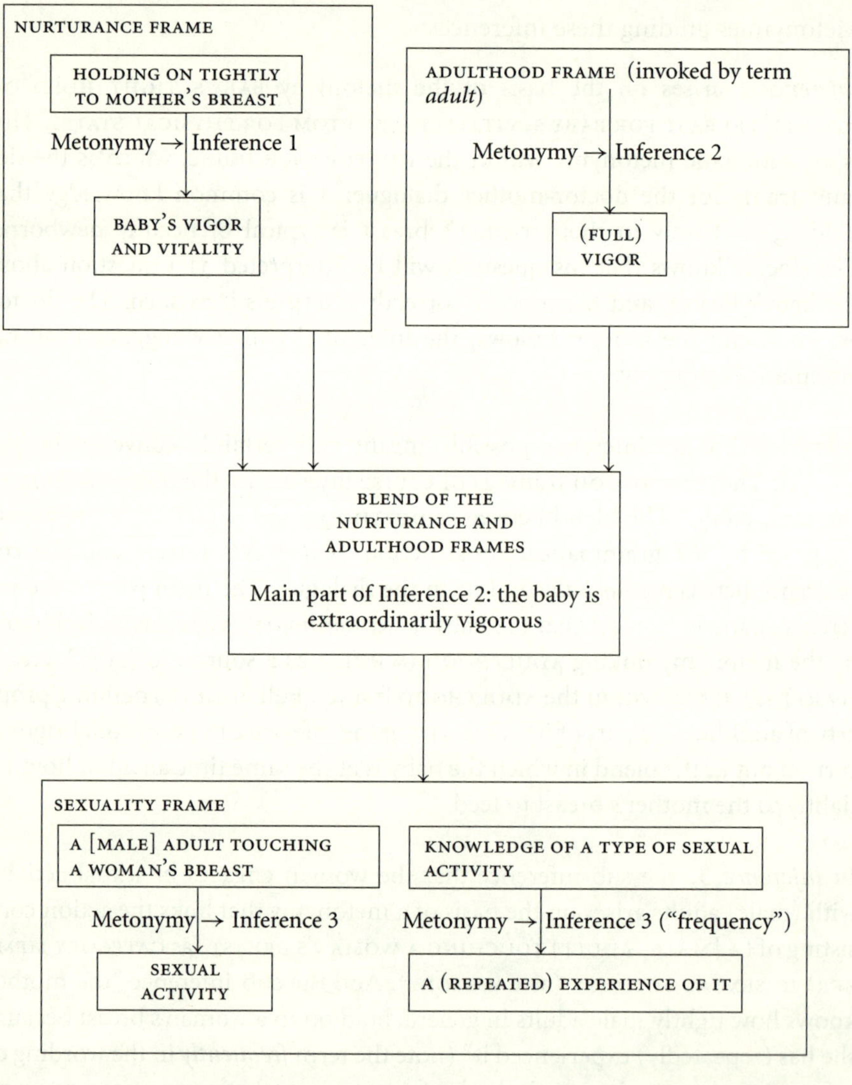


**Figure 1.** Frames and metonymies operating in the pediatrician-mother anecdote

### 3.2 The ironic doctor

This anecdote is also from Arana (2000: 22).

Context
The patient, a woman, is the type that never trusts a doctor. She asks an impolite question and receives an ironic reply, which she takes literally.

Text

Patient: *Excuse me, but have you been to medical school to get your M.D. degree?*
Doctor: *No, madam, I just got it at a lottery.*

(After this, the patient files a complaint writing, in all seriousness, that she cannot understand how a government-supported health center, "which is paid for with our tax money," has hired a doctor who obtained his degree at a lottery. As this case shows, the main thrust of an ironic remark may fail to be grasped by an obtuse addressee.)

Some possible inferences

a. Meant and conveyed by the patient:
   1. The patient has serious doubts about the doctor's qualifications.

b. Meant (ironically) and conveyed (literally) by the doctor:
   2. Doctors' degrees are won at lotteries.

c. Meant but not conveyed by the doctor:
   3. Believing that a doctor's degree can be won at lotteries is an absurd belief.
   4. Believing that a doctor's degree can be awarded to a person who did not go to medical school is an absurd belief.
   5. *The belief that a doctor can get his degree without attending a school of medicine is as absurd as the belief that a doctor can get his degree as a lottery prize.* (Main inference intended by the doctor.)

Frame adjustment
*Frame overlap*, *frame blend* and *frame shift*. The MEDICAL EDUCATION frame unexpectedly overlaps with the LOTTERY frame, both in the REALITY frame or mental space, to create a counterfactual blend of both frames, which, in the

frame of REALITY, invokes the ABSURDITY frame. The main inference is, thus, due to a shift to the latter frame. However, this shift, intended by the doctor, is not carried out by his literal-minded patient.

The MEDICAL EDUCATION and the LOTTERY frames are separately included in the REALITY supra-frame. But the blend of these frames that we find in this joke is inevitably confronted with the REALITY supra-frame or mental space, which shows that participating at a lottery is not equivalent to studying at a medical school as a condition for obtaining a medical degree; therefore, inference 2 is a counterfactual proposition in REALITY space. And when one reasons within the reality frame, this blend automatically invokes the notion of *absurdity*. One of the things that enters the ABSURDITY frame is the belief in the truth of counterfactual situations.[11] Two instances of this belief, which metonymically activate the whole frame, are the belief that doctor's degrees are given out at lotteries, and the belief that a doctor's degree can be awarded to a person who did not go to medical school.

Metonymies guiding these inferences:

*Inference 1* arises on the basis of the metonymy CONDITION FOR RESULT. This metonymy operates within the MEDICAL EDUCATION frame. A pre-condition for obtaining a medical degree is attending medical school. If the fulfillment of the condition is questioned, so is the fulfillment of the result.

*Inference 2* arises on the basis of the metonymy RESULT FOR CONDITION. Winning a doctor's degree at a lottery (result) stands for its condition (the fact that medical degrees can be earned just by buying a lottery ticket). This metonymy, thus, operates within a counterfactual blend between the MEDICAL EDUCATION and the LOTTERY frames. The blend is possible because there is an overlap (a shared sub-schema) between both frames: both exhibit a connection between a (pre)condition and a result.

*Inference 3* arises on the basis of the metonymy ENTITY FOR ITS CONVENTIONAL PROPERTY. The entity here is a propositional entity (the plainly counterfactual belief that doctor's degrees can be given out as lottery prizes); the "defining property" here is a property (absurdity) that is definitionally predicated of this entity in reality space; this property is mentally activated by the mental activation of the entity. As a result the ABSURDITY frame is also invoked.[12]

*Inference 4* arises, on the one hand, on the basis of the same metonymy, ENTITY FOR ITS CONVENTIONAL PROPERTY. The entity here is a propositional entity, i.e. the belief (a plainly counterfactual belief) that doctors can get their degree without going to medical school. And the conventional property of this belief is again ABSURDITY.

*Inference 5* arises on the basis of metonymy-based inferences 3 and 4: if the belief that medical degrees are obtained at lotteries is absurd, and the belief that you can become a doctor without going to medical school is absurd, then both beliefs are equally absurd.

Figure 2 illustrates the foregoing analysis. It should be read from its bottom-most part upwards. The LOTTERY frame is reproduced here to show

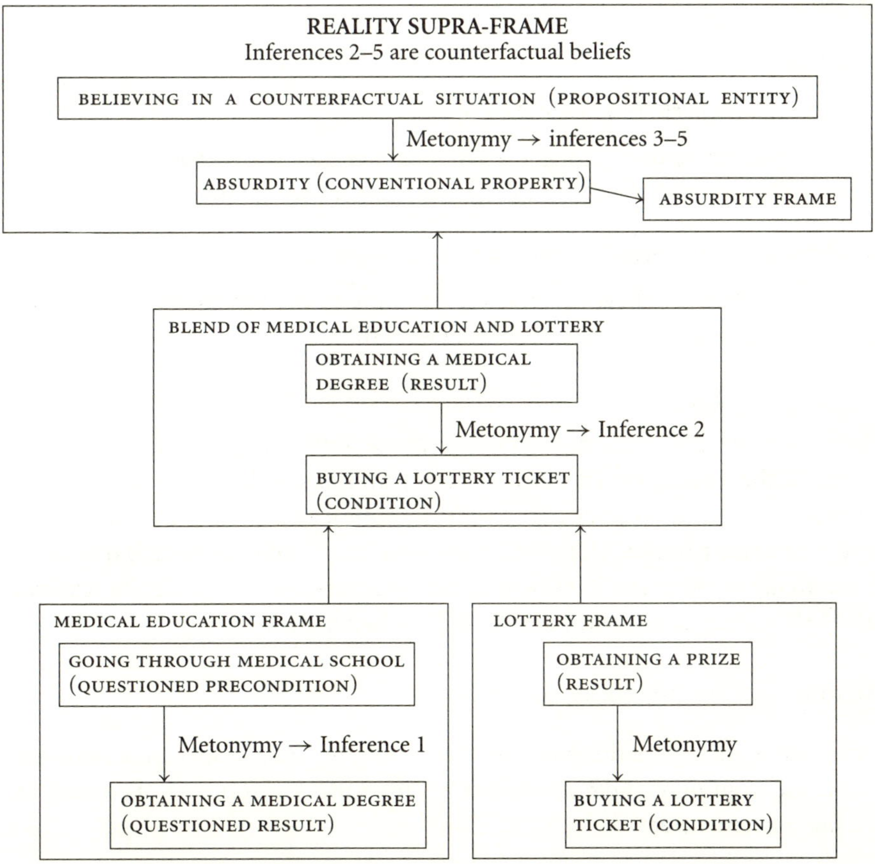


**Figure 2.** Frames and metonymies operating in the ironic doctor anecdote

that the same metonymic connection between a result and a condition is preserved in the blend of the two frames.

### 3.3 Clubs and kindness

The following joke attributed to W. C. Fields is taken from Attardo (1990: 355).

Context
No context is provided

Text

Speaker A: *Do you believe in clubs for young men?*
Speaker B: *Only when kindness fails.*

Inferences

a. Meant and *perhaps conveyed* by Speaker A:[13]

   1. Speaker A wants to know whether Speaker B believes in the convenience, usefulness, etc. of (social) clubs for young men.

b. Meant and (eventually) conveyed by Speaker B:

   2. Speaker B believes in the use of clubs to hit young men only when kindness fails in case of conflict with them.

Frame adjustment
*Frame overlap* due to homonymy and *frame shift*. The CLUB frame (a sub-frame of the SOCIAL INSTITUTIONS frame) overlaps with the CONFLICT frame (a sub-frame of the HUMAN INTERACTION frame), and the interpretation shifts to the CONFLICT frame. The overlap between CLUB and CONFLICT is due to the homonymy of the form *clubs*, which can correspond to two different lexemes: 'club-1' (a social institution) and 'club-2' (a heavy stick).[14]

Metonymies guiding these inferences

*Inference 1* arises on the basis of the metonymy ARGUMENT FOR PROPOSITION: the argument *clubs* stands for a whole proposition such as 'clubs are useful/convenient/etc.'[15]

*Inference 2* arises on the basis of a number of metonymies.

First, there is a PART OF A FRAME FOR A WHOLE FRAME metonymy. This metonymy is triggered by the word *kindness*, i.e., KINDNESS, a possible behavior in the HUMAN INTERACTION frame, activates the whole frame. The HUMAN INTERACTION frame contains the CONFLICT frame as a sub-frame.

Second, the words *when kindness fails* trigger another PART FOR WHOLE metonymy but this time within the CONFLICT frame, which is already implicit in the HUMAN INTERACTION frame: STRATEGY (IN A CONFLICT) FOR CONFLICT. Acting with kindness towards an opponent is one of the possible alternative strategies in a conflict. The mention of the strategy, and what is more, of the possibility that it may fail, invokes the whole CONFLICT frame.

Third, once the CONFLICT frame is activated, *failure* of the "soft" strategy (acting with kindness to the opponent) invokes the application of the "tough" strategy (exerting violence on the opponent), because this failure is the condition for the application of the alternative strategy. The underlying metonymy is a CONDITION FOR RESULT (PART FOR PART) metonymy within the CONFLICT frame: THE FAILURE OF THE SOFT STRATEGY STANDS FOR THE APPLICATION OF THE TOUGH STRATEGY.

Fourth, once the APPLICATION OF THE TOUGH STRATEGY sub-frame is activated, of the two lexemes conventionally sharing the morpho-phonological sequence /klʌb/ (and the morpho-graphological sequence <*club*>), the lexeme with a SOCIAL INSTITUTION sense is discarded, and the lexeme with the sense PHYSICAL OBJECT USED FOR HITTING is activated. This lexical and semantic shift is achieved on the basis of INSTRUMENT (club) for ACTION (hitting with a club), and on the basis of the metonymy TYPE (*i.e.* using a tough strategy) FOR TOKEN (hitting the opponent). Hitting the opponent is one of the possible tokens of a tough strategy. The re-interpretation of *clubs* thus brings about the specification of the tough strategy as the use of clubs (sticks) for hitting.

Given the complexity of the inferential chains in the previous joke and in the following anecdote (3.4), no figures have been provided illustrating the metonymic basis of the inferences and the connections among them, because such figures, though perfectly feasible, would be very complex and would, therefore, take up too much space.

## 3.4 A parliamentary repartee

### Context

The anecdote is usually reported as taking place in the mid-1930s in Spain, during a parliamentary session. An opposition M.P. concludes his savagely aggressive speech against the Prime Minister with a seriously offensive accusation. The M.P. has no evidence for his accusation; he merely intends to unsettle the Prime Minister. Yet the latter retorts very cleverly. His strategy consists of accepting, for the sake of irony, the truth of the literal interpretation of the M.P.'s utterance, thereby triggering a very different set of inferences.

Text
Opposition M.P. (referring to the Prime Minister): *But what can we expect, after all, of a man who wears silk underpants?*
The Prime Minister (rising calmly): *Oh, I would never have thought the Right Honorable's wife could be so indiscreet!*

Inferences:

a. Meant and conveyed by the opposition M.P.
   1. The Prime Minister is a homosexual.
   2. The Prime Minister is unfit for office.

b. Meant and conveyed by the Prime Minister.
   3. The M.P.'s wife shares a secret with the Prime Minister.
   4. She has told the M.P. the secret.
   5. She knows that the secret consists in the fact that the Prime Minister always wears silk underpants.
   6. *She has had a sexual affair with the Prime Minister, and is, thus, an adulteress* (main inference)

c. *Perhaps* meant and *perhaps* conveyed by the Prime Minister.
   7. The Prime Minister is, after all, despite his supposed dressing habits, not a homosexual.
   8. The M.P. is a cuckolded husband.
   9. The M.P. knew that he was a cuckolded husband before uttering his words.
   10. Through his words, the M.P. has publicly admitted that the Prime Minister is not a homosexual.
   11. Through his words, the M.P. has publicly admitted that he is a cuckolded husband.
   12. Through his words, the M.P. has publicly shown himself to be an utter fool.

Frame adjustment

*Frame overlap* and *frame shift*. The UNDERWEAR frame overlaps with the HOMOSEXUALITY frame. This frame, in turn, overlaps with the DISCRETION frame, which finally shifts to the ADULTERY, HETEROSEXUALITY, and STUPIDITY frames. That is, the M.P. implies that the Prime Minister is a homosexual, by accusing him of wearing silk underwear (HOMOSEXUALITY). And the Prime Minister attributes the knowledge of this fact to an indiscretion of the M.P.'s wife, thereby linking this information about his supposed homosexuality to the woman's indiscretion (DISCRETION frame). But then the most likely explanation for the M.P.'s wife's knowing such intimate details of the Prime Minister's life is that she has had a sexual affair with him, i.e., that she has been an adulteress, that her husband has been cuckolded (ADULTERY), and that the Prime Minister is a heterosexual (HETEROSEXUALITY). A further possible major inference resulting from the previous inferences is that the M.P. has acted very foolishly (STUPIDITY) by revealing these facts in Parliament.

Metonymies guiding these inferences

*Inference 1* is due to the metonymy BEHAVIOR (wearing silk underpants) FOR KINDS OF PEOPLE CONVENTIONALLY ASSOCIATED (in the Spain of the 1930s) WITH THAT BEHAVIOR (i.e. women or homosexuals).

*Inference 2* arises from the metonymy linking an ENTITY to one of its CONVENTIONAL PROPERTIES (women and homosexuals were then thought to be unfit for performing important social functions).

*Inference 3* arises on the basis of the metonymy RESULT (being discreet/indiscreet) FOR (PRE)CONDITION (knowing a secret). One can only be discreet/indiscreet if one knows a secret.

*Inference 4* arises on the basis of the metonymy CAUSE (the wife's indiscreet behavior) FOR EFFECT (the fact that the M.P. knows the secret). It also arises on the basis of another metonymy of the type RESULT (the fact that the M.P. has publicly revealed the secret) FOR PRECONDITION (knowing or having been told about the secret).[16]

*Inference 5* arises on the basis of the following metonymies:

ENTITY (the propositional entity consisting of the fact that the Prime Minister wears silk underpants) FOR ONE OF ITS CONVENTIONAL PROPERTIES (being secret). Information about a person's choice of underwear is considered private. This metonymy identifies the private information as the secret that the M.P.'s wife has imprudently disclosed.

FACT (knowing the underwear worn by a person) FOR ONE OF ITS CONVENTIONAL EXPLANATIONS (seeing the man undress). She has had access to this intimate information because she has seen him undress.

The first part of *inference 6* also arises on the basis of the metonymy FACT (seeing someone undress) FOR ONE OF ITS CONVENTIONAL EXPLANATIONS (having a sexual affair with that person). One of the explanations of the fact that a woman has seen a man undress is that she has had, or has been about to have, a sexual encounter with that man. The second part of this inference is due to the metonymy DEFINITION (a married woman having sex with a man other than her husband) FOR DEFINED (the behavioral category called ADULTERY). Spelling out the definitional properties of a category (of behavior, in this case) can automatically invoke the category.

*Inference 7* arises on the basis of the metonymy BEHAVIOR (having sex with a woman) FOR KINDS OF PEOPLE CONVENTIONALLY ASSOCIATED WITH THAT BEHAVIOR (heterosexuals). Note that this is the same metonymy that led to the offensive inference intended by the M.P. and listed above as inference 1, except with source and target specified by different domains. The Prime Minister thus seems to have, very skillfully, used exactly the same metonymy as the one used by the opposition M.P. to suggest exactly the opposite inference.

*Inference 8* arises on the basis of the metonymy DEFINITION (one's wife having a sexual affair with another man) FOR DEFINED (the category of cuckolded husbands).

*Inference 9* comes about on the basis of inferences 4, 5, 6 and 8, all of which contribute the defining properties of cuckoldry. Inference 4 is the most relevant of all as a *direct* basis for inference 9, since it makes clear that the M.P. knows the secret, spelled out in detail by Inferences 5, 6 and 8. From inference 4, inference 9 arises thanks to the metonymy KNOWING A FACT (knowing the secret) FOR KNOWING ITS SALIENT IMPLICATIONS (e.g. knowing that the M.P. is a cuckolded husband).

*Inferences 10 and 11* arise on the basis of a similar metonymy: STATING A FACT (stating the secret (publicly)) FOR STATING ITS SALIENT IMPLICATIONS (stating, among other implications, that the Prime Minister is not a homosexual and that the M.P. is a cuckolded husband).[17]

*Inference 12* arises on the basis of two metonymies:

MEMBER (stating publicly that one is a cuckolded husband) FOR CATEGORY (acting against one's interest). In the culture of the time, revealing publicly that one has been cuckolded was regarded as an instance (a "member") of the category "self-damaging behavior".

MEMBER (acting against one's interest) FOR CATEGORY (acting foolishly). Damaging oneself (especially if one is not aware of what one is doing) is an instance ("member") of the category "foolish behavior").

## 4. Conclusions

Metonymy has been shown, at least as far as the above sample of jokes and anecdotes is concerned, to be at the basis of *all* of the pragmatic inferences that can be drawn from these humorous pieces. One may disagree with the exact naming of the metonymies proposed above, but it is undeniable, in my view, that in each of them, the domain, concept or frame presented as *source* is normally a mental activator of the domain, concept or frame presented as target. Therefore, a general conclusion that emerges from this brief study is that conceptual metonymies often provide "ready-made" pointers towards plausible inferential pathways in the interpretation of a joke or an anecdote, and, in fact, in the interpretation of any other kind of discourse. These pointers, which are normally automatic, contribute greatly to the ease and speed of interpretation. A reader or hearer of these stories might have drawn other inferences in addition to the ones provided above. But my guess is that they would have been drawn on the basis of *some* metonymy. A similar claim is made by Coulson and Oakley (this volume), who stress the fundamental role of metonymy in maintaining connections between distant mental spaces in reasoning. Metonymies (and metaphors) also constrain the range of possible inferences to be drawn from an explicit proposition, a point clearly made by Ruiz de Mendoza (1997), and Ruiz de Mendoza and Pérez Hernández (this volume).

Metonymy thus seems to constitute the very *skeleton* of pragmatic inferencing. Now, does this mean that pragmatic inferencing can be reduced to metonymic reasoning? There are other important aspects of pragmatic inferencing that cannot simply be accounted for in terms of metonymic connections, but rather in terms of pragmatic principles and rules necessary for a complete understanding of pragmatic inferencing processes. My analyses of the inferences apparently occurring in the understanding of the jokes and anecdotes presented above have attempted to discover which clues or "pointers" the utterances in question provide for the comprehender, and it appears that the nature of these clues is metonymic in all cases. But I have not addressed the general principles that help hearers choose and navigate among several possible inferences based on the same utterance. These general pragmatic principles, studied particularly by scholars working in a relevance theoretic framework, cannot be reduced to metonymy. Therefore, my answer to this question is, at least for the time being, negative.

Finally, another important conclusion from this study is the further support it lends to the cognitive linguistic claim that metonymies have a substantive status as cognitive mechanisms. Note that one and the same metonymic principle or pattern (e.g. RESULT FOR CONDITION) may be accessed directly to derive very different specific inferences, as the sample analysis showed.[18] This is evidence of the stability of *conceptual* metonymies as part of our cognitive equipment. Therefore, even though the interpretation of a metonymic linguistic *expression* is often subject to general pragmatic principles, as Papafragou (1996) contends, these pragmatic principles are, as Ruiz de Mendoza (1998) convincingly argues in his critical comments on Papafragou, effectively implemented by means of independently motivated conceptual metonymies.

## Notes

* I am grateful to my anonymous reviewers for their useful suggestions and to the editors of the volume for their careful work.

1. I have discussed in detail most of these problems and properties, except for the "functional domain" and the "pragmatic link" notions (see below) in Barcelona (in press).

2. Most inference-prompting metonymies do not involve substitution of source by target, but activation of the latter by the former, as in Panther and Thornburg's example (this volume) *General Motors had to stop production*, which yields the implicature 'General Motors stopped production'. This implicature is prompted, according to Panther and Thornburg, by the metonymy OBLIGATION FOR ACTION FOR ACTION. As an anonymous reviewer of the present volume correctly points out, the target does not eliminate the source, but is rather "added" to the proposition. However, I support Panther and Thornburg's claim that this addition is prompted by the metonymic connection between source and target.

3. In Barcelona (n.d.) and Barcelona (2002) I have proposed that the cognitive domain mentioned in the definition should be a "functional cognitive domain" (i.e. a frame or ICM), and not just a taxonomic domain. In both papers, and in Barcelona (in press), I have also pro-

posed that the mapping in metonymy is unidirectional and *asymmetrical*, whereas the one in metaphor is unidirectional and *symmetrical*. By "symmetrical" I mean that each source element has in its frame a structurally equivalent role to its counterpart in the target (e.g., in the LOVE IS A JOURNEY metaphor, the lovers have a role in the "romantic love frame," which is structurally equivalent to the role of the travelers in the "journey frame").

4. The difference between "purely schematic" and "typical" metonymies lies in the fact that the target in the former is a "primary" domain or subdomain of the source, whereas the target in the latter is a comparatively more "secondary" domain or subdomain of the source, or is outside it, as in PART FOR WHOLE metonymies. In (3) PHYSICAL OBJECT is a primary subdomain in BOOK, whereas SEMANTIC CONTENT is comparatively a more secondary (or less primary) subdomain. Purely schematic, typical and prototypical metonymies constitute a continuum of metonymicity. Purely schematic metonymies are contextual semantic values occurring in the "literal" use of expressions, which points to the artificiality of the strict literal-figurative distinction. For details, see Barcelona (in press).

5. These two metonymies are "active zone" metonymies in which the "active zone" of the notion BOOK is different in each case.

6. The reader is reminded that the lists of inferences analyzed in the ensuing case studies does not exhaust the full set of the inferences that might be drawn on the basis of some metonymy. We should also distinguish, in principle, the inferences that seem to have been actually made by the direct participants in the stories, from those made by indirect participants (i.e. their observers) or by the listeners or readers of these stories, as they are narrated. I include in my analysis both types: the inferences *intended* or made by the actual direct participants, and those made by other participants, or by readers or listeners. Another important caveat is that the order in which the inferences are presented does not mean that they are necessarily arrived at sequentially. Nor by numbering do I commit myself to a specific real-time ordering of the inferences, even though this ordering appears to reflect the conceptual ordering among them, i.e., inference 1 below appears to set up one of the conceptual frames needed for inference 2, just as the latter sets up one of the frames needed for inference 3.

7. Under a slightly different interpretation, the mother intentionally blends the baby's vigor, vitality and eagerness to feed with the vigor, firm grasp of her breasts and desire of a sexually aroused adult. This less likely interpretation would not necessarily diminish the woman's naiveté (she may just have thought this blend an effective way of forcefully picturing her baby's strength, without thereby intending to convey the third inference).

8. See Turner and Fauconnier (1995) and Fauconnier (1997); see also Turner and Fauconnier (2000), and Coulson and Oakley (this volume) for the important role of metonymy in blending, and Barcelona 2000, for its basic role in metaphor.

9. This activation of a frame (a whole) by mentioning an item of its conventional vocabulary (a representative part) is in turn a ubiquitous metonymy (see Lakoff & Turner 1989: 108).

10. As stated above, what I call a "frame blend" in my analysis of this anecdote and in that of the other jokes and anecdotes can be analyzed in terms of Turner and Fauconnier's model of conceptual integration. The mother's reply in the dialogue with the pediatrician would be analyzed as an instance of the integration of three "input spaces" (adulthood, nurturance,

sexuality) into a blended space. In my analysis, I have represented the sexuality frame outside the blend to highlight the suggestion that the inference that the mother engages in frequent sexual activity may be a later by-product of the blend between adulthood and nurturance. In the conceptual integration model, the main inference would occur in the blended space. I have shown that this inference is facilitated by metonymic connections imported from the input spaces or frames, such as BABY'S TIGHT HOLD ON MOTHER'S BREASTS FOR BABY'S VITALITY, or ADULTHOOD FOR FULL VIGOR. For more examples of the important role of metonymy in blending, see Coulson and Oakley (this volume).

11. An anonymous reviewer challenges the absurdity frame. The ABSURDITY frame is a very general conceptual frame that includes people's knowledge of what qualifies as absurd: unreasonable, foolish, or ridiculous situations, behaviors, ideas, beliefs, etc. For instance, paying a lot of money for an object one does not need at all, or welcoming the Queen of England in one's pajamas. Many absurd situations or beliefs are at the same time counterfactual, such as the idea that people can fly simply by moving their arms up and down. This frame can be invoked directly by such words as *absurd, ridiculous, outlandish*, etc. or indirectly, as in this case, by mentioning a typically absurd situation.

12. This metonymy often reflects personal stereotypes. For instance, in a recent interview in a regional newspaper in Spain (*La Verdad*, Murcia, 16/6/2000), David Byrne complains about being known only as the "ex-leader of *Talking Heads*," the rest of his career being overlooked. This example shows that an entity can automatically invoke its conventionally salient property.

13. Speaker B may have realized this straightforward interpretation yet he may have ignored it on purpose, or (which is much less likely) he may simply have failed to notice it.

14. These two lexemes, *club* ('association') and *club* ('a heavy stick') actually have a Scandinavian origin: the Old Icelandic form *klubba, klumba* 'club (stick), a mass of anything,' which was introduced in Middle English, and which was a cognate to Old Swedish *klubb* 'club, lump, log,' which in dialectal variants could also mean (metaphorically) 'a lump of people, a knot of people.' All of these forms are in turn cognate to *clamp, clamber, clasp,* and *clump*, all of which retain the ideas of 'grasping,' 'holding together,' and 'mass'. In the 17th century the term *club* was re-introduced from this Swedish dialect with the metaphorical meaning 'a lump of people,' i.e. an association. Source: Skeat (1993 [1884]). But the two senses are now so different, and are felt to be so unrelated, that Skeat himself treats them as homonymous lexemes, rather than as two senses of one and the same lexeme. I have followed him here. However, present day standard dictionaries differ in their treatment of this form, though most tend to follow the homonymy position.

15. According to Langacker this metonymy (an "active zone" metonymy in which a participant stands for its active zone, consisting of a relationship in which it participates) motivates "raising" constructions. It also motivates other constructions in which the subject NP is covertly propositional: *A car is a good idea today* (i.e., 'Having/using, etc. a car is a good idea today'); *This knife is convenient* ('Having/using, etc. this knife is convenient') (Langacker 1999:327–332).

16. If I am to trust my sources, the M.P. was actually a married man at the time of this exchange, which explains his speechlessness in the face of the retort.

17. Another possible inference is that the M.P., after being told the secret by his wife, does not realize *all* of its negative implications for himself. This would show him as doubly foolish: first for not grasping these implications and second for unwittingly stating them publicly.

18. Ruiz de Mendoza and Pérez Hernández (this volume) claim that metaphor and metonymy are two fundamental explicature-deriving mechanisms. Most of the inferences I have presented in my paper are implicatures, whose derivation has been shown to be regularly facilitated by metonymic connections. So metonymy is instrumental in obtaining both types of "pragmatic implications", to use Ruiz de Mendoza and Pérez Hernández's terms.

## References


Arana, José Ignacio de (2000). *Diga treinta y tres: Anecdotario médico.* Madrid: Espasa Calpe.

Attardo, Salvatore (1990). The violation of Grice's maxims in jokes. *Berkeley Linguistics Society, 16*, 355–362.

Barcelona, Antonio (2000). On the plausibility of claiming a metonymic motivation for conceptual metaphor. In A. Barcelona (Ed.), *Metaphor and Metonymy at the Crossroads: A Cognitive Perspective* [Topics in English Linguistics 30] (pp. 31–58). Berlin and New York: Mouton de Gruyter.

Barcelona, Antonio (2002). Clarifying and applying the notions of metaphor and metonymy within cognitive linguistics: an update. In R. Dirven & R. Pörings (Eds.), *Metaphor and Metonymy in Comparison and Contrast* [Cognitive Linguistics Research 20] (pp. 207–277). Berlin and New York: Mouton de Gruyter.

Barcelona, Antonio (in press). Metonymy in cognitive linguistics. An analysis and a few modest proposals. In H. Cuyckens, T. Berg, R. Dirven, & K.-U. Panther (Eds.), *Motivation in Language: Studies In Honor of Günter Radden.* Amsterdam and Philadelphia: John Benjamins.

Barcelona, Antonio (n.d.). *The distinction between metaphor and metonymy: A question of (a)symmetry?* Paper presented at the Conference on Researching and Applying Metaphor. University of Manouba, Tunis, April 5, 2001.

Fauconnier, Gilles (1997). *Mappings in Thought and Language.* Cambridge: Cambridge University Press.

Fillmore, Charles (1985). Frames and the semantics of understanding. *Quaderni di Semantica, 6–2*, 222–254.

Grice, H. Paul (1975). Logic and conversation. In P. Cole & J. L. Morgan (Eds.), *Speech Acts* [Syntax and Semantics 3] (pp. 41–58). New York: Academic Press.

Horn, Lawrence (1984). Toward a new taxonomy for pragmatic inference: Q-based and R-based implicature. In D. Schiffrin (Ed.), *Meaning, Form, and Use in Context: Linguistic Applications* (pp. 11–42). Washington, DC: Georgetown University Press.

Kövecses, Zoltán & Radden, Günter (1998). Metonymy: Developing a cognitive linguistic view. *Cognitive Linguistics, 9*, 37–77.

Lakoff, George & Turner, Mark (1989). *More than Cool Reason: A Field Guide to Poetic Metaphor*. Chicago and London: The University of Chicago Press.

Langacker, Ronald W. (1993). Reference-point constructions. *Cognitive Linguistics, 4*, 1–38.

Langacker, Ronald W. (1999). *Grammar and Conceptualization*. Berlin and New York: Mouton de Gruyter.

Marín Arrese, Juana I. (1998). What's so funny? Cognitive and pragmatic aspects of humor. In I. Vázquez Orta & I. Guillén Galve (Eds.), *Perspectivas Pragmáticas en Lingüística Aplicada* (pp. 67–73). Zaragoza, Spain: Anubar.

Panther, Klaus-Uwe (1994). Sentence types, speech acts and metonymy. *Cognitive Linguistics: Explorations, Applications, Results* 2. Hamburg University.

Panther, Klaus-Uwe & Thornburg, Linda (1998). A cognitive approach to inferencing in conversation. *Journal of Pragmatics, 30*, 755–769.

Papafragou, Anna (1996). On metonymy. *Lingua, 99*, 169–195.

Raskin, Victor (1979). Semantic mechanisms of humor. *Berkeley Linguistics Society, 5*, 325–335.

Raskin, Victor (1985). *Semantic Mechanisms of Humor*. Dordrecht: Reidel.

Ruiz de Mendoza, Francisco (1998). Understanding through metonymy: The role of metonymy in communication and cognition. In B. Penas (Ed.), *The Pragmatics of Understanding and Misunderstanding* (pp. 150–171). Zaragoza, Spain: Universidad de Zaragoza, Servicio de Publicaciones.

Ruiz de Mendoza, Francisco (1997). Cognitive and pragmatic aspects of metonymy. In A. Barcelona (Ed.), *Cognitive Linguistics in the Study of the English Language and Literature in English*. Monograph issue of *Cuadernos de Filología Inglesa, 6*(2) (pp. 161–178). Murcia, Spain: University of Murcia.

Skeat, Walter W. (1993 [1884]). *Concise Dictionary of English Etymology*. Ware, Hertfordshire: Wordsworth.

Sperber, Dan & Wilson, Deirdre (1986/1995). *Relevance: Communication and Cognition*. Oxford: Blackwell.

Thornburg, Linda & Panther, Klaus (1997). Speech act metonymies. In W.-A. Liebert, G. Redeker, & L. Waugh (Eds.), *Discourse and Perspectives in Cognitive Linguistics* [Current Issues in Linguistic Theory 151] (pp. 205–219). Amsterdam and Philadelphia: John Benjamins.

Turner, Mark & Fauconnier, Gilles (1995). Conceptual integration and formal expression. *Metaphor and Symbolic Activity, 10*, 183–203.

Turner, Mark & Fauconnier, Gilles (2000). Metaphor, metonymy, and binding. In A. Barcelona (Ed.), *Metaphor and Metonymy at the Crossroads: A Cognitive Perspective* [Topics in English Linguistics 30] (pp. 133–145).

Wilson, Deirdre (1997). Linguistic structure and inferential communication. Plenary lecture delivered at the *16th International Congress of Linguists*, Paris, July 25, 1997.

Part II

# Metonymic inferencing and grammatical structure

# A construction-based approach to indirect speech acts*

Anatol Stefanowitsch

## 1. Introduction

The central issue concerning indirect speech acts (ISAs) has always been the question of how the hearer arrives at the interpretation intended by the speaker. Traditionally, scholars have held that in order to interpret an ISA, the hearer has to do a certain amount of inferencing, i.e., that the propositional content and the illocutionary force of the indirect speech act are arrived at via a stepwise application of inferencing rules of some sort (Searle 1975; Grice 1975; Sperber & Wilson 1986). More recently, it has been suggested that the ISA activates one part of a cognitive model that then metonymically evokes the whole model or some other part of it (Thornburg & Panther 1997; Panther & Thornburg 1998; Panther & Thornburg this volume, cf. also Gibbs 1994: 351ff.). For example, the cognitive model for a 'giving' event includes the core idea of an act of giving, but also various peripheral ideas, e.g. that the hearer is willing and able to perform the act, that the speaker wants something the hearer has, etc. By referring to any part of the model (e.g. *Will/can you give me that book?, I want that book*, etc.), the speaker can evoke the whole model (PART FOR WHOLE), or the core of the model (PART FOR PART).

Researchers in both paradigms have recognized that indirect speech acts can have different degrees of conventionality. For example, the utterances *Can you close the window?* and *It's cold in here* can both be used as requests to close the window. Both are traditionally assumed to be *indirect* requests, but the first type of expression is *conventionally* used as a request, while the latter is not. This distinction between conventionalized and non-conventionalized indirect speech acts is long-standing and has been discussed, among others, by Searle (1975), Morgan (1978), Bach and Harnish (1979), and Clark (1979).

In this chapter I propose a new approach to the distinction between conventionalized and non-conventionalized indirect speech acts. I argue that conventionalized ISAs can be analyzed as constructions in the sense of Construction Grammar, i.e., that their illocutionary force is directly linked to their form (and they are thus not really 'indirect' speech acts at all). I then show how Panther and Thornburg's theory of speech act metonymies nevertheless provides the motivation for the similarity in form between the conventionalized indirect speech acts and the direct speech act on which they seem to be based. Finally, I review neurolinguistic evidence concerning the interpretation of ISAs, and show how it could be accounted for by the analysis of conventionalized ISAs as constructions.

## 2. Some basic tenets of Construction Grammar

Construction Grammar is a theory of language that views the *construction* as the fundamental principle of grammatical organization, where 'construction' is defined as follows (Goldberg 1995: 4):[1]

> C is a construction iff$_{def}$ C is a form–meaning pair ‹$F_i$, $S_i$› such that some aspect of $F_i$ or some aspect of $S_i$ is not strictly predictable from C's component parts or from other previously established constructions.

In the definition above, 'meaning' must be understood in a broad sense, as encompassing aspects traditionally dealt with in semantics as well as those traditionally dealt with in pragmatics. In other words, a construction is any formal element that is directly associated with some meaning or, crucial for the analysis proposed in this paper, pragmatic function (cf. Lakoff 1987: 474). Such a formal element could be (i) a single morpheme, like *give* 'transfer to'; (ii) a fully or partially filled idiom, like *What gives?* 'What is going on,' or *SUBJ be given to VERB-ing* 'SUBJ habitually performs VERB-ing' (as in *Sam is given to quoting Yeats*); and (iii) an abstract syntactic pattern such as the English ditransitive construction [*SUBJ V OBJ*$_1$ *OBJ*$_2$] 'SUBJ causes $OBJ_1$ to receive $OBJ_2$' (as in *Billy gave Diane the ball*). Note that it is the construction itself that imparts a meaning of transfer (or 'causing to receive'), and not just the verb; the meaning of transfer is present even with verbs that do not evoke a transfer frame. Consider a sentence like *Billy threw Diane the ball. Throw* simply means something like 'propel (with force) through the air,' but if used in the ditransitive construction it takes on the meaning 'cause someone to receive something (by propelling it through the air).' Thus, *Billy threw Diane the ball* cannot mean

'Billy threw the ball at Diane' or 'Billy threw the ball in the direction of Diane,' but only 'Billy threw the ball intentionally in such a way that Diane could catch it' (cf. Goldberg 1995: 34f.).

In Construction Grammar it is assumed that any given expression will instantiate several constructions at once (Goldberg 1996: 68): the sentence *The doctor kicked his wife the ball* instantiates the subject-predicate construction (i.e. [SUBJ PRED]), the ditransitive construction (i.e. [SUBJ V $OBJ_1$ $OBJ_2$]/'SUBJ causes $OBJ_1$ to receive $OBJ_2$'), the past tense construction (i.e. [V-*ed*]/'past'), two types of noun phrase construction ([*the* N] and [POSS N]), and the lexical constructions (i.e. words) *ball*, *doctor*, *his*, *kick*, *the*, and *wife*. In Construction Grammar terms, an expression is a well-formed expression of a language if it is an instantiation of the combination of existing constructions (including morphemes and lexemes) of that language (sometimes described as the *unification* of constructions). Construction Grammar, then, is non-derivational, since constructions are seen as basic units rather than the result of an interaction between lexical items and syntactic rules, and it is non-modular, since constructions directly link form and meaning/use.

Crucially, Construction Grammar does not view the set of constructions making up a particular language as an unstructured list of items. Instead, constructions are seen as forming a highly structured inventory; four types of *inheritance links* between constructions are posited.

First, there are *polysemy links*, which show the relation between different extensions from some central meaning (Goldberg 1995: 75). For example, the ditransitive construction mentioned above is linked by a polysemy link to formally identical constructions with the meanings 'X *intends to* cause Y to receive Z,' as in *Jim baked Mary a cake*, 'X *enables* Y to receive Z,' as in *Jim allowed Mary some cake*, 'X causes Y not to receive Z,' as in *Jim denied Mary cake*, etc.

Second, there are *metaphorical extension links*, which show relations between two senses of a construction that are based on conceptual metaphors (Goldberg 1995: 81). For example, the ditransitive construction is linked by a metaphorical extension to a formally identical construction meaning 'X *communicates* Y to Z,' as in *Jim told Mary a story* (based on the conduit metaphor, cf. Lakoff & Johnson 1980).

Third, there are *instance links*, which show the relation between a general construction and a more specific instance of this construction (Goldberg 1995: 79). For example, the ditransitive construction is an instance of the subject-predicate construction; it has a subject and a predicate that share the properties of subjects and predicates in general, but it adds its own specifications, namely the exact type of verb phrase instantiating the predicate (i.e. [$_{VP}$ V NP NP]), as well as a particular configuration of semantic roles (i.e. ‹agent, recipient, theme›).

Finally, there are *subpart links*, which show the relation between one construction and another that is a proper subpart of the first. For example, a simple transitive construction of the type *Jim kicked the ball* can be described as a subpart of the ditransitive construction (*Jim kicked Mary a ball).*

## 3. Indirect speech act constructions

In this section I will argue that conventionalized ISAs such as those given in (1) must be considered constructions in their own right, i.e. form-meaning pairs whose properties cannot be strictly predicted from other constructions or general principles in the grammar of English (I will refer to such constructions as ISA constructions):

(1) a. Can you pass the salt?
b. Would you mind closing the door?
c. I'd like a cheeseburger with fries.

I will then argue that these ISA constructions are nevertheless *motivated* by other constructions and general principles. Drawing on the theory of Speech Act Metonymies (Thornburg & Panther 1997; Panther & Thornburg 1998), I will suggest a new type of inheritance link to be added to the apparatus of Construction Grammar: the metonymic link ($I_{My}$). This link allows us to capture the (partial) motivation behind ISA constructions, while at the same time acknowledging their independent status. I will also argue that non-conventionalized ISAs are different from ISA constructions. While the latter, being constructions in their own right, do not require inferencing on the part of H (although see further below), the former do require such inferencing.

In order to demonstrate the need for positing ISA constructions in the first place, it must be shown that conventionalized ISAs fit the definition given in Section 2 above, i.e. that they do in fact have formal or semantic properties that are not strictly predictable from other constructions of English.

### 3.1 Unpredictable semantic properties of indirect speech acts

Both conventionalized and non-conventionalized indirect speech acts differ in meaning from the direct speech act whose form they seem to share – this is what makes them ISAs in the first place. The whole point about a sentence like

*Can you pass the salt?* is that it has the form of a question, but is not uttered to *mean* a question, but instead is (typically) uttered to mean a request.

However, the fact that a particular type of ISA has a different meaning than its direct counterpart is not enough to argue for its status as a construction; it must also be shown that this meaning is not predictable. The question how indirect speech acts convey their intended meaning has been variously answered in terms of Gricean implicatures (e.g. Searle 1975), inferencing on the basis of 'mutual contextual beliefs' (Bach & Harnish 1979), conversational postulates (Gordon & Lakoff 1975), conventions of use (Searle 1975; Bach & Harnish 1979; Morgan 1978), or abstract performative verbs in their semantic structure (e.g. Sadock 1974). All but the last two theories claim that the meaning of ISAs is completely predictable on the basis of the construction they are based on and general principles of communication. If these theories are right, then there is no semantic justification for positing ISAs, conventionalized or not, as constructions in the sense of Construction Grammar.

In addition to differences in terms of illocutionary force, there is typically a restriction on the semantic roles of requests that is not present in the corresponding direct constructions. For example, the subject of *Can you X? or Would you mind X?* must be an agent, and the object (if present), must be a patient. Thus, (2a) could be a question or a request, but (2b) could only be a question:

(2) a. Can you close the window?
    b. Can you see the window?

However, this restriction follows plausibly from our knowledge of what is or is not a reasonable request; in other words, if it is predictable that *Can you X?* or *Would you mind X?* can convey requests, then the semantic restrictions on their subjects are also predictable.[2]

I will return to the issue of whether or not the meaning of ISAs is generally predictable. For now, suffice it to say that this is a very contentious issue, and one that is extremely difficult to resolve. We should therefore look for formal arguments for construction status first (since formal properties tend to be less open to debate or interpretation).

## 3.2 Unpredictable formal properties of indirect speech acts

An argument for the status of conventionalized ISAs as constructions on the basis of formal properties requires two kinds of evidence. First, it must be shown that they differ formally from the direct speech act whose general form they share. For example, it must be shown that although indirect requests like

*Can you X?* have the same structure as questions, they have some additional properties that questions do not have, or that they do not have some of the additional properties of questions. Second, it must be shown that conventionalized ISAs differ formally from other ISAs with the same illocutionary force. For example, it must be shown that the formal properties that distinguish a request like *Can you X?* from the corresponding question are not properties of indirect requests in general.

Both types of evidence do, in fact, exist. Beginning with the first type, it has been noted that while conventionalized indirect requests typically allow the preverbal occurrence of request markers like *please* or *kindly*, the corresponding direct constructions do not (cf. e.g. Sadock 1974: 104):[3]

(3) a. Can you open the door?
⇒ Open the door! / Are you capable of opening the door?
b. Can you please/kindly open the door.
⇒ Open the door! / *Are you capable of opening the door?

(4) a. Would you mind opening the door?
⇒ Open the door! / Do you believe it would have a negative psychological effect on you if you opened the door?
b. Would you mind please/kindly opening the door?
⇒ Open the door! / *Do you believe it would have a negative psychological effect on you if you opened the door?

Thus, there is clear evidence that conventionalized indirect requests differ formally from the direct question whose form they appear to share. The existence of such differences has been recognized by proponents of a purely pragmatic analysis of ISAs (such as Searle 1975 or Bach & Harnish 1979), but has not been satisfactorily accounted for (a point which we will return to presently). Before doing so, however, we must address a potential counterargument against using facts about *please* and *kindly* as evidence for a special formal status of conventionalized ISAs at all. Recall that in order to argue convincingly that conventionalized ISAs are constructions, it is not sufficient to show that they have formal properties that distinguish them from the direct speech act whose general form they share. We must also show that they differ formally from non-conventionalized ISAs, which have no claims to construction status. After all, the formal differences between ISA constructions and their direct counterparts could potentially be linked directly to their illocutionary force. More precisely, since *please* is commonly considered to be a request marker, we might be tempted to link its distribution to the use of an utterance as a request. Preverbal *please* (and adverbs like *kindly*) can occur with a wide variety of formal structures, as long as they are used as requests:

(5) a. You can please/kindly give that back now.
  b. You will please/kindly close the window.
  c. (For the hundredth time,) I please/?kindly want the salt.

However, note that there are many ISAs that can be unambiguous requests in a particular situation, but that cannot occur with preverbal *please* (and in many cases cannot occur with *please* at all). Example (5c) is already somewhat odd for many speakers without the material in parentheses, and the following examples are clearly out:

(6) a. *It's please/kindly cold in here. ~ *It's cold in here, please.
  b. *You please/kindly can't keep that. ~ *You can't please/kindly keep that. ~ ??You can't keep that, please.
  c. *This sauce could please/kindly do with some salt. ~ ?This sauce could do with some salt, please.

Thus, it is a non-predictable (if motivated) property of the utterances in (3a), (4a) and (5a–c) that they can occur with preverbal *please* and *kindly*.

A second difference between conventionalized and non-conventionalized ISAs is that in the former a conditional modal can be used to express not conditionality but politeness (cf. Sadock 1974: 105):

(7) a. Will you close the door? ~ Would you close the door?
  b. When will you close the door. ~ *When would you close the door?

Example (7a), a conventionalized indirect request, can alternate between *will* and *would* with no difference in meaning (other than the difference in politeness). In contrast, the two variants in (7b) have completely different meanings. The variant with *will* could mean 'At what point in the future will you close the door,' or it could be a non-conventionalized request to close the door. The variant with *would* can mean 'What conditions have to be fulfilled for you to close the door' or 'At what point in time did you usually close the door,' and it cannot be a request.

A third difference between conventionalized and non-conventionalized requests is that only the former can occur with a preposed subordinate clause giving the speaker's reason for making the request (Sadock 1974: 105):

(8) a. Since I've got my hands full, will you close the door?
  b. *Since I've got my hands full, when will you close the door?

I will briefly return to this criterion in connection with the concept of speech act metonymy below.

In sum, conventionalized indirect requests have at least three formal properties that distinguish them both from the direct speech act on which they seem to be based and from non-conventionalized indirect speech acts with the same illocutionary force: they can occur with preverbal *please* or request adverbs; conditional modals express politeness instead of conditionality; and they can have a preposed subordinate clause stating the reason for the request.[4] Note that they share the first and the third property with direct requests:

(9) a. Please/kindly close the door!
    b. Since I've got my hands full, close the door!

As mentioned above, at least one of these formal properties, the possibility for preverbal *please* to occur, has been acknowledged by proponents of a purely pragmatic analysis, e.g. Searle (1975) and Bach and Harnish (1975). Thus, before we are fully justified in assigning construction status to conventionalized requests on the basis of these formal properties, we have to ensure that they cannot be accounted for by such a purely pragmatic analysis.

Searle's explanation consists of two parts; first, he argues that *please* "explicitly and literally marks the primary illocutionary point of the utterance as directive, even though the literal meaning of the rest of the sentence is not directive" (Searle 1975: 68). As was pointed out above, this observation does not account for the fact that preverbal *please* can occur in conventionalized indirect requests, but not in non-conventionalized ones. Searle also seems to be aware of this fact (Searle 1975: 75). However, he does not offer an explanation; instead, he simply observes that "certain forms will tend to become conventionally established as the standard idiomatic forms for indirect speech acts" (Searle 1975: 76). Thus, if there is an explanation implicit in Searle's discussion at all, it is the circular statement that conventionalized indirect requests accept preverbal *please* because they are conventionalized.

Bach and Harnish (1979: 188f.) also criticize Searle's account, but their own suggestion is hardly more enlightening. They simply suggest that the occurrence of preverbal *please* in indirect requests is always ungrammatical and that indirect requests with preverbal *please* are "examples of syntactic liberty [...], ungrammatical but usable sentences that are perfectly acceptable to fluent speakers" (Bach & Harnish 1979: 199). Even if we ignore the problems inherent in the notion of "ungrammatical but usable and acceptable sentences," note that it does not account for the crucial fact that preverbal *please* can occur in conventionalized, but *not* in non-conventionalized indirect requests; why is 'syntactic liberty' not possible with the latter?

Since conventionalized ISAs differ formally both from their direct counterparts and from non-conventionalized ISAs in ways that are not strictly predictable and that cannot be explained by purely pragmatic analyses, we are now justified in assigning them construction status. For example, I posit that (3a), (4a), and (5c) are instantiations of the ISA constructions represented informally in (10a), (10b) and (10c) respectively:

(10) a. [SUBJ$_{2P}$ *can* VP]/'s is telling H$_{SUBJ.2P}$ to do A$_{VP}$'
b. [*Would* SUBJ$_{2P}$ *mind* VP$_{ing}$]/'s is telling H$_{SUBJ.2P}$ to do A$_{VP}$'
c. [SUBJ$_{1P}$ *want* OBJ]/'s is telling H to give OBJ to S$_{SUBJ.1P}$'

Note that the analysis of conventionalized ISAs as constructions is more than a simple renaming. At the very least, it places them in a framework in which unpredictable formal and semantic properties have an explicit theoretical status (unlike in Searle's account), and do not have to be explained away (unlike in Bach and Harnish's account). It also allows us to be explicit about the semantic relationship between direct requests and conventionalized indirect requests, and it allows us to relate formal similarities between these two types of requests to these shared semantic properties. Finally, as the next section will show, it allows an explicit account of the way in which conventionalized indirect speech acts are related to the direct speech acts whose form they superficially share.

Returning to the examples in (10), note that these are intended as simplified representations that can manifest themselves in a variety of syntactic patterns; e.g. (10a) accounts for both *Can you pass me the salt* and *You can pass me the salt* (the difference in pragmatic meaning between interrogatives and declaratives is a separate issue). Of course, the semantic glosses in (10) are only approximations; clearly, there is a difference for example between (10a) and (10b). Such differences have been posited in the form of Gibbs' *obstacle hypothesis* (and confirmed experimentally; for a summary, cf. Gibbs 1994). Roughly, this theory claims that many indirect speech acts are associated with a particular belief on the part of S as to what potential reasons H may have for not complying. A more precise semantic gloss for (10b) would be 'S is telling H$_{SUBJ.2P}$ to do A$_{VP}$ and S believes H may not be willing to comply.' Such beliefs are an important part of the specification of ISA constructions; I will return to the issue below.

### 3.3 The metonymy link

In light of the vast literature on indirect speech acts, the above account may seem somewhat lacking in explanatory value. After all, it simply pairs semantic/pragmatic functions with certain syntactic patterns, without making any attempt to motivate the latter in terms of the former or to account for the fact that all the ISA constructions listed here have roughly homonymous syntactic patterns that function as questions or statements. In other words, the analysis sketched out here so far does not explain why the particular ISA constructions under discussion share their basic formal properties with particular types of questions/statements, rather than any other (arbitrarily chosen) pattern.

There are two issues that need to be addressed. First, what happens in the present account to the long and impressive series of inferential steps that a hearer must take under the traditional view in order to arrive at the correct interpretation of *Can you pass the salt?* (cf. e.g. Searle 1975, who needs 10 steps to arrive at the intended meaning)? Second, if those inferences are dispensed with, is there any motivated link between, for example, *Can you pass the salt?* in its interrogative and in its requestive meaning? I will dispose of the first issue in a somewhat cavalier fashion, by simply pointing out that such inference processes were never very plausible to begin with, and that there is ample psycholinguistic evidence for their non-existence (e.g. Gibbs 1994; Clark 1979). I will however, come back to this issue briefly in my conclusion.

Let me turn instead to the second issue in more detail. Obviously, no account of ISA constructions would want to deny that there is some relation between the 'indirect' and the 'direct' meaning of a construction. I believe that Panther and Thornburg's theory of speech act metonymies provides a way of capturing this relation that can fruitfully be adapted to a constructional account.

In a series of publications, Panther and Thornburg have developed an account of the interpretation of indirect speech acts in terms of what they call *speech act scenarios*, essentially *idealized cognitive models* of certain culturally entrenched activities, that include not only an event itself, but also knowledge about preconditions, results and consequences of this event. For requests, such a scenario would include the following kinds of knowledge (Panther & Thornburg 1998: 759):

(11) Simplified scenario for requests

BEFORE: H can do A. S wants H to do A.
CORE: S puts H under a (more or less strong) obligation to do A.

RESULT: H is under an obligation to do A.
AFTER: H will do A.

This is a very abstract cognitive model, which can be combined with cognitive models of different events, depending on the situation and the specific content of a request. For example, if S requests H to *give* her something, then both S and H need to share a GIVE schema, i.e. specific knowledge about giving events and their participants, a 'giver,' a 'recipient,' and a 'thing-given.' This knowledge must be integrated into the abstract scenario shown above. Such knowledge includes presuppositions about the thing-given, namely that it exists and that the giver has access to it, and it includes knowledge about motivations, namely that the recipient wants to have the thing-given. These aspects of the giving event will be integrated with the BEFORE of the request scenario. The GIVE schema also includes knowledge about what counts as an act of giving (this will be integrated with the CORE and the RESULT), and what the consequences of such an act are (the recipient now has access to the thing-given (this will be integrated with the AFTER) (cf. Thornburg & Panther 1997: 211f. for detailed discussion).

The basic insight of Panther and Thornburg's approach is that a cognitive model integrating a speech act scenario and an event schema can serve as the conceptual basis for interpreting (and producing) a wide variety of indirect speech acts: an utterance that refers to any aspect of the model can metonymically evoke the whole model. The following are some examples of such utterances:

(12) a. BEFORE: Can you pass me the salt?
I need the salt.
I want the salt.
b. CORE: I'm asking you to pass me the salt.
Could I ask you to pass me the salt?
c. RESULT: You must give me the salt.
d. AFTER: Will you pass me the salt?
That's my salt!

Panther and Thornburg point out that the metonymic approach accounts for the fact that the closer to the core of the request scenario an utterance is, the more likely it will be understood as a request (cf. Panther & Thornburg 1998: 761ff. for evidence from conversational data).

Note that utterances referring to the various parts of the request scenario are essentially conventionalized indirect speech acts, although they are conventionalized to varying degrees. However, the model can also account for non-conventionalized indirect speech acts. An utterance like *I always eat my egg with salt*, for example, can be understood as a request to pass the salt even though it does not directly evoke any aspect of the request scenario. The reason is that it evokes a possible motivation for S's wanting the salt, which will then evoke the BEFORE component of the request scenario. Panther and Thornburg distinguish utterances that directly evoke a part of the speech act scenario (which they refer to as *metonymic functions*) from those that indirectly evoke a part of it (which they refer to as *indexical functions).*

Panther and Thornburg's model provides the missing piece for the analysis of ISA constructions: their motivation. As mentioned in the overview of its basic tenets, Construction Grammar does not view the linguistic system as an unstructured collection of constructions, but as a highly structured inventory of constructions that inherit aspects of form and/or meaning from one another in intricate ways. In the case of the ISA constructions discussed above, I propose that *metonymic links* provide the motivation for the partial structural identity with the direct construction. These metonymic links are themselves structured by the request scenario as defined by Panther and Thornburg. The relationship between the question *Can you X?* and the request *Can you X?* can be represented as shown in Figure 1.

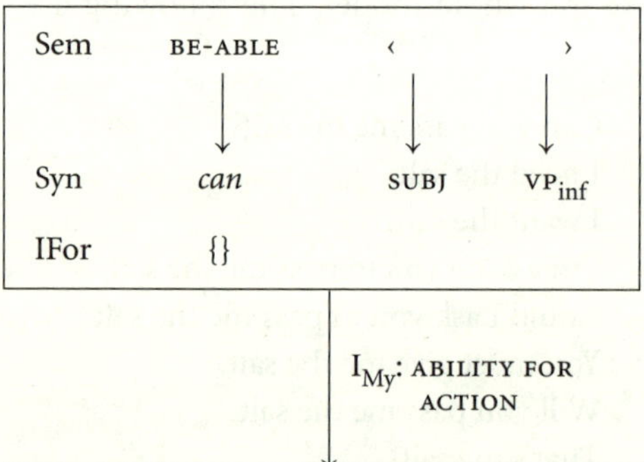


**Figure 1.** The *Can-you-X* construction

The 'direct' construction at the top does not specify anything beyond its syntax (Syn), i.e. the fact that it needs a subject and a verb phrase, and part of the semantics (Sem), namely that *can* means 'be able.'[5] The semantic roles of the subject and (if present) the object(s) or obliques will be specified by whichever verb heads the VP, and the illocutionary force (IFor) will be specified by the discourse context in which the construction is used. If it is unified with the interrogative construction (or rather, the subject-auxiliary inversion construction), it will most likely be a question; if it is unified with the declarative construction, it will most likely be a statement. However, it could – under the right circumstances – have almost any illocutionary force.

The ISA construction at the bottom inherits the formal specifications, but it does not inherit the semantics of *can* (I will leave open the question whether *can* is actually completely empty, or whether it retains a weak trace of its meaning). The ISA construction also adds the specification that the subject must be 2nd person, and that it must have the semantic role of ‹agent›. Contrary to the direct construction, the ISA construction inherently specifies the illocutionary force. This inherent specification of the illocutionary force also accounts for the formal properties that it shares with direct requests (preverbal *please*, etc.).

The metonymic link captures the motivation of the ISA construction in terms of the request scenario: an aspect of the BEFORE component (that H *can* do A) stands for an aspect of the AFTER component (that H *will* do A). However, the fact that the ISA is shown as a separate unit captures the fact that it has construction status despite the existence of a motivating link, and thus allows us to state its unpredictable formal properties. In other words, the ISA has construction status in spite of the theoretical possibility to derive its meaning from the request scenario on-line (as must in fact be done in the case of non-conventionalized ISAs).

Note that the notion of speech act metonymy also allows us to motivate one of the formal properties of direct requests and conventionalized indirect requests (both of which we can now characterize as *request constructions*, i.e. constructions that have the illocutionary force *request* directly associated with them). Recall examples (8a, b), which show that request constructions can have a preposed subordinate clause stating the hearer's reason for making the request. This fact can now be restated more insightfully: any construction that *directly* evokes the core of the speech act scenario (i.e. any request construction) can occur with a subordinate clause referring to the periphery of the scenario, while non-conventionalized indirect speech acts which refer to the a more peripheral component cannot take such a clause. Take examples

(13a, b), where the subordinate clause encodes aspects of the BEFORE component (asterisks represent unacceptability under a request reading):

(13) The BEFORE component

a. (H can do A)
Since you're sitting right next to the window...
...would you mind closing it? ~ ...can/could you close it? ~ ...I want you to close it.
*...it's cold in here. ~ *...when will you close it? ~ *...I need it closed.

b. (S wants H to do A)
Since I can't get to the window...
...would you mind closing it? ~ ...can/could you close it? ~ ...I want you to close it.
*...it's cold in here. ~ *... when will you close it? ~ *...I need it closed.

Similarly, in (14) the subordinate clause encodes the RESULT component:

(14) The RESULT component
(H is under an obligation to do A)
Since you are supposed to close the window anyway...
...would you mind closing it (now)? ~ ...can/could you close it (now)? ~ ...I want you to close it (now).
*...it's cold in here. ~ *... when will you close it? ~ *...I need it closed.

Finally, in (15) the subordinate clause encodes the AFTER component:

(15) The AFTER component
(H will do A)
Since you will (eventually) close the window anyway...
...would you mind closing it (now)? ~ ...can/could you close it (now)? ~ ...I want you to close it (now).
*...it's cold in here. ~ *... when will you close it? ~ *...I need it closed (now).

The motivation for the facts in (13–15) is presumably that it is strange to evoke a request scenario weakly via a speech act metonymy in the preposed subordinate clause, and then follow it with an utterance that evokes it just as weakly or even more weakly. Under these circumstances, the contents of the *since*-clause can no longer be construed as a reason for the illocutionary point of the main clause.

Returning to the issue of how ISAs mean what they mean, note that on the present account the construction *as a whole* carries the illocutionary force 'request,' while at the same time it does not convey the 'literal' meaning of ability (i.e., the semantics of *can* as an individual item in this construction is (almost) zero). Thus, the ISA construction loses the meaning of the 'direct' construction. This does not have to be the case for every ISA construction. Consider the case of the *Would you mind X?* construction. In this case, the direct construction's meaning of asking about the hearers potential objections to the activity denoted by the VP is retained in the ISA construction, which simply adds the inherent specification of the illocutionary force. This state of affairs is shown in Figure 2.

This type of analysis captures the fact that many ISAs seem to retain the meaning of the direct construction in addition to their illocutionary function. Recall the *obstacle hypothesis* mentioned above: speakers often select request constructions that make reference to the most likely obstacle to fulfillment, in this case the hearer's willingness.

An alternative to the analysis presented here would be to assume an on-line motivation of *all* indirect speech acts in terms of speech act metonymies. However, such an analysis would leave the unpredictable formal properties of the type of conventionalized ISA discussed above unaccounted for. Thus, the linguistic evidence alone is sufficient to support the analysis presented here. However, additional evidence for such an analysis comes from neurolinguisics.

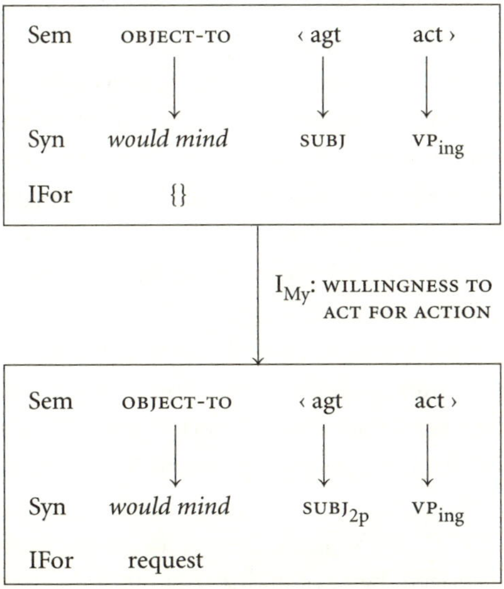


**Figure 2.** The *Would-you-mind-X* construction

## 4. Neurolinguistic evidence

The research on indirect speech acts has focused on individuals with right-hemisphere damage (RHD), since it has repeatedly been observed that while for such individuals the core linguistic abilities are typically intact, they have difficulties interpreting various types of non-literal meaning. The general expectation would thus be that they would have a tendency to interpret ISAs literally, i.e. give them a direct interpretation even where the context encourages an indirect interpretation.

There are five studies in particular that are relevant to the present discussion (Hirst et al. 1984; Foldi 1987; Weylman et al. 1989; Stemmer 1994; Stemmer et al. 1994; and Brownell & Stringfellow 1999), though they have slightly different foci. In the following discussion, I will be concerned with the evidence they provide for the following questions: (i) Do RHD individuals have difficulties interpreting ISAs (I will touch on the issue of production at several points, but the literature is sparser here)? (ii) If so, are there differences between conventionalized and non-conventionalized ISAs? (iii) If RHD individuals have difficulties, what is the nature of these difficulties? I will also briefly discuss how individuals with left-hemisphere damage (LHD), i.e. aphasics, perform on some of the same tasks.

Hirst et al. (1984) found that RHD individuals do not in fact tend to give *conventionalized* ISAs (of the form *Can you X?*) a direct interpretation. When asked to judge the appropriateness of videotaped role-plays, they were equally likely to judge direct *and* indirect interpretations as appropriate in a situation where the context strongly suggested a direct interpretation. For example, for the utterance *Can you play tennis?*, uttered in a situation where S and H are sitting in the living room reading, they accepted as appropriate a verbal response (where H would say "Yes") in 75% of the cases, and a physical response (where H would get up and start playing tennis in the living room) in 70% of the cases (this difference was not significant).

On the other hand, they were vastly more likely to accept an indirect interpretation where the context suggested one. For example, for the utterance *Can you pass the salt?* in a situation where S and H are sitting at the dinner table, they judged a verbal response as appropriate in 5% of the cases, but a physical response in 97% of the cases.

Clearly, then, RHD individuals have difficulties with conventionalized ISAs, but not in the expected way of taking them literally. Instead, the results are opposite to the expectation: they clearly know the pragmatic meaning of ISAs, and they apply it even in a context that by its incongruity makes an indirect interpretation highly implausible.

Of course, Hirst et al.'s results cannot be generalized to all ISAs since they used one of the most conventionalized ISA constructions available. The question remains how RHD individuals perform with non-conventionalized ISAs. The answer is provided in a similar study by Foldi (1987), in which sequences of line drawings were used as stimuli rather than role plays. Presented with a mixed set of ISAs consisting mostly of *non-conventional* ISAs (e.g. *Will your tray hold all these dishes?* or *Do you have everything to wash the car?*), RHD patients showed a significant preference for direct interpretations as opposed to both a group of aphasic individuals (see below) and the control group (Foldi 1987:96). From the examples given, it seems that the contexts in Foldi's study allow both interpretations without producing the kind of incongruity found in Hirst et al.'s examples, although they make an indirect interpretation much more plausible.

Finally, Weylman et al. (1989) showed that in a task with verbal stimuli (i.e. with verbal rather than visual descriptions of situations) RHD individuals interpreted ISAs with different degrees of conventionalization (*Can you X?, Are you able to X?, Is it possible for you to X?*) indirectly more often than the control group in a context that encouraged a direct interpretation (*ibid.*: 585). This study thus confirms Hirst et al.'s results. Weylman et al. found that RHD individuals showed no sensitivity to different degrees of conventionalization in one task, and very little sensitivity in a second task (*ibid.*: 588). Superficially, this may seem to contradict Foldi's results. However, note that Weylman et al.'s examples are all fairly conventionalized expressions; at the very least they are clearly more conventionalized than Foldi's examples.

With regard to production, Brownell and Stringfellow (1999:460f.) found that RHD individuals are able to produce ISAs, but that they have difficulties varying the directness of their requests, especially with regard to the degree of imposition on the hearer. Similarly, Stemmer (1994) and Stemmer et al. (1994) showed that RHD patients have a tendency to overuse non-conventionalized ISAs (in the form of hints), again, disregarding what would be appropriate in a given context.

In sum, RHD individuals clearly have difficulties with ISAs. In the case of expressions typically associated with conventionalized ISAs, their difficulty lies in determining when the indirect reading is not intended. In the case of non-conventionalized ISAs, their difficulty lies in discovering the intended meaning. It seems, then, that RHD individuals have problems generally with taking context into account in order to arrive at a plausible interpretation of an utterance. I will return to this point in the next section.

Before I do so, however, I will briefly turn to aphasics' performance on interpreting ISAs. For conventionalized ISAs, Hirst et al. (1984) show that anterior LHD individuals are much more likely to assume a direct interpretation where the context suggests one (34% direct vs. 8% indirect), although they seem significantly impaired even with the direct interpretation. They are also much more likely to assume an indirect interpretation where the context suggests one (12% direct vs. 92% indirect). For a mixed set of ISAs consisting mainly of non-conventionalized ISAs, LHD individuals showed no particular preference for direct or indirect interpretations (Foldi 1987:96). In Weylman et al.'s verbal task, LHD individuals preferred indirect interpretations in direct contexts to about the same degree as RHD patients (about a quarter of the time), but in indirect contexts they performed much worse with ISAs having a low degree of conventionality than for highly conventionalized ones.

Thus, LHD individuals seem to be fairly good at taking context into account in order to arrive at the intended interpretation, although, of course, they are impaired by the difficulties that they have with syntax and (literal) semantics. It seems that at least in some situations, a highly conventionalized form helps them interpret an utterance.

## 5. Discussion and conclusions

The neurolinguistic evidence, while still sketchy in part, makes clear at least one thing: ISAs are always produced and interpreted by on-line inferencing. However, the inferencing process is *not* one of deriving the non-literal, indirect meaning of a construction from its literal meaning.

If this were the case, RHD individuals should have a uniform tendency to interpret ISAs literally. Instead, the process is simply one of interpreting what a speaker is trying to communicate on the basis of the meaning of the sentence uttered and the context in which it is uttered. The meaning of a sentence is the combined meaning of all constructions (syntactic, argument-structure, lexical, etc.) that it instantiates. Since expressions may instantiate alternative constructions at the same time, interpreting a speaker's communicative intention often involves disambiguating homonymous expressions in terms of the constructions they instantiate. The problem a hearer is faced with when hearing strings like (16a–c) is *not* to process its 'literal' meaning, determine that the utterance does not lend itself to a literal interpretation, and then infer possible 'non-literal' meanings:

(16) a. Can you close the window?
b. Would you mind telling me the time?
c. I would like a cheeseburger.

Instead, the problem faced by the hearer is to realize that each of these expressions is ambiguous in terms of the conventional meanings attached to the constructions they instantiate, and to use context in order to determine which of their conventionalized meanings is the one intended by the speaker, in the same way as a hearer faced with (17) must determine which of the conventionalized meanings of *bank* is intended:

(17) Sam went to the bank to take out a loan.

The RHD individuals clearly know that expressions like (16a) have two meanings: recall that they accept both verbal replies (*yes* or *no*) or physical activities (closing the window) as appropriate responses. However, they are not able to disambiguate between them on the basis of the non-linguistic context (they do not find it odd to play tennis in the living room). In a similar fashion, they are not able to produce requests that are appropriate to the context. Instead, they often tend to use ISA constructions regardless of the situation, like Brownell and Stringfellow's patient JM, who consistently produced conventionalized ISAs, even in contexts where normal controls unanimously preferred direct requests: "It is as if she generated a single request frame and applied it consistently" (Brownell & Stringfellow 1999: 460).

Of course, the existence of ISA constructions, i.e. of constructions that inherently specify their illocutionary force, does not entail that *all* constructions work in this way. The sentences in (18) are not ambiguous between a 'direct' and an 'indirect' interpretation:

(18) a. It's cold in here.
b. I wonder if it is already past seven.
c. I love cheeseburgers.

Yet, given the right context, they can have the same interpretations as (16a–c) respectively. In this case, there *does* need to be some inferencing, i.e. the hearer does need to ask herself 'Why is the speaker telling me this?' How this inferencing is done is essentially an open question. It is clear, however, that RHD individuals have great problems with it, and *do* tend to interpret utterances like those in (18) literally, even where the context leaves no doubt that they are to be understood as requests.

The idea of metonymic reasoning cannot be proved or disproved by the neurological evidence as it currently stands. It is very useful, however, since it draws attention to the fact that 'inferencing' consists of the activation of related aspects of culturally entrenched models. It allows us to capture neatly the motivation behind conventionalized as well as certain non-conventionalized ISAs. One piece of evidence at least for the special status of non-conventionalized ISAs that directly invoke a part of the request scenario is that RHD individuals seem to have less trouble with these (cf. Weylman et al. 1989) as opposed to non-conventionalized ISAs that do not directly invoke part of the scenario (cf. Foldi 1987). We might argue in this case (although further evidence is certainly needed), that the existence of conventionalized metonymic links between independently existing constructions also facilitates inferencing processes that make use of these metonymic links in interpreting utterances that do not instantiate ISA constructions.

## Notes

* I would like to thank the participants of the panel "Metonymy and Pragmatic Inferencing" at the IPrA Conference 2000 in Budapest, in particular Klaus-Uwe Panther, Linda Thornburg, and David Zubin, for fruitful comments on an earlier version of this paper, for posing tough questions, and for pointing out weaknesses in my argumentation. All remaining weaknesses are, of course, mine alone.

1. There is a set of fundamentally similar, closely related theories that share this view of language and are referred to as 'Construction Grammar' (e.g. Lakoff 1987; Fillmore 1988; Fillmore & Kay 1993; Kay & Fillmore 1999; Goldberg 1995). The discussion in this section essentially follows the exposition in Goldberg (1995).

2. Note that here and elsewhere, the notion of predictability is used in the sense of the definition quoted at the beginning of Section 2. A property of a construction is referred to as *predictable* if it is expected on the basis of the properties of its component parts and general 'rules' (e.g. other constructions or pragmatic principles) of the language in question.

3. Note that this is not true of sentence-initial or sentence-final *please*, which under certain conditions can occur with questions too, at least if followed/preceded by an intonation break, as in *Please, is it true that you are planning a new movie at the moment*. It seems that this is only possible where the hearer is under an extremely weak obligation to answer the question; the *please* seems to function as a request to answer the question, thus the example just given means 'Please tell me, is it true....'

4. There is a further formal property with respect to which conventionalized indirect requests resemble direct requests but not questions or non-conventionalized indirect requests:

their subject is restricted to a particular person (second person in *Can you X?* and *Will you X?*, first person in *I want X*, etc. This difference, unlike the others, is predictable from the request function of these expressions.

5. I will leave open the question whether the direct speech acts here and below are actually constructions themselves, or whether their form and meaning can be completely predicted from the constructions that they consist of (the specific lexical items used, the subject-predicate construction, the subject-auxiliary inversion construction, etc.).

## References


Bach, Kent & Harnish, Robert M. (1979). *Linguistic Communication & Speech Acts.* Cambridge, MA, and London: The MIT Press.

Brownell, Hiram & Stringfellow, Andrew (1999). Making requests: Illustrations of how right-hemisphere brain damage can affect discourse production. *Brain and Language, 68*, 442–465.

Clark, Herbert H. (1979). Responding to indirect speech acts. *Cognitive Psychology, 11*, 430–477.

Fillmore, Charles (1988). The mechanisms of 'Construction Grammar'. *Berkeley Linguistics Society, 14*, 35–55.

Fillmore, Charles & Kay, Paul (1993). Construction Grammar. Ms. University of California, Berkeley.

Foldi, Nancy S. (1987). Appreciation of pragmatic interpretations of indirect commands: Comparison of right and left hemisphere brain-damaged patients. *Brain and Language, 31*, 88–108.

Gibbs, Raymond W., Jr. (1994). *The Poetics of Mind: Figurative Thought, Language, and Understanding.* Cambridge: Cambridge University Press.

Goldberg, Adele (1995). *Constructions: A Construction Grammar Approach to Argument Structure* [Cognitive Theory of Language and Culture]. Chicago and London: The University of Chicago Press.

Goldberg, Adele (1996). Construction Grammar. In K. Brown & J. Miller (Eds.), *Concise Encyclopedia of Syntactic Theories* (pp. 68–71). Oxford: Pergamon.

Gordon, David & Lakoff, George (1975). Conversational postulates. In P. Cole & J. L. Morgan (Eds.), *Speech Acts* [Syntax and Semantics 3] (pp. 83–106). New York: Academic Press.

Grice, H. Paul (1975). Logic and conversation. In P. Cole & J. L. Morgan (Eds.), *Speech Acts* [Syntax and Semantics 3] (pp. 41–58). New York: Academic Press.

Hirst, William, Le Doux, Joseph, & Stein, Susanna (1984). Constraints on the processing of indirect speech acts: Evidence from aphasiology. *Brain and Language, 23*, 23–33.

Kay, Paul & Fillmore, Charles (1999). Grammatical constructions and linguistic generalizations: The *What's X doing Y?* construction. *Language, 75*, 1–33.

Lakoff, George (1987). *Women, Fire, and Dangerous things: What Categories Reveal About the Mind.* Chicago and London: The University of Chicago Press.

Lakoff, George & Johnson, Mark (1980). *Metaphors We Live By.* Chicago and London: The University of Chicago Press.

Morgan, Jerry L. (1978). Two types of convention in indirect speech acts. In P. Cole (Ed.), *Pragmatics* [Syntax and Semantics 9] (pp. 261–280). New York: Academic Press.

Panther, Klaus-Uwe & Thornburg, Linda (1998). A cognitive approach to inferencing in conversation. *Journal of Pragmatics, 30*, 755–769.

Sadock, Jerrold M. (1974). *Toward a Linguistic Theory of Speech Acts.* New York: Academic Press.

Searle, John R. (1975). Indirect speech acts. In P. Cole & J. L. Morgan (Eds.), *Speech Acts* [Syntax and Semantics 3] (pp. 59–82). New York: Academic Press.

Sperber, Dan & Wilson, Deirdre (1986). *Relevance: Communication and Cognition.* Oxford and Cambridge, MA: Blackwell.

Stemmer, Brigitte (1994). A pragmatic approach to neurolinguisics: Requests (re)considered. *Brain and Language, 46*, 565–591.

Stemmer, Brigitte, Giroux, Francine, & Joanette, Yves (1994). Production and evaluation of requests by right hemisphere brain-damaged individuals. *Brain and Language, 47*, 1–31.

Thornburg, Linda & Panther, Klaus (1997). Speech act metonymies. In W.-A. Liebert, G. Redeker, & L. Waugh (Eds.), *Discourse and Perspective in Cognitive Linguistics* [Current Issues in Linguistic Theory 151] (pp. 205–219). Amsterdam and Philadelphia: John Benjamins.

Weylman, Sally T., Brownell, Hiram H., Roman, Mary, & Gardner, Howard (1989). Appreciation of indirect requests by left- and right-brain-damaged patients: The effect of verbal context and conventionality of wording. *Brain and Language, 36*, 580–591.

# Metonymies as natural inference and activation schemas

## The case of dependent clauses as independent speech acts

Klaus-Uwe Panther and Linda L. Thornburg

For Juliane House on the occasion of her 60th birthday

## 1. Introduction

The syntactic correlates of speech acts are typically independent sentences such as *I will submit this article on time* (promise) or *Give me more time to finish this article* (request). Many speech acts are however realized as non-sentential constituents such as *Happy birthday!* (nominal expression) or *Sorry!* (adjective) that deviate from the sentential prototype. An especially interesting class of speech acts is exemplified by the expressions in (1)–(10) below – with data from English, German and French – that look like *dependent clauses* introduced by a syntactically subordinating conjunction. Moreover, in German, such expressions exhibit dependent clause, i.e. verb-final, word order, as seen in (7)–(9). Interestingly, these apparent dependent clauses can however "stand alone" and function as independent speech acts.

*English*

(1) **If** you will come to order. [request]

(2) Why, **if** it isn't Susan! (Quirk et al. 1985: 842) [expression of surprise]

(3) **If** you would like a cookie. [offer]

(4) **That** you should say such a thing! [expression of indignation]

(5) **That** you dare to show your face here! [reproachful indignation]

(6) **For** you **to** even think that! [indignation]

*German*

(7) **Wenn** Sie jetzt bitte zahlen wollen. [request]
'If you will please pay the bill now.'

(8) **Daß** (mir) niemand den Saal verläßt! [prohibition]
'Nobody should leave this room!'

(9) **Ob** er wohl kommen wird? [question]
'I wonder whether he will come.'

*French*

(10) **Que** personne ne sorte. (Grevisse 1993:624) [prohibition]
'Nobody should leave.'

The expressions in (1)–(10) raise an intriguing question: How is it that the more or less conventional pragmatic forces with which they are associated result from what they literally convey (see also Okamoto, this volume, for a similar problem in Japanese)? In presenting our approach to answering this question we will focus on but one exemplar type in English – "independent" clauses beginning with *if*, like those in (1)–(3).

## 2. A cognitive approach to independent *if*-clauses

Our approach to independent *if*-clauses is "cognitive" in that it is based on conceptual, semantic, and functional principles. Our goal is to provide an explicit description of these clause types, to show that their pragmatic functions follow naturally from what is literally expressed, and that in many cases they constitute independent grammatical "constructions" in the sense of Goldberg (1995). We contend that the uses of these *if*-clauses are not arbitrary but that their particular pragmatic forces are *motivated*. We incorporate into our analysis an approach to speech acts as *scenarios* having metonymic structure, which we have developed in prior work (Thornburg & Panther 1997; Panther & Thornburg 1998; see also Stefanowitsch, this volume). We also make use of the theory of *mental spaces* (Fauconnier 1985; Fauconnier & Sweetser 1999: Ch. 1; also see Coulson & Oakley, this volume), a framework whose goal is to connect cognitive structure with linguistic structure.

## 2.1 The conceptual space of the independent *if*-clause

We begin with our characterization of the conceptual space of the independent *if*-clause. In the mental spaces framework, the conjunction *if* is what is called a *space builder* – that is, *if* is an overt means by which a speaker induces a hearer to set up a new mental space defined as a cognitive domain of structured information and inferences. Our characterization of this space is given in (11).

(11) The Conceptual Space of the *if*-clause

WHAT IS EXPLICITLY EXPRESSED:

- a hypothetical/possible situation or state of affairs, p

WHAT IS IMPLICATED/METONYMICALLY ACTIVATED:

- some consequence, q, that, in a given context, may follow from p;
- an assessment of the truth of p, and by extension, q, e.g., true > possible/nonactual > doubtful > false;
- an evaluation of p, and by extension, q, e.g., good/desirable > neutral > bad/undesirable;
- an emotional attitude towards p, and by extension, q, e.g., surprise, awe, wonderment, gratitude, indignation, bitterness, indifference.

What an independent *if*-clause explicitly expresses is merely a hypothetical or possible situation or state of affairs, which we refer to as p. However, we claim that the conjunction *if* – as a space builder – allows the hearer to access additional conceptual material that is metonymically or inferentially linked to p: e.g., some consequence, q, that may follow from p; the speaker's assessment of the truth of p as well as an evaluation of p; and lastly, an emotional attitude towards p that the speaker may have.[1]

Since *if*-clauses create a mental space that is distinct from *reality space*, the distance between the two conceptual spaces can be exploited for various pragmatic purposes. We propose, for example, that by locating the imposition of a request within the hypothetical space of an *if*-clause – instead of in reality space – a speaker can minimize potential face-threat. Because of this distancing capability, *if*-clauses can serve the purpose of negative politeness in directive speech acts (cf. Brown & Levinson 1987).

## 2.2 A scenario approach to speech acts

In prior research (Thornburg & Panther 1997; Panther & Thornburg 1998) we have defined speech acts and their felicity conditions in terms of scenarios –

that is, as complexes of conceptually contiguous elements that bear metonymic relations to each other and to the scenario as a whole.[2] In Figure 1 we give a simplified representation of one such scenario – the Request Scenario.

In Figure 1 the BEFORE component states preconditions and motivations for performing a request. These subcomponents of the BEFORE component are aligned respectively along the Background and Motivation branches of the scenario. The CORE and its immediate RESULT define the essential features of the request and the immediate pragmatic outcome of a felicitous performance of a request, respectively. The AFTER component describes the intended consequences of a request that lead to the realization of the propositional content of the request. The AFTER may or may not be followed by other CONSEQUENCES, e.g., the realization of a request may evoke some feeling in the speaker such as gratitude, relief, etc. These subcomponents are aligned along the Realization branch of the scenario. Thus, all subcomponents of the Request Scenario are linked to the CORE and to each other along and across the three branches. We propose that the activation of one (sub)component in a scenario offers the potential of activating – automatically or inferentially – other or even all components of the scenario. In what follows we apply the Request Scenario to the analysis of a portion of our data; other scenarios will be presented in later sections of the paper.

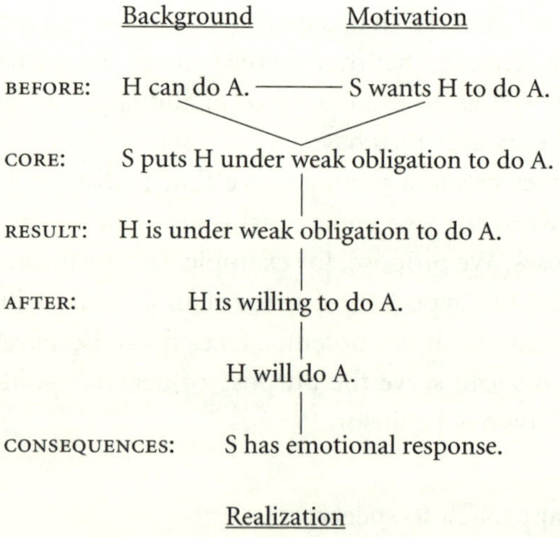


**Figure 1.** The *Request* Scenario

## 3. Analysis of data[3]

For each of the examples in the data set, we analyzed the pragmatic force with respect to (i) the content of the proposition in the *if*-clause in terms of its mental space structure, (ii) potential metonymic links to various speech act scenarios, and (iii) the degree of conventionalization, i.e. whether or not the pragmatic force of the *if*-clause is cancelable. To illustrate, consider example (1). *If you will come to order* is conventionally understood as a request to come to order.[4] To account for that fact, we begin with an analysis of the hypothetical space triggered by *if* along the lines we have proposed in (11). First, we note that the proposition within the clause, given in (1a):

> Hypothetical space for *If you will come to order*
>
> (1) a. Proposition p: you will come to order

explicitly refers to the addressees' action in terms of *future* time frame and *willingness* to undertake the action.[5] Secondly, we assume that there is a strong metonymic link between the hearers' willingness to perform the action and the *ability* to do so. Thirdly, because the hypothetical *if* space allows for potential consequent propositions in some context, in the context of a noisy classroom, say, in which a teacher utters *If you will come to order*, it is possible to infer the consequent given in (1b):

> (1) b. Inferable q: ... then I will begin the lecture.

The potential consequent proposition q in (1b) refers to the speaker's imminent undertaking of an action. Fourthly, we can also infer then that the speaker *evaluates* the hypothetical proposition in the *if*-clause as desirable (and therefore also q as desirable) and that the satisfaction of that desire will lead to the speaker's consequent action.

Our analysis of the content of the hypothetical space of the *if*-clause – that is, its knowledge, inferential and activation structure – yields several elements that can be linked to the components of the Request Scenario as represented in Figure 2: *If you will come to order* contains *explicit references* to the hearers' willingness and to a future action as well as derivable *implicit references* to the hearers' ability to undertake the action and to the speaker's desire for the action. All of these explicit and implicit elements in the *if*-space correspond to subcomponents of the Realization, Background and Motivation branches of the Request Scenario, and together activate the remainder of the scenario – namely, the CORE and the immediate RESULT represented in the shaded box.

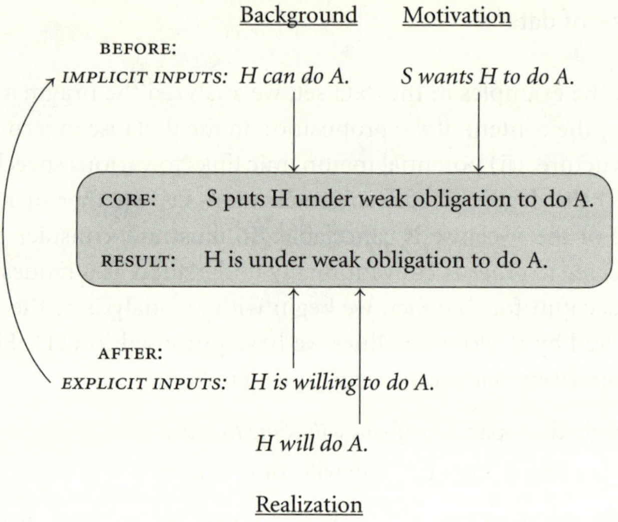


**Figure 2.** Inputs to the *Request* Scenario (utterance (1))

Having accounted for the request interpretation of *If you will come to order*, we further note that this reading is difficult – if not impossible – to cancel, as tested in (1c), which yields a pragmatic contradiction:

(1) c. Cancelability: #If you will come to order ... but I'm not asking you to do that.

Lastly, we note that the independent *if*-clause is a good candidate to be conventionalized for the expression of *polite* requests because it creates its own mental space distinct from, and therefore "distant" from, reality space. The POLITENESS IS DISTANCE metaphor predicts that a request originating in hypothetical space would be more polite than a corresponding request in reality space. Indeed, *If you will come to order* is more polite than *You will come to order.*

At this point we would like to note that example (1) illustrates the use of an independent *if*-clause for a deontic communicative function. This turns out to be but one major function. The results of our pilot study indicate that independent *if*-clauses can also be used for expressive and for epistemic purposes (see Okamoto, this volume, for a discussion of similar pragmatic functions associated with reanalyzed [S *koto*] constructions in Japanese). We consider each in turn.

## 3.1 Deontic function

In this section of the chapter we present additional *if*-clause data that have predominantly deontic pragmatic force. That is to say, what the *if*-clause implicates requires that the world should change in such a way so as to match what is metonymically evoked. As Searle (1983: 7 *et passim*), among others, has put it, the "direction of fit" in these cases is from the world to words, the so-called "so be it" use of language. In using *if*-clauses to issue directives or commissives or to express wishes, a speaker uses language to talk about the way the world will or should change to fit some propositional content.

### 3.1.1 *Directives*

We present here additional examples of *if*-clauses with directive illocutionary force:

(12) "This is awful," Julia exclaimed in consternation. "Do please tell her to stop crying, Don Felipe. I can't bear it. **If you could explain it isn't that I really want to go home.** I just have to." [LOB.P1]

For the *if*-clause in (12) our intuition is that the speaker is making a request of the addressee.[6] At issue is how we derive the pragmatic request force from what looks like a truncated conditional sentence. Using the methodology outlined and demonstrated above, we first note that the mental space triggered by *if* contains the hypothetical proposition:

(12) a. Proposition p: you could explain it isn't that I really want to go home

Embedded within the *if* space is another hypothetical space that is evoked by the modal *could*. This second hypothetical space contains the proposition that the addressee *is able* to perform an action of explaining.

Secondly, given the context, a potential consequent proposition q in this doubly hypothetical space that very likely follows from the *if*-clause is:

(12) b. Inferable q: ... then I would be so grateful to you.

This potential consequent proposition q (an expression of the speaker's contingent gratitude) in (12 b) strongly implicates that the speaker desires that the addressee do some explaining. It follows then that the speaker evaluates the hypothetical action contained in p – explaining – as being *desirable*.

Thus the *if*-clause in (12) has three elements in the doubly hypothetical space that can be inputs to the Request Scenario in Figure 3: one explicitly refers to the ability of the hearer to perform the action and the other two implicitly evoke the speaker's anticipatory gratitude for and desirability of the action. As subcomponents of the Request Scenario, they activate the remainder of the scenario, as represented in the shaded box:

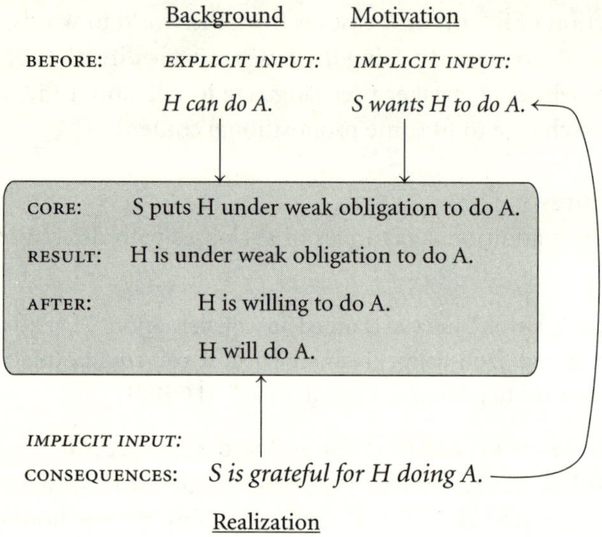


**Figure 3.** Inputs to the *Request* Scenario (utterance (12))

The request reading of (12) is fully conventionalized and uncancelable without pragmatic infelicity, as shown in (12c):

(12) c. Cancelability: #If you could explain it isn't that I really want to go home ... but I'm not asking you to explain ...

In example (13) we find a different type of directive. Here the speaker appears to *suggest* to the addressee that the two of them go up to the addressee's room.

(13) "I have made a discovery, sir. It may be of no account, but I think that you will find it – interesting. **If we could go up to your room, sir....**" Nick wondered if he was about to be touched by a blackmailer, but the young man sounded genuine enough. [LOB.P1]

In the conceptual space created by *if*, the proposition, given in (13a):

(13) a. Proposition p: we could go up to your room

expresses, in an additional hypothetical space created by the form *could*, the ability of both the speaker and the addressee to perform the action mentioned. Furthermore, a potential consequent proposition q likely to follow from p in this context is:

(13) b. Inferable q: ... then I will reveal to you my interesting discovery.

The potential consequent proposition in (13b) strongly implicates a benefit to the hearer – that is, the speaker evaluates the action in p as good for the hearer. As with example (12), the doubly hypothetical space of the *if*-clause in (13) has two elements that can be inputs to a speech act scenario, which we represent in Figure 4: one that explicitly refers to the *ability* of the hearer to perform the action and another that implicitly evokes a *benefit to the hearer* in undertaking the action. Thus, in example (13) the activated speech act scenario is that of a suggestion, whose face-threat is minimized by the metaphorical distance of the *if*-clause:

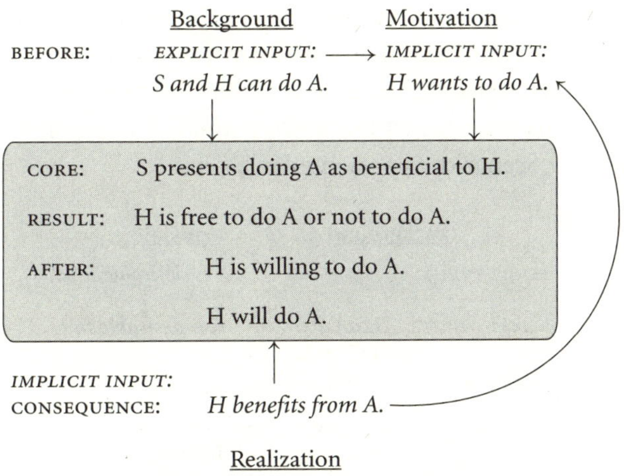


**Figure 4.** Inputs to the *Suggestion* Scenario

In the context of (13), the suggestive force is uncancelable:

(13) c. Cancelability: #If we could go up to your room, sir ... but I'm not suggesting that we do.

### 3.1.2 *Offers*

Our LOB data yielded no examples of *if*-clauses with the force of an *offer* comparable to our constructed example in (3). Yet this example strikes us as plausible and we include it in our analysis, reproduced here as (14):

(14) If you would like a cookie.

In the conceptual space of the *if*-clause, possible inferable consequences of (14) are:

(14) a. ... then I can give you one.
b. ... then I will give you one.

In (14a) the proposition *I can give you one* is interpretable as being a subcomponent of the Background branch in the Offer Scenario (at the same time a BEFORE subcomponent), whereas the proposition *I will give you one* in (14b) is interpretable as being a subcomponent of the Realization branch in the Offer Scenario (simultaneously an AFTER component). Also in the conceptual space of the *if*-clause is the possibility of elaborating the proposition *you would like a cookie* into the proposition p':

(14) c. Proposition p': you would like me (speaker) to give you a cookie

This expanded proposition p' contains as a sub-proposition A, the speaker's action of giving the hearer a cookie. Quite naturally, this action is interpretable as being both desirable to the hearer and within the speaker's capability. Thus, several propositions inferable within the hypothetical space of the *if*-clause give access to the Offer Scenario, as presented in Figure 5:

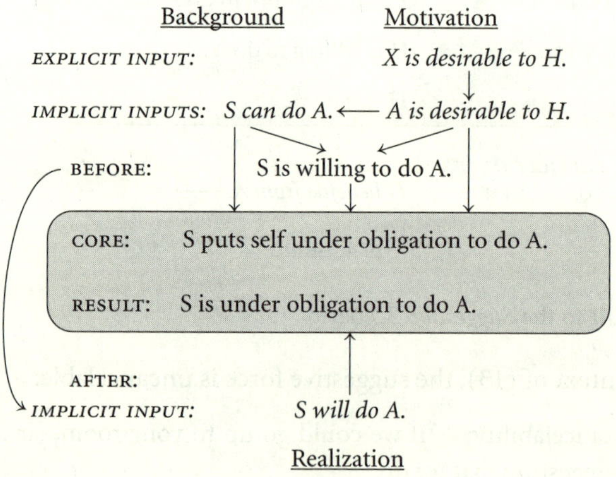


**Figure 5.** Inputs to the *Offer* Scenario

Cancelability of the offer interpretation of (14) seems impossible:

(14) d. Cancelability: #If you would like a cookie ... but I'm not offering you one.

### 3.1.3 *Wishes*

We turn now to examples of *if*-clauses that have the force of a wish expression.

(15) 'That girl's nothing but a load of trouble, I'm warning you.' 'Kitty's all right,' Bone contradicted flatly. 'It's her boy-friend that's the trouble. **If we could get rid of him...**' Harry nodded his grizzled head like an old hound. [LOB.L1]

(16) "But meanwhile, I must find her. **If only I had a clue where to look for her.**" "Has it occurred to you that when you told her about us it was such a shock to her that she has run away." [LOB.P1]

We think both these examples have the force of a wish expression.[7] However, the wish interpretation is weaker in (15) and cancelable; in contrast, *if only* in (16) makes the wish interpretation conventional and thereby uncancelable.

In (15) the hypothetical proposition:

(15) a. Proposition p: we could get rid of him

explicitly denotes the possibility for the interlocutors to carry out an action in future time, an action that is doubly hypothetical by virtue of both *if* and *could.* This gives rise to the inference that the action has not yet occurred.

Given the context in (15), an inferable consequence might be:

(15) b. Inferable q: ...then our troubles would be over.

– a satisfactory outcome from which it is possible to infer that the speaker evaluates the sub-proposition p'

(15) c. Sub-proposition p': we get rid of him

as desirable. In the hypothetical space of (15), then, we can identify four components that are inputs to the Wish Expression Scenario depicted in Figure 6: (i) the explicit reference to the *possibility* to undertake an action *to get rid of him*; (ii) the inference that the action has not occurred; (iii) implicit reference to the *desirability* of the action; and (iv) implicit reference to resulting feelings of *satisfaction.*

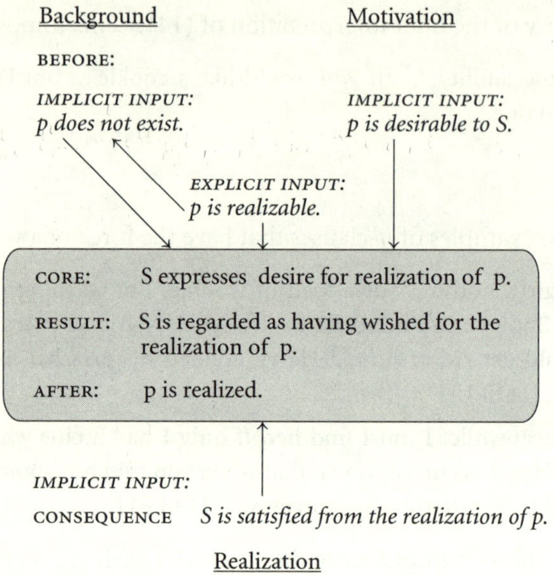


**Figure 6.** Inputs to *Expression-of-Wish* Scenario: (p = some state of affairs)

As mentioned earlier, the *wish* force of (15) seems cancelable; in other words, the wish sense is not part of the conventional meaning of the *if*-clause:

(15) d. Cancelability: If we could get rid of him but I'm not saying I *wish* we could get rid of him – I'm just entertaining the thought.

The cancelability of (15) contrasts with examples like (16) containing *if only*. The proposition in this example presented in (16a):

(16) a. Proposition p: I had a clue where to look for her

is counter-factual at the time of speaking. The focus particle *only* singles out one proposition to the exclusion of others – it highlights the importance or relevance of that proposition for the speaker; *only*, then, triggers an implicature of emotional involvement and high desirability with respect to the proposition. The *wish* interpretation is not cancelable in this case, as seen in (16b):

(16) b. Cancelability: #If only I had a clue where to look for her, but I don't wish I had a clue where to look for her.

We also note that in (16) the proposition is non-factual but also potentially fulfillable. This contrasts with examples (17) and (18) in which the propositions refer to non-occurrent past events that have no possibility of future realization.

(17) Tom, she thought. **If only I could have asked Tom's advice.** But now it's too late for that. [LOB.L1]

(18) Watching him go, unable to speak, she felt that part of her was leaving with him. She couldn't hate him... **If only he would have confided in her, given some explanation.** Now there was nothing – not even friendship. [LOB.P1]

The Wish Scenario for (17) and (18) – in contrast to that given in Figure 6 – would contain a background assumption: Some state-of-affairs is impossible. Furthermore, the unfulfillability of such wishes implicates the absence of emotional satisfaction. The emotions that are likely to be associated with unfulfillable wishes are strongly negative, such as regret, bitterness, anger and so on – which likely characterize examples (17) and (18).

We now briefly summarize Section 3.1. We discussed *if*-clauses whose predominant function is deontic – serving to metonymically convey requests, suggestions, offers, and wishes. We saw that the conceptual distance created by the space builder *if* is exploited in the cases of other-directed speech acts like directives and commissives to minimize negative face-threat. We also saw that the metonymically evoked pragmatic forces of these clauses tend to be uncancelable suggesting that they are highly conventionalized; i.e., the scenarios associated with them are automatically activated. In such cases the *if*-clause can be said to have achieved the status of a construction.

## 3.2 Expressive function

As we saw with unfulfillable wishes like (17) and (18), it is difficult to know if the speech act was predominantly deontic – the expression of a wish – or primarily an expression of emotion. In what follows we will focus on *if*-clauses whose *primary* function seems to be the expression of a strong emotional attitude with regard to some state of affairs.

### 3.2.1 *Negative p*

We begin with example (2) from Quirk et al. (1985), reproduced here as (19a). We also provide some examples from the OED given in (19b–f). All of them contain exclamation marks and/or other devices indicating that the *if*-clauses are uttered with attendant emotions.

(19) a. Why **if it isn't Susan!** (Quirk et al. 1985: 842)

b. **If he is not equipped for a housebreaker!** [1702 Vanbrugh False Friend iii. ii]

c. And, so help me never! **if his nibs didn't go and dossed with her the same night.** [1846 Swell's Night Guide 49]
d. **'If it ain't Frisco Red!'** exclaimed one prone figure. [1914 Sat. Even. Post 4 Apr. 10/1]
e. 'Oh, Gee, well, ain't that the limit?'.. **'If you aren't the grouch.'** [1925 T. Dreiser Amer. Trag. I. xvii. 145]
f. Well, by jing, **if it ain't Tom.** [Ibid. II. iii. 184]

We first note that this type of *if*-clause has the highest degree of syntactic and pragmatic independence. That is, they don't have plausible implicit consequent propositions, except perhaps for absurdities like that in (19f'):

(19) f'. Inferable q: ?Well, by jing, if it ain't Tom, then I'll eat my hat!

Secondly, we note that all the propositions in (19a–f) assert at the moment of speaking a non-factual state of affairs, for example *it ain't Tom*, when in fact it is precisely Tom. In other words, what the speaker does not do is simply assert what is empirically true in reality space, which for (19f') might be:

(19) f". Well, by jing, it is Tom!

Why might a speaker choose an *if*-clause containing a non-factual proposition for the purpose of exclaiming what is empirically true rather than a "simple" declarative sentence? Our analysis – represented schematically in Figure 7 – is the following: In speaking within hypothetical space – which the *if*-clause makes possible – the speaker places those propositions that correspond to his/her expectations of what constitutes a normal course of events. In hypothetical space, someone that you do not expect to see is not present; thus, *it ain't Tom* would be a true proposition in the hypothetical space of the speaker in (19f) prior to seeing Tom. In encountering Tom, the speaker expresses the proposition in his hypothetical space – i.e. his world of ordinary expectations – that Tom is not present. Tom's unexpected appearance in reality space is the very contradictory of the *it ain't Tom* proposition in hypothetical space. The clash between expectation and reality surprises the speaker, an emotion that is expressed in the uttering of the hypothetical proposition, which is now no longer true.[8]

It seems that the expression of an emotional attitude such as surprise or amazement cannot be canceled in these cases involving contradictions between *if* space and reality space.

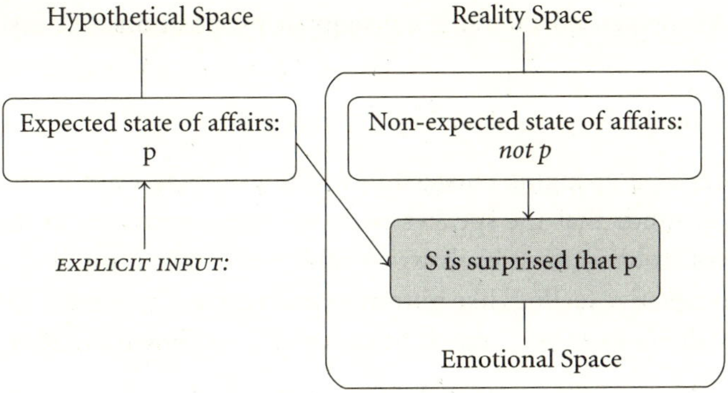


**Figure 7.** Input to the *Exclamatory if not p* Scenario:

A slightly different case is (19e), which seems rather to express irony. In (19e) we find that what is posited as expected in the speaker's hypothetical space is the norm:

(19) e'. posited norm: *you aren't the grouch*

By using an *if*-clause in this case the speaker can achieve multiple effects: avoid directness, metonymically implicate the contradictory in reality space, namely, *you are the grouch* (implicating "it is so"), convey a normative evaluation – one shouldn't be a grouch – and express a negative emotion such as dissatisfaction.

### 3.2.2 *Positive p*

Unlike the examples discussed thus far in Section 3.2, example (20) does not contain a negative proposition in the *if*-clause:

(20) 'You must think I like the military sticking its nose in.' I said bitterly: 'We spend our lives running things the quiet way. Then the army arrives – a blow, a false word – bang – suddenly there are shots. All right. **If that's the way they want it.** But don't ask me to clean up the mess.' [LOB.K1]

Here the speaker uses the hypothetical space of an *if*-clause to convey the positive proposition:

(20) a. Proposition p: that's the way they want it

This implicit assertion has a words-to-world direction of fit – it describes a state of affairs. But it also functions to metonymically evoke the speaker's disagreement with the proposition, namely, that that's not the way the speaker wants it.[9] Moreover, an inferable consequent proposition that easily follows from (20a) is:

(20) b. Inferable q: ... then they can have it.

which expresses a grudging concession to the way they want it and provides additional grounds that the speaker evaluates the proposition as undesirable, out of his control and most likely irreversible, and – like unfulfillable wishes – gives rise to negative feelings like bitterness and regret. This dissatisfaction with the state of affairs does not seem to be cancelable, as shown in (20c):

(20) c. Cancelability: #If that's the way they want it, fine, it's also my profoundest wish.

The examples in (19) and (20) have been presented with the claim that their primary function is the expression of an emotional attitude with regard to a state of affairs – i.e. some "it is so" description. In the cases in (19), the *if*-clause provides a mental space for conveying an expected state of affairs that is contradicted in reality space. Because of the discrepancy between what is hypothetically denied but empirically true, the construction is a potential vehicle for the expression of attitudes like surprise or amazement, a use which is conventional. In contrast, in cases like (20), the construction is used to conventionally signal disapproval of what is conceded in hypothetical space, an emotional attitude that results from the speaker's opposition to what he/she concedes.

## 3.3 Epistemic function

### 3.3.1 *Reasoning from premises*

In this last part of our data analysis we show how a speaker may use an *if*-clause for predominantly epistemic, i.e. reasoning, purposes. In these cases the direction of fit is from "words-to-world" – using language to convey the sense of "it is so." In the first set of examples below the main function of the *if*-clause is to introduce a premise on the basis of which non-expressed conclusions can be drawn. Consider (21) and (22):

(21) So it had been chance that saved the organisation. **If Rickie Oppenheimer hadn't picked up the wrong valise...** But Rickie shouldn't have been carrying a brief-case that morning. Every other time he'd left it in the office at the Blue Bottle Club. Monday night he'd broken a long-standing habit. [LOB.L1]

(22) Judging from the spot where it lay it had been planted between the underside of the mattress and one of the cross-supports. **If I hadn't re-made the bed... if Sonia and I hadn't made love...** Sonia. Nothing else accounted for the presence of that hellish box. I'd left her alone in the bedroom when we awoke from the brief sleep of exhaustion. [LOB.L1]

We note first that the *if*-clauses in (21) and (22) – unlike those in (19) – have a *low* degree of pragmatic independence; rather, they give the impression of being highly elliptical *if*-clauses. Secondly, they are classical cases of counterfactuals. In uttering a counterfactual premise in hypothetical space – as represented in Figure 8 – the speaker pragmatically activates the shared background knowledge in reality space that the proposition is false and at the same time invites the hearer to consider the counterfactual proposition as a premise from which to reason to unstated consequences.

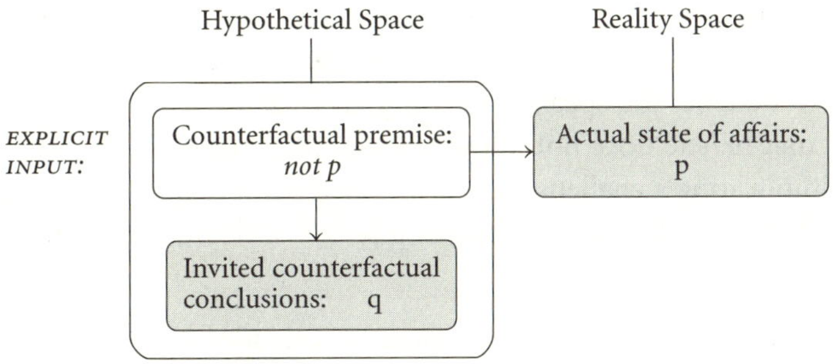


**Figure 8.** Input to the *Reasoning* Scenario

Example (23) is similar to (21) and (22) in inviting the reasoner to complete the conditional by drawing conclusions from the premise it expresses.

(23) Farland summed up. Quite fair to hold out on Winter. It seems he's keeping things back. **If he knows about the knife... And if he knows that Wally did attack the girl...** There were voices in the hall and Winter entered with the visitor.

In this example, however, the premise is not counterfactual but merely not known to be true. Nevertheless, despite the lack of certainty about the truth of p, the reasoner seems to believe that it is rational to assume that p. What we see in (23) is a kind of hedged assertion or reasonable supposition that p. Note, however, that the (weak) assertive force can be canceled very easily, as in (23a) and (b):

(23) a. If he knows about the knife... But I don't believe he really knows about it...
b. And if he knows that Wally did attack the girl... But I don't think he knows that Wally attacked the girl...

### 3.3.2 *Challenging prior assumptions*

Example (24) is quite different from the preceding cases in having a fairly autonomous status:

(24) "I've told you I have no idea who this warning could have been for. **If it was a warning.**" "Did anyone turn up at her place," he probed patiently, "soon after she was dead?" [LOB.L1]

As for the examples in (19), for (24) there do not seem to be any plausible consequent propositions that follow from the *if*-clause. Our proposal for the conceptual structure of (24) is represented in Figure 9. That is, given a context in reality space in which some proposition like 'it was a warning' is generally assumed to be true, the speaker, in using an *if*-clause, conveys in hypothetical space that he/she does not know *whether* the proposition is true, thereby strongly implicating a challenge to the *assumed* truth of p in reality space.[10]

Indeed, the implicature raised by *if p* seems difficult, if not impossible, to cancel:

(24) a. Cancelability: "I've told you I have no idea who this warning could have been for. **If it was a warning. #But I think it was a warning.**"

We briefly summarize the analysis of data in this last section regarding the use of *if*-clauses in relation to reasoning. We saw that in posing within an independent *if*-clause a premise whose truth value is not known – as in (23), a speaker can implicate in hypothetical space a weak assertion, which is cancelable, as

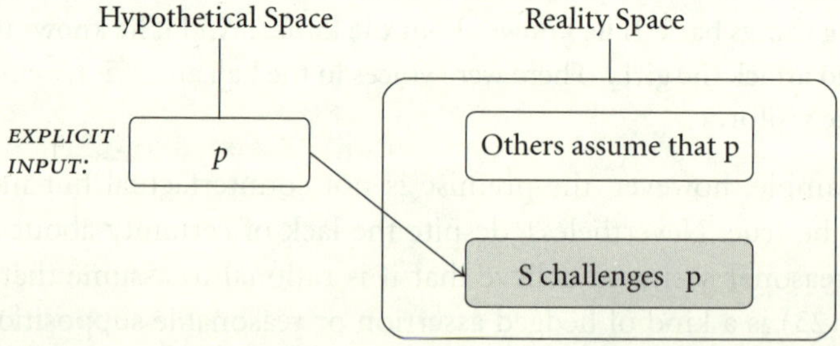


**Figure 9.** Input to the *Challenge-to-p* Scenario

well as implicate unstated conclusions. But in posing a premise within an *if*-clause whose truth value is known to be counterfactual – as in (21) and (22) – or assumed to be true – as in (24), the speaker has access to two mental spaces at once: the hypothetical space created by *if* and the reality space in which the opposite state of affairs holds. *If* plus a past counterfactual implicates a line of reasoning leading to a false conclusion while simultaneously metonymically evoking an opposite line of reasoning leading to a known conclusion – an economical way of reviewing two chains of events: what might have happened and what in fact happened. On the other hand, *if* plus a premise assumed by others to be true conventionally conveys that the speaker questions that assumption.

## 4. Summary and conclusions

When independent *if*-clauses are used as directives and commissives, *if* creates a hypothetical space that is metaphorically mapped onto negative politeness where "non-reality" corresponds to "non-imposition." Within that polite space, mentions of ability, willingness, benefit, future action, etc. are interpreted as BEFORE and AFTER components of speech act scenarios and thus function as conceptual metonymic links to these scenarios.

When independent *if*-clauses are used to express wishes, *if (only)* simply creates a hypothetical world that may even be counterfactual. Within that space, mention of e.g. possibility can metonymically evoke the wish scenario as a whole in which the speaker "implores" the world to change in such a way as to match a description. In the case of unrealizable wishes, the *if*-clause can also convey strong emotional attitudes (regret, despair). In the use of an independent *if*-clause to express surprise, amazement, irony, etc., *if p* describes an expected state of affairs in hypothetical space that contrasts with its metonymically linked opposite state of affairs in reality space.

When independent *if*-clauses are used epistemically, *if* establishes a hypothetical space for reasoning to an unknown conclusion. Especially interesting are the cases when the *if*-clause is used to reason with a counterfactual premise known to be false or to challenge a proposition assumed by others to be true. In these cases what is expressed in the *if* space is metonymically linked to an opposite state of affairs in reality space.

We conclude that the pragmatic speech act forces conventionally associated with the deontic, expressive, and epistemic functions of independent *if*-clauses are not arbitrary pairings of pragmatic meaning with linguistic form, but rather are motivated largely by metonymically based pragmatic inferences.

## Notes

1. We regard the components "assessment of the truth of p" and "evaluation of p" to be an elaboration of Fillmore's notion of *epistemic stance* (cited in Sweetser 1996:318) – "the speaker's mental association with or dissociation from the world of the protasis [...]."

2. Ruiz de Mendoza Ibáñez and Pérez Hernández (this volume) would call relations between parts of a scenario and the whole scenario 'source-in-target' metonymies.

3. The majority of our data were collected from the Lancaster-Oslo-Bergen-Corpus [LOB], which consists of contextualized naturalistic language. We extracted from the results of our search only those examples of *if*-clauses lacking an apodosis plus the surrounding context of each. Additional data were taken from the CD-ROM version of the *Oxford English Dictionary*.

4. Stefanowitsch (this volume) would treat such examples as constructions with a fixed conventional illocutionary meaning.

5. We take the meaning of *will* in this context to be ambiguous. Cf. Sweetser (1996:329ff.) for discussion of the meaning of *will* in protases.

6. This intuition is supported by the *please* test. That is, *please* can be inserted into the *if*-clause making the utterance a request.

7. Example (15) could also be construed as a suggestion, which we don't consider here.

8. A Gricean analysis might argue that the speaker has flouted the Maxim of Quality: that is, in asserting what is empirically not the case, a speaker implicates "the most obviously related proposition [...] the contradictory of the one he purports to be putting forward" (Grice 1975:53). This argument seems to apply where irony is the intended contextual effect as in (19e), but does not seem to account for the exclamatory force of the other examples in (19).

9. See Voßhagen (1999) on the notion of opposition as a metonymic principle.

10. Examples of the type in (24) are probably quite numerous. We surmise that they will contain adverbs such as *really*, *ever*, etc. to signal that the speaker is in doubt about the truth of the hypothetical proposition, e.g.:

(i) If it was actually Mary (and not Sheila, Linda, etc.).
(ii) If she really did write that letter (as they claim).
(iii) If he ever did propose to her (as she claims).

Another characteristic of this type of *if*-clause is that it is used for "afterthoughts"; i.e., it cannot be used to initiate a conversation but rather expresses a reaction to some assumed state of affairs.

## References

Brown, Penelope & Levinson, Stephen C. (1987). *Politeness: Some Universals in Language Use* [Studies in Interactional Sociolinguistics 4]. Cambridge: Cambridge University Press.

Fauconnier, Gilles (1985). *Mental Spaces: Aspects of Meaning Construction in Natural Language*. Cambridge, MA: The MIT Press. Reprinted 1994, Cambridge: Cambridge University Press.

Goldberg, Adele (1995). *Constructions: A Construction Grammar Approach to Argument Structure* [Cognitive Theory of Language and Culture]. Chicago and London: The University of Chicago Press.

Grevisse, Maurice (1993). *Le Bon Usage*. Paris and Louvain-la-Neuve: Duculot.

Grice, H. Paul (1975). Logic and conversation. In P. Cole & J. L. Morgan (Eds.), *Speech Acts* [Syntax and Semantics 3] (pp. 41–58). New York: Academic Press.

Panther, Klaus-Uwe & Thornburg, Linda (1998). A cognitive approach to inferencing in conversation. *Journal of Pragmatics, 30*, 755–769.

Quirk, Randolph, Greenbaum, Sidney, Leech, Geoffrey, & Svartvik, Jan (1985). *A Comprehensive Grammar of the English Language*. London: Longman.

Searle, John R. (1983). *Intentionality: An Essay in the Philosophy of Mind*. Cambridge: Cambridge University Press.

Sweetser, Eve (1996). Mental spaces and the grammar of conditional constructions. In G. Fauconnier & E. Sweetser (Eds.), *Spaces, Worlds, and Grammar* [Cognitive Theory of Language and Culture 2] (pp. 318–333). Chicago and London: The University of Chicago Press.

Sweetser, Eve & Fauconnier, Gilles (1996). Cognitive links and domains: Basic aspects of mental space theory. In G. Fauconnier & E. Sweeter (Eds.), *Spaces, Worlds, and Grammar* [Cognitive Theory of Language and Culture 2] (pp. 1–28). Chicago and London: The University of Chicago Press.

Thornburg, Linda & Panther, Klaus (1997). Speech act metonymies. In W.-A. Liebert, G. Redeker, & L. Waugh (Eds.), *Discourse and Perspectives in Cognitive Linguistics* [Current Issues in Linguistic Theory 151] (pp. 205–219). Amsterdam and Philadelphia: John Benjamins.

Voßhagen, Christian (1999). Opposition as a metonymic principle. In K.-U. Panther & G. Radden (Eds.), *Metonymy in Language and Thought* [Human Cognitive Processing 4] (pp. 289–308). Amsterdam and Philadelphia: John Benjamins.

# Metonymic pathways to neuter-gender human nominals in German

Klaus-Michael Köpcke and David A. Zubin

## 1. Introduction: remarkable syntax in a text by Karl Waggerl

At the end of his tale about the three pledges of love, Karl Waggerl finishes with the rather peculiar sentence in (1):[1]

(1) … als er in die Stube kam, da lag sein Mädchen auf der Bahre. Da wußte er, daß sie es war, die er dreimal geliebt und dreimal verraten hatte, und nun steckte sein Messer mitten in ihrer weißen Brust.
[…] when he entered the main room, there lay his girl on the bier. And then he knew that she was the one[2] whom he had loved three times, and three times betrayed, and now there was his knife, thrust in the middle of her white breast.

As the underlining indicates, Waggerl switches back and forth between *fem*- and *neut*-gender in apparent anaphoric reference to the noun *Mädchen*.[3] Our goal in this paper will be to provide a general context in which this apparent anomaly is explained. In the process we will first briefly review the state of research on the semantics of nominal classification in German, and then provide evidence for both the historical and current productivity of *neut*-gender classification for human beings, and females in particular, before returning to the Waggerl text. As the discussion moves through these three steps the functional role that *metonymy* plays will become apparent, first as part of the diachronic lexical processes that result in *neut*-gender human nouns, and then in the pragmatics of referential tracking. In developing the argument we will follow Lakoff's analysis and commentary on metonymic ICMs (Lakoff & Johnson 1980: Ch. 8; Lakoff 1987: Ch. 5). Four of Lakoff's (1987: 84–85) points about metonymy are particularly pertinent to our analysis:

a. A metonymic relation is dependent on a *background metonymic model*, a species of ICM (Idealized Cognitive Model). In many cases this ICM embodies *a socio-culturally defined stereo-* or *archetype.*
b. In the ICM there is an element A closely associated with an element B, and [in discourse/situational context].[4] B will uniquely determine A.
c. B is [communicatively] useful for the given purpose in context.[5]
d. "Most metonymic models are, in fact [...] models of *individuals*."

To these four points we add (e), which follows from point (c) and examples in Lakoff and Johnson (1980: Ch. 8):

e. Some property evoked by B is relevant to the speaker's current discourse intent, and often is carried into the resulting discourse representation.[6]

In particular we will suggest, as depicted in Figure 1, that there is a background metonymic model embodying a socio-cultural stereotype of (sexual) innocence, social naiveté, dependent social status, etc., associated with a class of *neut*-gender nominals referring to human females. Since this is a model of an individual, B is the stereotype, and A is the discourse (or situational) referent. Furthermore, by metonymically identifying the referent through the stereotype, the speaker succeeds in mapping properties of the stereotype onto the referent. The cue for evoking this mechanism is the incongruence between a *neut*-gender nominal or pronoun as the referring expression, and the female sex of the referent. In contrast, the use of a *fem*-gender referring expression establishes a direct deictic link to the referent in the discourse world, by virtue of the *congruence* between the grammatical gender of the referring expression and the sex of the referent (hence "natural" gender), with no intervening metonymic model.

There is, however, a consequence of contrasting *fem*-gender and *neut*-gender reference to females in the same context. This consequence is depicted in Figure 1 in the markedness relationship between *fem*-gender as the unmarked (non-metonymic) referential form for females, labeled (α) in the figure, and the metonymic use of *neut*-gender, labeled (β). Note that *fem*-gender, as the unmarked member of the opposition, may take on a *contextually* marked value, labeled (α′) in the diagram. This is another female stereotype, one of sexual experience, social maturity, sophistication, etc. When *neut*-gender is used to evoke the neuter-metonymic model (β) in a particular context, the other, *fem*-metonymic model (α′) may be contextually evoked when *fem*-gender referring expressions are also used.

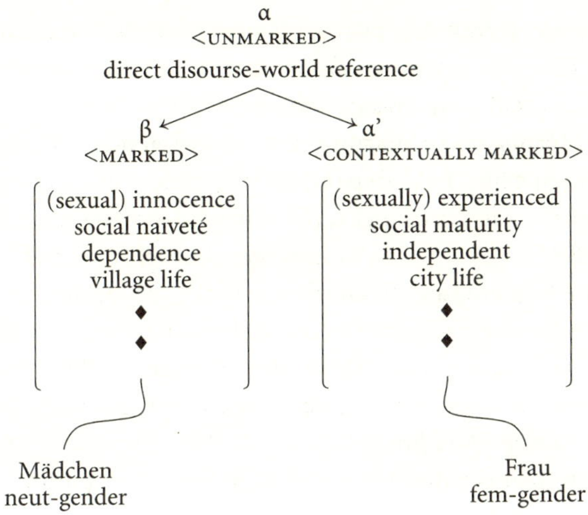


**Figure 1.** Markedness relations among female-reference nominals.[7]

In order to follow up on this hypothesis we will begin with a brief review of what is known about the semantics of nominal classification in German.

## 2. The semantics of nominal classification in German

There has been a great deal of research in this area, reviewed in such places as Wienold (1967), Zubin and Köpcke (1984, 1986), Claudi (1985), Corbett (1991), and Köpcke and Zubin (1996), but such research has tended to be anecdotal rather than systematic, and limited to a biased sample of high-frequency nouns. In our own previous work (Köpcke 1982; Köpcke & Zubin 1983, 1984, 1996; Zubin & Köpcke 1981, 1984, 1986, in preparation) we have been able to demonstrate the existence of underlying patterns of semantic motivation for gender assignment.

### 2.1 Some principles of gender assignment in the German lexicon

We have argued for the following general principles underlying gender assignment in folk-taxonomic domains in the German lexicon (cf. Zubin & Köpcke 1986):

a. **Superordinate terms** are primarily *neut*-gender, for example, *das Obst* 'fruit', *das Gemüse* 'vegetable', *das Auto* 'automobile', *das Motorrad* 'motorcycle', *das Kraftfahrzeug* 'motor vehicle'.
b. **Basic level terms** are primarily *masc*- or *fem*-gender, the choice often depending on specific field-dependent principles. For example, fruit types are *fem*-gender (*die Birne* 'pear', *die Apfelsine* 'orange'); vegetable types are *masc*-gender (*der Spargel* 'asparagus', *der Brokkoli* 'broccoli') or *fem*-gender (*die Tomate* 'tomato', *die Zucchini* 'zucchini'), depending on the plant part from which the vegetable is derived.[8] Referring expressions for cars are productively *masc*-gender (*der BMW, der Mercedes C200*) while corresponding referring expressions for motorcycles are productively *fem*-gender (*die BMW, die Harley-Davidson).*
c. **Subordinate terms** inherit their gender from the dominating basic-level term. For example beer subtypes (*das Pilsner, das Dortmunder*) inherit *neut*-gender from the basic-level term *das Bier*. Wine subtypes (*der Riesling, der Burgunder*) inherit *masc*-gender from the basic-level term *der Wein*. Soda subtypes (*die Cola, die Fanta)* inherit their *fem*-gender from the basic-level terms *die Brause* and *die Limonade.*[9]

## 2.2 Empirical support for non-arbitrary gender assignment in German

But just how inclusive are such gender-motivating principles in the lexicon? In order to test the generality of semantic principles, and of corresponding phonological principles, we have constructed an extensive cross-sectional random sample of the nominal lexicon in German (Zubin & Köpcke, in preparation), based on the *Duden Universalwörterbuch* (1983). In the analysis of this sample we created a measure of *cognitive entropy* on a scale ranging from 0 (no semantic association at all) to 5 (the nominal receives its gender based on a fully productive semantic principle); intermediate steps correspond to increasing degrees of generality of the basis for gender assignment.[10] This was coupled with a corresponding measure of formal entropy, again ranging from 0–5. The combined mean entropy for nominals is about 5.0 indicating that on the average, gender assignment is fully motivated through a combination of semantic, phonological and morphological factors. Some nouns have an entropy as high as 10, indicating the cooperation of fully productive semantic and formal factors. And very few nouns in the sample have negative entropy (which indicates an anomalous gender assignment in conflict with overall semantic and phonological factors).

## 3. German *neut*-gender classification for human beings

### 3.1 Historical development and current productivity

Several of our studies include diachronic data showing that there is a general drift toward greater semantic motivation in the evolution of gender assignment in the lexicon. For example, the *neut*-gender human nouns – the topic of this paper – have their beginnings as a lexical field in the lexicon with nouns such as those in Table 1.

**Table 1.** The *neut*-gender nominal cluster for humans in the period between Middle High German and Early New High German

| Lexeme | Diachronic Source (MHG > ENHG) | Current Meaning |
|---|---|---|
| *das Aas* | 'rotting body' | 'nasty woman' |
| *das Luder* | 'bait' | 'loose woman' |
| *das Mädchen* | 'little girl' < Magd | 'girl' (basic-level term) |
| *das Mensch** | der Mensch 'human being' | 'loose, useless woman' |
| *das Reff* | 'skeleton' | 'skinny old woman' |
| *das Weib* | 'woman' (basic-level term) | '(ugly, old) woman' |

**Das Mensch* is a *neut*-gender alternate that first appeared in the 16th century.

As the middle column suggests, such *neut*-gender nouns have a wide variety of etymological sources, with only a minority of them originating with female human reference. For example, *das Luder* referred to meat used as bait for trapping animals. One can only speculate about the origins of the cluster. But the following nouns form a plausible basis:

a. *das Weib* has had *neut*-gender since its Germanic origins and was the basic-level term for 'woman' until the 16th century, when it was gradually replaced by *die Frau* and began to take on its pejorative meaning. The parallel semantic shift of other nouns such as *die Dirne* ('girl' > 'prostitute') points to a general culture-historical basis for the shift (cf. Grimm & Grimm 1984).
b. *der Mensch* developed a *neut*-gender alternate in the 16th century. Initially this alternate made sex-neutral generic reference to humans, evident in citations from Luther, but then became increasingly restricted in reference to women, first as a completely neutral referring expression (parallel to *das Weib*), but then developing pejorative and objectifying affect in the 17/18th century (cf. Grimm & Grimm 1984).

c. das Mädchen gradually replaced *die Magd* as the basic-level term for 'girl' in the 17/18th century.[11] There was no corresponding shift of *der Junge* or *der Knabe* 'boy' to *das Jüngchen* or das *Knäblein* as basic-level terms.

In the transitional period leading up to Early New High German the small group of nouns in Table 1, perhaps led by *das Mensch* and *das Weib*, developed form-meaning correspondences that brought them into a lexical cluster through a variety of processes detailed in Table 3. This small cluster was characterized by semantic/pragmatic downgrading on the one hand, and *neut*-gender on the other. The 19th and 20th centuries have seen a dramatic increase in the size of the cluster, leaving no doubt about its productive potential. In our sample of about 100 *neut*-gender human nominals from this period, many have entered the German lexicon in the last 50 years, some of these quite recently. A few recent additions are given in Table 2.

Nowhere is semantic motivation in the lexicon stronger than in the domain of nominals referring to human beings. Human sex is the basis for the typological distinction between gender systems, as in Indo-European or Australian languages such as Dyirbal (Dixon 1968, 1982) and other non-gender noun class systems such as those in Swahili/Bantu (Contini-Morava 2001) or Navajo/Athapaskan (Young & Morgan 1987) that do not function to distinguish sex. Indeed human sex is the basis for the linguistic term 'gender' itself. In German *masc*- and *fem*-gender are highly productive for nominals referring to human males and females, respectively.[12] Yet in the German lexicon there are long-noted exceptions to sex-based assignment, some already noted above in Tables 1 and 2. A systematic examination of such human-reference nouns shows that *neut*-gender nominals are not randomly distributed and have formed a cluster in the lexicon with some modest productivity, as illustrated

**Table 2.** Productivity of the *neut*-gender cluster

| Lexeme | Diachronic Source (< 5–50 years) | Current Meaning |
|---|---|---|
| *das Bunny* | English: Playboy club bunny | 'club hostess in costume' |
| *das Groupie* | English | 'female rock-band fan' |
| *das Model** | English | '(clothing, photo) model' |
| *das Pin-up* | English | 'pinup' (picture, woman) |
| *das Video-Chick* | English | 'female participant in MTV video' |

*Pronounced [mádəl]. The lexeme *Modell* [modél] is older and has a more complex history.

**Table 3.** Diachronic mechanisms in the evolution of human-reference *neut*-gender nominals

| Process Type | Neuter Examples | Literal Meaning |
|---|---|---|
| Animal metaphor | *das Bunny* | 'little rabbit' |
| | *das Schwein* | 'pig' |
| | *das Schaf* | 'sheep' |
| Shape metaphor | *das Klappergestell* | 'flimsy rack' |
| | *das Knochengerüst* | 'bony scaffold' |
| Objectification/ dehumanization | *das (Sexual-)objekt* | 'sexual object' |
| | *das Element* | 'element' |
| | *das Model* | 'model' |
| | *das Ding* | 'thing' |
| Diminuative/ trivialization | *das Entlein* | 'duckling' |
| | *das Hürchen* | 'little whore' |
| | *das Hausmütterchen* | 'little house-mother' |
| Metonymy | *das Frauenzimmer* | 'women's parlor' |
| | *das Callgirl, Covergirl* | 'call girl, cover girl' |
| | *das Ding* | 'thing'* |
| | *das Ekel* | 'disgust' |
| | *das Flittchen* < vb *'flittern'* | 'little flitterer' |
| | *das Loch* | 'hole' |
| Archetype† (fairy-tale based) | *das Aschenputtel* | 'Cinderella' |
| | *das Schneewittchen* | 'Snow White' |
| | *das Rotkäppchen* | 'Little Red Riding Hood' |

*Also, euphimistic reference to vulva, penis.
†Giesela Breitling, writing in *Die Tageszeitung* 3/8/1991, captures the current cultural relevance of fairytale archetypes: "Sie [die Märchenfiguren] sind eingewoben in ein kunstvolles Gebilde aus Geschichten, von denen wir ein Echo vernommen haben in unserer Kindheit, als wir einige dieser Geschichten in kindgemäß zurechtgestutzter Fassung gelesen hatten oder vorgelesen bekamen. [...] – Aschenbrödel, Schneewittchen, Schneeweißchen und Rosenrot –, diesen Griseldis-Figuren, diesen Idiotinnen an Gefühl und Verstand: *richtungsweisende Disziplinierungsinstrumente, die uns Unterwürfigkeit und Schweigen als weibliche Kardinaltugenden angedient haben*" [italics ours].

in Table 2. The nominals in this cluster have the diachronic sources depicted in Table 3.

### 3.2 Metonymic motivation of German neut-*gender nouns*

At this point we turn to the central role that metonym*y* plays as a source of *neut*-gender for human-reference nouns discussed in Section 3.1. Many are based on metonymically structured perspectival ICMs, as defined in Figure 2.

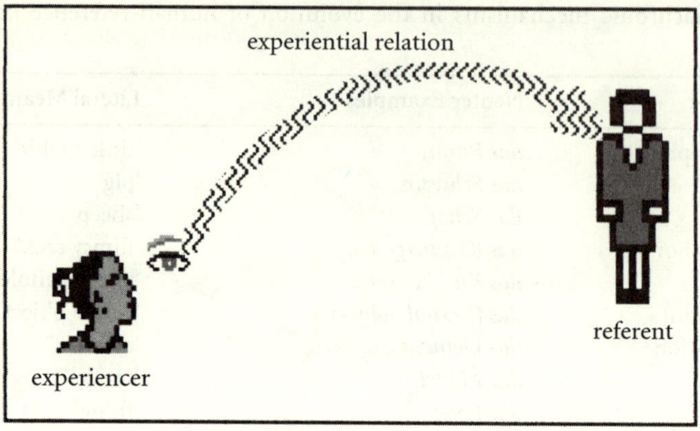


**Figure 2.** Perspectival metonymically-structured ICMs.

These are an elaboration of the basic metonymic ICM presented in Figure 1. The ICMs are *perspectival* in that they contain not only a referent (an object of perspective) and a stereotype, but also an experiencer and an experiential relation that may have affective content in what Langacker (1990) identifies as a subjective viewing arrangement.[13]

There are at least four subtypes of perspective in these ICMs, as depicted in Table 4.

**Table 4.** Types of perspective in the metonymically structured ICMs for downgrading women

| PERSPECTIVES | CHARACTERIZATIONS |
|---|---|
| Type A | The experiencer expresses negative affect such as disapproval, rejection, scorn, dislike, trivialization toward the referent. This ICM is evoked by *neut*-gender nominals such as *Weib* 'woman', *Reff* 'skeleton', *Luder* 'bait', *Ferkel* 'piglet', and *Aas* 'rotten body'. |
| Type B | The experiencer treats the referent as a visual object. This ICM is evoked by *neut*-gender nominals such as *Mannequin, Model, Pin-up, Revuegirl,* and *Centerfold.* |
| Type C | The experiencer treats the referent as an object of inspection or analysis, which typically implicates depersonalization. This ICM is evoked by nominals such as *Objekt* 'object', *Subjekt* 'subject', *Wesen* 'being'. |
| Type D | The experiencer views the referent as the embodiment of (presexual) innocence and conformity to (stereotypic) social values. |

In all, we have identified nine subtypes of metonymic grounding that account for about 80% of our exhaustive sample of *neut*-gender human nouns:

a. **Body part, physical characteristic.** In some cases the metonymic source is transparent, as with *das Mannweib* ('butch,' lit. 'man-woman'); in others the metonymic source is synchronically obscure, as with *das Besteck* 'set of instruments'.
b. **Dress, accompanying objects.** This includes nouns like *das Rotkäppchen* (lit. 'red cap', i.e. 'little red riding hood'), which evokes a piece of clothing, and *das Nummerngirl* (lit. 'number girl', i.e. 'woman who holds sign on shows'), which evokes a held object.
c1. **Characteristic activity, behavior.** This includes monolexemic nouns like *das Groupie*, which evoke a specific type of behavior, and compound nouns such as *das Klageweib* (lit. 'weeping woman') that actually describe behavior.
c2. **Behavior based on animal metaphor.** The initial referential transfer for these nouns is based on an animal metaphor that (stereotypically) describes characteristic behavior. Metonymic reference to a person is then accomplished by using the metaphor to evoke this behavior. Examples are *das Schaf* ('sheep'), which evokes passive dependent behavior or disposition, and *das Schwein* ('pig'), which evokes sloppy and or socially offensive behavior.
d. **Status.** Some *neut*-gender nouns evoke the social or personal status of the referent, sometimes through an animal metaphor. Examples are *das Mündel* ('ward'), evoking legal dependency, and *das Küken* ('chick'), evoking physical immaturity (as well as other properties).
e. **Intersubjective reaction.** In this type the structure of the background metonymically structured ICM is especially apparent. Some *neut*-gender nouns in the group, such as *das Ekel* ('disgusting person,' lit. 'disgust'), evoke the affective reaction directly.[14] Others such as *das Miststück* ('piece of dung') evoke an object or situation that gives rise to the affective reaction. In these cases there is an initial metaphor underlying the metonymic relation.
f. **Representation.** In this type the nominal evokes a representation (picture, doll, puppet, etc.) of a human being. In some cases both the source and the target of the metonymic relation may be referred to, e.g. *das Centerfold*, which may refer both to the picture in the center of the magazine, and to the person who is depicted there.
g. **Archetype.** In this type a social archetype is named in order to evoke characteristic behavior, appearance, etc. *Das Flintenweib* ('gun-woman'), for

example, describes the archetype of a frontier woman with gun in hand in order to evoke aggressive, uncompromising behavior.

h. **Instance.** These are nominals that to a greater or lesser extent segregate an individual from a group or collection. Depersonalization is often a perlocutionary effect of this metonymic process. Examples are *das Unikum* ('original') and das *Weibsstück* ('hussy,' lit. 'piece of woman').

i. **Location.** These nominals evoke reference to a characteristic location. The classic example is *das Frauenzimmer* ('skirt,' lit. 'woman's room'), which has followed a complex diachronic metonymic pathway: (a) the 19th century women's parlor; (b) women gathered in such a parlor; (c) women of a class to participate in parlor gatherings; (d) a single woman as in (c); and finally (e) a shift from positive to negative affect in the metonymically structured ICM.

Whatever their metonymic source, the examples given in (a)-(i) above all depend on the perspectival metonymic ICM structure depicted in Figures 1 and 2. For example, *das Ekel* 'disgusting person' evokes a perspectival ICM in which the experiencer feels disgust in the presence of the object of experience. *Flintenweib* 'gun-woman' evokes a cultural stereotype of the hardy independent frontier woman when used as a referring expression. In general the examples discussed in this section are characteristic of the approximately 100 nouns in our database of *neut*-gender downgrading human nominals.

## 4. Metonymic processes in discourse: the Waggerl text

We now turn to the final issue: given that there is a nominal cluster in the lexicon that continues to attract human *neut*-gender nominals, and given that the processes underlying the growth of this cluster are supported by metonymic ICMs, we may pose the question, to what extent do these lexical structures play a role in discourse processes, in particular in lexical choice and in pronominal anaphora (see also Ruiz de Mendoza & Pérez Hernández, this volume)?[15]

We will illustrate the impact that these lexical structures have on discourse processes in the short story *Legende der drei Pfänder der Liebe* ('The Legend of the Three Pledges of Love') by Karl Waggerl. The story tells of a young village pot-maker who leaves his girl and goes off to sell his wares in the surrounding towns. She gives him three pledges of love: a hair ribbon, a ring, and a knife. On his travels he camps alone, as promised, and each night he is visited by a mysterious woman who sleeps with him. Each morning he gives this woman one of the love pledges from his girl at home, and on the third night the knife. On the way home he finds the ribbon and the ring, and begins to wonder. Upon entering his house he finds his girl there with the knife in her breast, and realizes that his girl and the mysterious woman are one and the same.

A few pertinent highlights will help to make clear the role that gender plays in structuring the story. First, the story evokes two contrasting archetypes (cf. Figure 1): the sexually innocent naive female bound to village life and morality (β ICM), lexicalized with the *neut*-gender noun *Mädchen*, and the sexually experienced, citified, independent, amoral female (α′ ICM), lexicalized with the *fem*-gender noun *Frau*. Second, in section A of the story (see Appendix) in which the girl is the object of perspective, anaphoric pronouns are consistently *neut*-gender. In section B in which the woman is perspectivized, anaphoric pronouns are consistently *fem*-gender.

Finally comes the somewhat unusual syntax of section C, with which the issues of this paper were introduced: "Da wußte er, daß sie es war, die er dreimal geliebt und dreimal verraten hatte." On a syntactic level the *es* is an expletive pronoun in a cleft construction; i.e. a purely syntactic unit presumably incapable of referring. But on a pragmatic level, such expletive pronouns can be at least quasi-referential.[16] In the sentence at hand, *es* can be secondarily taken to evoke the *neut*-archetype (β in Figure 1), which then metonymically refers to the innocent village girl character.[17] The *sie*, on the other hand, evokes the marked *fem*-archetype (α′ in Figure 1), which in turn metonymically refers to the mysterious woman character.[18] A further complication is presented by the following relative clause – *die er dreimal geliebt und dreimal verraten hatte* – containing two verb phrases, coordinately conjoined to the relative clause head, the *fem*-gender pronoun *die*. Up to this point in the story, the referent of "dreimal geliebt" ('loved three times') is, from the young man's perspective, the mysterious woman; and the referent of "dreimal verraten" ('betrayed three times') is his village girlfriend. In other words, from his psychological perspective, these are two separate individuals. So who is the referent of the relative pronoun *die*? It cannot be either the girl or the woman, metonymically referenced through the two cultural archetypes, since each of the two predicates applies to only one of them. It can only be a direct, non-metonymic reference (α in Figure 1) to that female person in the story world who plays both the role of the girl and of the woman. The stylistic peculiarity of this sentence thus resides in the fact that with extreme syntactic compactness Waggerl evokes both culturally opposed archetypes for females, and then refers to the "real" person standing behind the archetypes.

## 5. Conclusion

The Waggerl story of the three pledges provides an extensive, systematic, and sophisticated exploitation of the group of ICMs for females presented in Figure 1, leaving open the question whether such exploitation is limited to specific literary genres such as the archaic folk tale. In conclusion we turn to some short passages from current journalistic cultural critique to show that the use of *neut*-gender terms for women, and the metonymic ICM they project onto, has current and wide cultural validity. We take up each of the four perspectival choices set out in Table 4.

**Perspective type A: disapproval, rejection, scorn.** The following passage contains a double perspective. It is a feminist portrayal of the conservative culture's attitude toward feminists, and their supposedly destructive effects on young men:

> Sexualverbot, Geschlechtertrennung und die Warnungen vieler Eltern vor dem Leben und Karriere zerstörenden bösen **Weib** prägten die hoffnungsvollen jungen Männer. (*Tageszeitung* 3/8/1991, p. 13)

The *neut*-gender term *Weib* is used by the feminist writer to satirize the use of this noun by conservatives to express their distaste for feminist actions and issues. Thus the passage illustrates both the use of this term by one segment of society to express scorn and rejection toward another, but also the use of the term by the target of scorn themselves to make fun of their tormentors.

**Perspective type B: visual object.** The following passage describes a poster model in terms of her physical appearance and her affects on the viewer in the context of advertising for a business specializing in physical appearance.

> Auf riesigen Plakaten hängt das '**Model** mit runden Formen, üppigem Busen und gesundem Selbstbewußtsein' in allen Schaufenstern der Hamburger Body Shop-Filialen. 'Schön ist, wer sich wohl fühlt', wirbt die Creme-und-Shampoo-Kette. (*Tageszeitung* 3/7/1998, p. 36)

The overall context makes clear that the model is presented as a visually attractive object. Even the expression "healthy self awareness" refers to her confident appearance, not to other, non-visual aspects of her person. Thus the context strongly supports the use of the *neut*-gender noun *das Model* and the metonymic model it projects onto.

**Perspective type C: object of analysis.** The following passage is taken from an analytic description of a painting:

> [...] eine nackte Frau beim Leser darzustellen: leuchtendes, von Licht getöntes **Inkarnat** vor dunklem Tizianrot." (*Die Zeit* 29, 7/17/87, p. 17)

The *neut*-gender noun *Inkarnat* literally denotes the flesh-toned colors used to depict the model's body, and thus metonymically refers to the model herself. The choice of noun and its context decompose her into the play of paint color on the canvas. The use of the noun *Inkarnat* in this context thus evokes the sense of extreme analytic distance from the described person as a human being.

**Perspective type D: innocence, conformity to stereotypic cultural values.** In this passage the feminist writer laments the stereotypic cultural values ("female cardinal virtues") embodied by fairytale archetypes such as Cinderella and Snow White.

> [...] **Aschenbrödel, Schneewittchen, Schneeweißchen** und **Rosenrot** – , diesen Griseldis-Figuren, diesen Idiotinnen an Gefühl und Verstand: richtungsweisende Disziplinierungsinstrumente, die uns Unterwürfigkeit und Schweigen als weibliche Kardinaltugenden angedient haben.
> (*Tageszeitung* 3/8/1991, p. 13)

The writer's point is that these archetypes are culturally current: listening to and reading stories with these characters during childhood has negative effects on the psyches of modern women.

The perspectives expressed in the metonymic ICM taken together form a linguistically marked category, marked by the *neut*-gender of their associated nominals. The increasing productivity of the ICM – evidenced by the consistent assignment of *neut*-gender to the influx of primarily English loans over the last 50 years – points to what appears to be a cultural distinction of current relevance in German society in which men are monovalent (they have one status: male) while women are bivalent: they are female, and they have specially marked perspectival values.[19]

## Notes

1. For a synopsis of the story, see the last section of the paper and the Appendix. Feminine gender referring expressions are marked with single underlining, neuters with double. The abbreviations *masc-*, *fem-*, and *neut-gender* are used to refer to the morphological and lexical gender properties of nouns, pronouns, and referring NPs in order to distinguish them from

both sex and the so-called "natural gender" of referents. The reader is asked to note the alternation between feminine and neuter gender in this passage.

2. lit: "… that she was it whom he had loved…"

3. In a standard syntactic analysis the clause "daß sie es war" is analyzed as an expletive construction, with the implication that the pronoun *es* is non-referential. In Section 4.2 we will argue that this pronoun is *simultaneously* licensed by the expletive construction *and* potentially referential, following functionalist analyses of such phenomena as impersonal and reflexive constructions. In functionalist approaches to syntax such as Construction Grammar, syntactic dependency and semantic/pragmatic value do not preclude each other.

4. Square brackets enclose expansion of Lakoff's points.

5. Lakoff's (1987:84) formulation: "Compared to A, B is either easier to understand, easier to remember, easier to recognize, *or more immediately useful for the given purpose in the given context*" [italics ours]. We make use here of the final alternative in the disjunction.

6. Examples from Lakoff and Johnson (1980:36–37) will illustrate:

a. We need a couple of *strong bodies* (B) for our team (A=strong people)
b. There are a lot of *good heads* (B) in the university (A=intelligent people)
c. She's just a *pretty face* (B) (A=good-looking woman)

Note that not only is the *content* of each of the metonymic B's appropriate to the context of utterance, and cannot be substituted in the others (e.g. ??? *We need a couple of pretty faces for our team*) but that this specific content surfaces in the interpretation of each of the utterances, e.g. strong bodies help the team succeed.

7. Unmarked referential forms (α) have *fem*-gender, and refer directly to discourse-world individuals. Marked (neuter) forms (β) evoke an intermediate scenario. Context may induce an intermediate scenario for *fem*-gender forms, labeled (α′).

8. While many basic-level nouns exhibit field-dependent gender assignment, others seem to have idiosyncratic gender. Basic-level terms for drinks exhibit all three genders. *Masc*-gender: *Wein* 'wine', *Schnaps* 'liquor', *Saft* 'juice'; *fem*-gender: *Milch* 'milk', *Limonade* 'soda'; *neut*-gender *Wasser* 'water', *Bier* 'beer'. But note that each is a hub for the productive assignment of gender to subordinate nominals, as pointed out below. The myth of extensively arbitrary gender assignment in German and other noun-class languages stems largely from almost exclusive attention being paid to a small set of high-frequency basic-level nouns.

9. An exacting analysis of gender in oral and written discourse reveals that soda types in fact vary between *fem*- and *neut*-gender. This variation is recent, and seems to stem from the competition of *Brause* and *Limonade* on the one hand and *(Mineral-)wasser* on the other for the dominating node in the lexical network.

10. In other words, the higher the numerical value on the cognitive entropy scale, the more semantically and/or formally motivated is gender assignment; conversely, the lower the numerical value, the higher the degree of arbitrariness of gender assignment.

11. It has often been argued that *Mädchen* and some of the other *neut*-gender human-referring nominals have *neut*-gender only because of their derivational suffix *-chen*, which is categorically associated with *neut*-gender, and do not have any semantic basis, other than

the diminutive meaning of the suffix itself. Proponents of such an hypothesis would have to explain (i) that such *chen*-suffixed nouns have become conventionalized for reference to females, and *not* to males; (ii) that *Mädchen* in particular has become the basic-level term for 'girl', while the corresponding *Jünglein* remains a semantic diminutive for *Junge* 'boy'; and that (iii) an increasing number of non-diminutive terms such as *Playmate*, *Groupie*, and *Video-chick* are receiving *neut*-gender assignment as they enter this lexical field. The form-obsessed analyst must face the possibility that the structuring of this field is driven by *pragmatic* forces and that word morphology is just a pawn in the process.

12. And *masc*-gender is highly productive for generic-reference nominals, one of the main sources of difficulty in attempts to make the language more sexually egalitarian (cf. Bußmann 1995).

13. This in contrast to Langacker's "optimal viewing arrangement," in which only the referent is in the scope of predication.

14. Note that the nominal expressing the emotion of revulsion itself is *masc*-gender: *der Ekel*.

15. Pronominal anaphora is of course important for the current study when it agrees in gender with its *neut*-gender antecedent.

16. In the so-called "weather" construction the *es* in *es regnet, schneit* ('it is raining, snowing') does not seem to evoke any referent. But in the context of other verbs the *es* is associated with a vague, indeterminate referent: *es hat eben geklopft* ('**someone** just knocked'); and in the context of an extraposed complement, the *es* is understood as cataphoric: *es gefiel ihm, **daß sie da war*** ('it pleased him **that she was there**').

17. That Waggerl would use a *double-entendre* at this point is characteristic of his mastery of the short story.

18. A further problem with this pronoun *sie* is the lack of gender agreement with its antecedent *sein Mädchen* (see Appendix). This is problematic for a derivation-based syntactic theory, which in characterizing agreement maps fully specified features of a head (noun) onto a target (pronoun), but not for a constraint-based theory such as HPSG, in which referential indices may be under pragmatic control. In commenting on:

(a) That dog is so stupid, every time I see *it* I want to kick *it*. *He*'s a damned good hunter, though.

Pollard and Sag (1994:73–74) note that "as illustrated in [a], a pronoun that refers to an entity already referred to by some earlier expression may have a new index with agreement features different from those of the earlier expression, *in order to serve some specific discourse purpose (in the present case, to signal a change of attitude toward the referent)*. In such cases, according to our definition, the earlier expression does not qualify as an antecedent; to put it another way, instead of being 'referentially dependent' on the earlier expression, such pronoun uses must be regarded as *deictic*" [italics ours].

19. A new archetype we have become aware of from current journalism, especially teen literature, is the sassy independent, unconstrained, sexually active, aggressive young woman who is free of the traditional constraints of womanhood, embodied e.g. in cartoon characters such as "das Tankgirl." The two nouns most closely associated with this archetype are *das Mädchen* and the borrowed noun *das Girl*, both *neut*-gender. It looks like youth culture

has "stolen" these nouns from the old archetype of dependence and sexual innocence, and appropriated them for their own archetype embodying strikingly contrasting values.

## References

Bußmann, Hadumod (1995). *Das* Genus, *die* Grammatik und – *der* Mensch: Geschlechterdifferenz in der Sprachwissenschaft. In H. Bußmann & R. Hof (Eds.), *Genus – zur Geschlechterdifferenz in den Kulturwissenschaften*, (pp. 115–160). Stuttgart: Kröner.

Claudi, Ulrike (1985). *Zur Entstehung von Genussystemen: Überlegungen zu einigen theoretischen Aspekten, verbunden mit einer Fallstudie des Zande.* Hamburg: Buske.

Contini-Morava, Ellen (2001). Noun classification in Swahili. University of Virginia, web-posted Ms. URL: jefferson.village.virginia.edu/swahili/swahili.html.

Corbett, Greville (1991). *Gender*. Cambridge: Cambridge University Press.

Dixon, R. M. W. (1968). Noun classes. *Lingua, 21*, 104–125.

Dixon, R. M. W. (1982). Noun classifiers and noun classes. In R. M. W. Dixon (Ed.), *Where Have All the Adjectives Gone? and Other Essays on Syntax and Semantics* [Janua linguarum, Series maior 107] (pp. 211–233). The Hague: Mouton.

Duden (1983). *Deutsches Universalwörterbuch*. Mannheim: Bibliographisches Institut.

Grimm, Jacob & Grimm, Wilhelm (1984 [1885]) *Deutsches Wörterbuch*. München: Deutscher Taschenbuchverlag.

Köpcke, Klaus-Michael (1982). *Untersuchungen zum Genussystem der deutschen Gegenwartssprache* [Linguistische Arbeiten 122]. Tübingen: Niemeyer.

Köpcke, Klaus-Michael & Zubin, David A. (1983). Die kognitive Organisation der Genuszuweisung zu den einsilbigen Nomen der deutschen Gegenwartssprache. *Zeitschrift für Germanistische Linguistik, 11*(2), 166–182.

Köpcke, Klaus-Michael & Zubin, David A. (1984). Sechs Prinzipien für die Genuszuweisung im Deutschen: Ein Beitrag zur natürlichen Klassifikation. *Linguistische Berichte, 93*, 26–50.

Köpcke, Klaus-Michael & Zubin, David A. (1996). Prinzipien für die Genuszuweisung im Deutschen. In E. Lang & G. Zifonun (Eds.), *Deutsch Typologisch: Jahrbuch des Instituts für Deutsche Sprache* (pp. 473–491). Berlin: Mouton de Gruyter.

Lakoff, George (1987). *Women, Fire and Dangerous Things: What Categories Reveal About the Mind.* Chicago and London: The University of Chicago Press.

Lakoff, George & Johnson, Mark (1980). *Metaphors We Live By*. Chicago: The University of Chicago Press.

Langacker, Ronald W. (1990). Subjectification. *Cognitive Linguistics, 1*, 5–38.

Pollard, Carl & Sag, Ivan A. (1994). *Head-Driven Phrase Structure Grammar*. Chicago: The University of Chicago Press.

Wienold, Götz (1967). *Genus und Semantik*. Meisenheim am Glan: Hain.

Young, Robert W. & Morgan, William, Sr. (1987). *The Navajo Language: a Grammar and Colloquial Dictionary.* Albuquerque: University of New Mexico Press.

Zubin, David A. & Köpcke, Klaus-Michael (1981). Gender: A less than arbitrary grammatical category. *Chicago Linguistic Society, 17*, 439–449.

Zubin, David A. & Köpcke, Klaus-Michael (1984). Affect classification in the German gender system. *Lingua, 63*, 41–96.
Zubin, David A. & Köpcke, Klaus-Michael (1986). Gender and folk taxonomy: The indexical relation between grammatical and lexical categorization. In C. Craig (Ed.), *Noun Classification and Categorization* (pp. 139–180). Amsterdam and Philadelphia: John Benjamins.
Zubin, David A. & Köpcke, Klaus-Michael (in preparation). *The Irrgarten: Natural Categories in Language: A Study of Nominal Classification Systems with Particular Reference to Gender in German.*

## Appendix

Excerpts from: Waggerl, Karl Heinrich. *Legende von den drei Pfändern der Liebe.* In: *Kalendergeschichten.* Insel-Verlag, no year.

Underlinings: ____ = feminine gender, ____ = neuter gender. Square brackets indicate bridging summary not in the original.

A Da war ein armer Mann, ein Kesselschmied in einem Dorf, der hatte ein Mädchen, mit dem er bald Hochzeit halten wollte. Und das war gut, denn das Mädchen liebte ihn mehr als alles in der Welt. Weil es aber nun am Geld für die Heirat fehlte, [zog] ... der Mann in die Fremde, um seine Kessel in den Dörfern zu verkaufen. ... Da weinte nun das Mädchen und bat ihn, zu bleiben. "Du wirst nicht wiederkommen," klagte es, "ach, du wirst mir untreu werden...!" ... Das Mädchen schwieg und verbarg seinen Kummer vor ihm. Aber als er auszog, gab es ihm drei Pfänder der Liebe mit auf den Weg [Haarband, Ring, und Messer ... Als er nach der Arbeit auf dem Markt sein Nachtlager fand], geschah

B es, daß sich in der Dunkelheit eine fremde Frau an sein Lager gesellte. "Du gefällst mir," flüsterte sie, "du junger Kesselschmied!" ...Er küßte die fremde Frau und vergaß alles und zog sie an sich. "Hast du kein Mädchen," fragte sie...? "Nein," antwortete der Mann ... Und vor Tag, als die Frau von ihm Abschied nahm, und als sie zu weinen anfing, da schenkte er ihr ein Band für das Haar zum Angebinde. ... [In der zweiten Nacht] kam abermals eine Frau aus der Stadt an sein Lager, die sagte ihm süße Worte ins Ohr und schlief bei ihm. "Hast du kein Mädchen daheim," fragte sie leise...? "Nein..." ...auch in der dritten Nacht schlief er nicht allein, und sie schien ihm die kostbarste von allen zu sein, diese Frau in der dritten Nacht. Die Frau schlang plötzlich die Arme um seinen Hals und küßte ihn und weinte bitterlich. ... "Ach," sagte die Frau, "ich bin todtrauerig. Sicher hast du ein Mädchen daheim, das dich so liebt wie ich und das vor Kummer stirbt...." Da verlangte der Mann nur noch heißer nach dieser Frau und schwor seine Liebe vor ihr ab... Und am Ende der Nacht bat ihn die Frau um ein Zeichen, daß sie an ihn denken könnte. ...er fand nur sein Messer in der Tasche, und das gab er ihr zuletzt, weil es blank und scharf war, ein hübches Ding. ...

C Nun...dachte er heimzukehren.... [Auf dem Heimweg findet er bei seinen Nachtlagern den Ring und das Band wieder]. In der letzten Nacht aber kam er endlich heim.... Und als er in die Stube kam, da lag sein Mädchen auf der Bahre. Da wußte er, daß sie es war, die er dreimal geliebt und dreimal verraten hatte, und nun steckte sein Messer mitten in ihrer weißen Brust.

A There was once a poor man, a village pot maker, who had a girl whom he soon wanted to marry. And that was fine, since the girl loved him more than anything in the world. But since there was not enough money for the wedding, the man went off from home in order to sell his pots in other villages. Now the girl cried and begged him to stay. "You'll never come back," she wailed, "you won't be faithful to me!" Then the girl was quiet and concealed her sorrow. But as he left, she gave him three pledges of (her) love to take with him, a hair ribbon, a ring, and a knife. When he had finished a day's work at the market

B and found a camp for the night, it happened that in the dark a mysterious woman came to be with him. "You're nice," she whispered, "you little pot maker, you." He kissed the mysterious woman and forgot everything and drew her to him. "Don't you have a girl?" she asked. "No," answered the man. And before morning, as the woman took leave of him, and as she began to cry, he gave her a ribbon to put in (her) hair. The second night a woman came again from town to his camp. She whispered sweet things in his ear and slept with him. "Don't you have a girl at home" she asked softly. No. ... Neither in the third night did he sleep alone, and she seemed to him the most precious of all, this woman in the third night. The woman suddenly threw (her) arms around his neck and kissed him and cried bitterly. "Ah!" cried the woman, "I'm so sad I could die. Surely you have a girl at home who loves you as I do and who will die of sorrow." Then the man desired this woman even more passionately and declared his love to her. And at the end of the night the woman begged him for a token for her to remember him by. But he could find only the knife in his pocket, and that he finally gave her, because it was shiny and sharp, a pretty thing. And now his thoughts turned to the trip home. [On the way

C he finds at his sleeping places the ring and the ribbon] The last night he finally arrived at home. And when he entered the main room, there lay his girl on the bier. And then he knew, that she was the one that he had loved three times, and three times betrayed, and now there was his knife, thrust in the middle of her white breast.

Part III

# Metonymic inferencing and linguistic change

# The development of counterfactual implicatures in English

## A case of metonymy or M-inference?

Debra Ziegeler

### 1. Introduction*

The analysis of counterfactual statements has provided the source for a diversity of studies in recent years, ranging from comparative cross-linguistic research (e.g. Kuteva 1998) to pragmatic approaches (e.g. Horn 2000; Van der Auwera 1997), but much of this work has focused almost exclusively on the counterfactual constructions found in the form of conditionals (see especially Athanasiadou & Dirven 1997; Fauconnier & Sweetser 1996). While conditional constructions are probably the most frequently cited environments for the expression of counterfactuality, counterfactual meaning is a form of inferential reasoning associated with a number of textual and contextual clues but not necessarily related to any particular grammatical construction. In this chapter, the objective is to examine such clues in order to determine if there are cognitive factors influencing the formation of a counterfactual implicature in the use of a modal expression of ability. The chapter further aims to assess whether the counterfactual meanings derive essentially from factors of formal complexity of expression or from the conceptually based pragmatic relations of contiguity, metonymy, or relevance.

The term 'counterfactual implicature' simply refers to a particular kind of pragmatic implicature that is counterfactual in nature. In earlier studies (e.g. Ziegeler 2000a) the creation of counterfactual reasoning was seen to be intricately bound up with the co-operative maxims of Grice (1975), in particular, the maxim of Quantity. However, in Levinson (1995), the maxim of Manner, underlying what he reconstructs as a heuristic label, *M*: 'marked descriptions warn "marked situation,"' is found to derive counterfactual implicatures in contrastive sets of marked and unmarked alternate expressions. One such pair expresses past ability, the marked alternate producing an inference of counterfactuality and the unmarked alternate producing an inference of actuality, now described as a metonymic device by Panther and Thornburg (1998, 1999): the POTENTIALITY FOR ACTUALITY metonymy. It will be seen that counterfactual implicatures are related to the Quantity maxim and can be created via metonymic inferences. However, if counterfactual inferences are derived from the markedness of a situation, as Levinson assumes, then it becomes necessary to explain the way in which the metonymic extensions of the type described by Panther and Thornburg can be reconciled with such an account.

In order to investigate the problem, historical factors will be used to test the validity of present-day constructed examples. Initially, the two alternating expressions of past ability are considered in the light of the two interacting Quantity implicatures, and as elements on Horn-scales of Quantity (Section 2). Grammatical environment is also seen to play a part in the types of inferences obtainable from such expressions, and it is shown that counterfactual expressions of past ability are restricted to perfective (Achievement or Accomplishment) predicates (Section 3). In Section 5 a historical survey is undertaken in which the grammaticalization path of *could* is traced diachronically and compared with that of *be able to* +*V*, and it is seen that for both the modal and the semi-modal, perfective predicates appear later than grammatically imperfective ones referring to states and generic attributes. A high frequency of imperfective predicates in earlier uses appears more conducive to the creation of Quantity 2 implicatures for both *could* and *was/were able to* and could suggest that Quantity 2 implicatures are basic to all such expressions, and Quantity 1 implicatures are derived at a later stage by cancellation of Quantity 2 implicatures. It is hypothesized that all modal and semi-modalized expressions can be located on Quantity scales, and therefore are susceptible to pragmatic conditioning by the grammatical environment in which they appear. As such, there is justification for proposing the influence of metonymy as a factor in the creation of counterfactual implicatures from modal expressions.

## 2. M-inferences and counterfactual implicatures

### 2.1 M-inferences and Quantity

The Quantity Maxim of Grice's (1975: 45) Co-operative Principle is subdivided into two tenets: (i) "Make your contribution as informative as is required for the current purposes of the exchange"; and (ii) "Do not make your contribution more informative than is required." These two principles, therefore, polarize the pragmatic control on the information quantity of the utterance resulting in a negative extension by the hearer in (i) and a positive extension in (ii). Thus, Quantity 1 (central to the 'Q(uantity)-Principle' in Horn 1984), maximizes the coding of expressive material in an utterance, inducing an interpretation that anything left unsaid is not true, or not known to be true or false (Atlas & Levinson 1981: 37–38), while Quantity 2 (subsumed into the 'R(elation)-Principle' of Horn 1984) minimizes the coding of information and invites inferences to include information not already supplied by the speaker.

Horn's Q- and R-Principles are further revised in Horn (1989: 384), in which they are seen to reduce most of the remaining maxims of Grice's Co-operative Principle to just two opposing forces that interact in numerous types of linguistic phenomena. Horn's treatment of Grice's maxims encompasses to a large extent the formal means of expressing propositions, in that what he labels 'pragmatic labor' in Horn (1984) is divided between pairs of expressions covering equivalent functional requirements in such a way that the briefer or more truncated of the two equivalents will R-implicate an unmarked, stereotypical meaning, while the more complex or prolix periphrastic counterpart will Q-implicate a marked meaning that could not be conveyed by the shorter form (*ibid.*: 197). For example, *Can you pass the hot sauce* is matched in opposition to *Do you have the ability to pass the hot sauce*, the former R-implicating a request for the hot sauce, and the latter Q-implicating a literal request for information about the hearer's personal skills and abilities.

Levinson (1995) revises the Manner maxim ('Be perspicuous') and Quantity maxims of Grice by relating them to three heuristics of utterance meaning: Q1: 'What is not said is not the case'; Q2: What is simply described is stereotypically and specifically exemplified'; and M: 'Marked descriptions warn "marked situation"' (*ibid.* 97). In Levinson's description, Q1 alludes to the first Quantity maxim of Grice, Q2 to the second, and M to the maxim of Manner (the latter subsumed by both the Q- and R-principles in Horn 1989). Q1 inferences are claimed to be applicable in sets of alternate items (of the kind found on Horn-scales) such as *all/some*, cardinal numbers, gradable properties like *hot/warm*, and modal adjectives like *possible/necessary*. However, for pairs like those in (1) below (*ibid.*: 105), denoting past ability, Levinson argues that it is not Q1 but rather M-inferences (as in (1b)) that complement Q2 inferences (as in (1a)):

(1) a. John could solve the problem (Q2 + > 'and he did')
b. John had the ability to solve the problem (M + > 'but he didn't').

According to Levinson (1987: 409), the contrast in inferences obtained from such a pair in (1) does not pertain to 'quantity' of information (although (1b) is visibly greater than (1a) in information quantity). Levinson (1995: 98 fn.) notes that Horn confounds M-inferences with the Q-principle and that the implicatures produced in the two cases are similar: in both M- and Q1 inferences, the implicature is to the negative of a stronger statement that could have been made. In Levinson's view, the trigger for the negative reasoning in (1b) is 'form of expression,' i.e., the formal markedness of (1b) (which, as Levinson (*ibid.*: 104) suggests, is iconic with the message conveyed) invites the inference to the marked, non-stereotypical, situation.

It is to be questioned whether the modal expressions in (1) are synonymous in function, and should be considered as marked and unmarked variants of the same concept in the same way as lexical items such as *drink/beverage*, or *house/residence* (Levinson 1995: 106). According to Visser's (1969–1973) records, sentences in which *could* was used as a modal referring to the ability of the subject were no longer found after 1775:

(2) What, could you gather no tidings of her? nor guess where she was?
1775. Sheridan, *The Duenna* III, ii
Visser (1969: 1743)

Visser suggests 'have you not been able to' as a present-day substitute for *could* in (2). However, the modal is used in a negative context, which enables the ability meanings to become more transparent even in Present-Day English (PDE) ('couldn't you gather any tidings of her' might also serve as a suitable substitute). According to Palmer (1986: 14), modals such as *could* and *would* cannot be used to refer to a single event in the past; e.g. **he ran fast and could catch the bus* (1986: 93). It will be seen later in this chapter that isolated sentences such as (1a), with a meaning of unambiguous past ability referring to single events, are rarely found in bare declarative main clauses, even in diachronic texts. Sentence (1a), then, is more likely to yield an R-based inference of future potentiality than of past ability, leaving the two sentences non-synonymous. The contrast expressed between the two forms, a modal and a semi-modal, periphrastic equivalent, may be related only to formal perceptual features, and functional diachronic factors should be considered instead as contributing to the present-day outcome. Such factors will be discussed further below.

## 2.2 Other possible candidates for M-inferences

Levinson carefully avoids the past ability expressions used by Horn (1984, 1989) to illustrate the operation of the R-principle. Horn also discusses the use of past ability expressions to provide the sources for implicatures, but in Horn's account, there is another more prolix, marked alternative of *could*, namely *be able to*, which may be seen to produce the same Q2 inferences claimed by Levinson (1995) for *could* in (1a):

(3) She was able to solve the problem.

which R-implicates:

(4) She solved the problem.

If, as Levinson seems to assume, *could* still contains senses of past ability in such sentences, then *was able to* ought to be substitutable in (1b) as a more lexicalized, periphrastic marked alternative as well (*be able to* was noted by Denison (1998: 171) as a suppletion for the use of *could* in assertive contexts). But in spite of its relative markedness, the inferences obtained are also Q2 or R-based implicatures, and are not complementary to those of *could*. Since (3) is also a relatively marked expression by comparison to (1a), it is questionable that relative markedness of formal expression is the only cause of the contrasting implicatures.

The counterfactual implicature derived from the use of such expressions must therefore be accountable to a more direct means of inferencing. Horn (1984: 21) also discusses the fact that R-based implicatures can be canceled in certain circumstances, and that the cancellation is obtainable without negation, using contrastive stress on the element in the sentence that derives the implicature, in this case, the expression of ability. Thus:

(5) She was *able* to solve the problem…

could imply to the hearer that she only had the ability to solve it, but did not actually solve it.

An appended clause introduced by an adversative conjunction such as *but* and followed by a negative can produce the same cancellation; e.g.

(6) She was able to solve the problem but (she didn't, as) she didn't have enough time.

The adversative clause discussed by Horn (1984) contributes to the conversion of an R-based implicature of the prediction of the complement proposition ('she solved the problem') to become a Q-based implicature of negative prediction ('she didn't solve it'). However, this is not a conversion from an unmarked form of expression to a marked one, of the type exemplified by Levinson, it is a clear example of a canceled R-based implicature. The expression of past ability is then restricted quantificationally either by prosodic variation or by the introduction of a clause expressing contrast. In the same way, Levinson's (1995) example can uphold a cancellation in the context:

(7) John had the ability to solve the problem, but (he didn't as) he didn't have his latest silicon-graphics software.

The use of *but* conventionally implicates a contrast in the clause it introduces, and therefore assumes a proposition of a contrary nature in the immediately preceding clause. If the implicature in (1b), then, is an M-inference of a counterfactual kind suggesting that John did not solve the problem (Levinson (1995: 97), then the use of the *but*-clause in (7) may appear redundant, as it explicitly asserts what is inferred in the first clause, and thus presents no contrast. In order to create a contrast, there must be some kind of expectation understood in the first clause of the possibility of John's solving the problem, which was defeated by the additional information supplied in the *but*- clause. The addition of a *but*-clause could be said to reinforce the implicature in (7) providing contrast only as a rhetorical device (Horn 1991); however, even as a rhetorical device this does not discount the likelihood of prediction being involved in the speaker's estimations of John's apparent ability. It would appear more logical to append a conjoining clause introduced by *and* as a reinforcement: *John had the ability to solve the problem and he didn't ...* ; but such a clause does not seem to follow logically, as the Q-implicature is not sufficiently conventionalized. The only explanation for the felicity with which a contrasting *but*-clause can follow such expressions is if the expression contained an element of prediction itself that required cancellation in the form of a contrasting assertion in order to reinforce the intended inferences of non-actuality of the predicated event.

## 2.3 Modality and Horn-scales

In examining modal expressions, the relation between Gricean implicatures and metonymic inferencing is best considered from the neo-Gricean approach adopted by Horn (1984, 1989), in which the modal expression may be located on Quantity scales (Horn 1972). The understanding of modality as a scalar item requires that the modalized utterance be regarded as a weaker version (*W*) of a non-modalized counterpart utterance (*S*), which is stronger in truth value and therefore higher on the scale of factuality; e.g. *She may be coming* (expressing possibility) is factually weaker than *She is coming* (expressing certainty), and the modalized element acts as a quantifier over the truth of the proposition it predicates. The complement of the modal, which may be expressed as a proposition *p*, is therefore the stronger proposition that the modal element (*m*) quantifies, and in an R-based implicature, the extension is towards the positive realization of *p*; i.e. (m [p] > p), forming a predictive statement of the potentiality of *p* that may be confirmed at a time later than the time of utterance. For example:

(8) She may be coming (m[p])
 > She is coming ([p])

However, in the construction of a Q-based implicature, the projection is toward the negative of the predictive statement in modalized expressions, and this results in the development of a type of counterfactual implicature (m[p] > ~p). Such a conversion can be made possible by the provision of additional information about the prediction, as illustrated in (6) and (7): [m [p] > p, but X] > [m [p] > ~p], where *X* stands for a clause containing an adversative or contrastive statement canceling the implied prediction of *p*, as illustrated in the *but*-clause in (7), and in (9):

(9) She may be coming (m[p]) (> she is coming ([p])),
 but she said she had a lot of work to do (but X)
 > she is not coming. [~p])

It could be argued that the R-based implicature of prediction in a modal expression such as *She may be coming* does not automatically cancel out with the provision of an adversative or contrastive clause in the context; e.g. *She could come, but she said she had a lot of work to do* is more expressive of the speaker's uncertainty than of knowledge that the prediction will not be fulfilled. This is because the modal has a non-past time reference, and therefore the speaker is not anticipated to have the same degree of knowledge of the outcome of the prediction as s/he would if the time reference were past. In present-day English, the preterite forms of modals retain very little of their past temporal meaning, but are reinforced by the use of the perfect auxiliary *have* to provide the same senses of past time reference that were once available in Old and Middle English. Hence *She could have come, but she said she had a lot of work to do* is more likely to express the speaker's knowledge that the prediction was not fulfilled than if the modal were in non-past form. The relation of the modal expressions with the propositions they quantify can be illustrated thus to show differences in temporal reference, where superscript *t* = reference time:

(10) a. non-past: $m^{t}$ [p] > p (by means of R-based implicatures); e.g. *She may be coming* ($m^{t}$ [p]) > *she is coming* (p)

b. past: $m^{t\text{-}n}$ [p] (but X) > ~p (by means of Q-based implicatures, or canceled R-based), e.g. *She might/could have come* ($m^{t\text{-}n}$ [p]) (but she said she had a lot of work to do) > *she didn't come* (~p).

The use of past time reference, for all intents and purposes, increases the hearer's evaluations of the speaker's capacity to provide more accurate information of the truth value of an utterance, and results in a higher probability of a counterfactual implicature as a result. In this way, the Quantity maxim is seen to interact with the maxim of Quality ('do not say that for which you lack adequate evidence'), the hearer believing there are grounds for the speaker's contribution to be backed by more accurate evidence, as is usually available when referring to past events. The most likely interpretation, then, with past time reference, produces a Q-based implicature of negative prediction.

## 2.4 The contribution of metonymic extensions

In example (5) above, a counterfactual implicature is produced simply by the use of contrastive stress on the modal element; in (6) the parenthesized material contains a negation of the R-based implicature in the preceding clause (*she didn't as ...*). Horn (1989: 389) suggests that R-based implicatures that need to be canceled by negation are already conventionalized, and the implicatum has become part of the literal meaning of the expression. It could be suggested, though, that (5) is a reduced form of (6), and that the entire modal expression in (5) together with its canceling adversative clause, *but she didn't*, could be understood as part of the meaning of (6), with only the contrastive prosodic stress remaining to mark the absent cancellation. In such cases there is a metonymic inference similar to the kind labeled by Panther and Thornburg (1999) as the POTENTIALITY FOR ACTUALITY metonymy. The POTENTIALITY FOR ACTUALITY metonymy is described by Panther and Thornburg (1998; 1999: 394) as a predicational metonymy, as opposed to the more frequently discussed referential metonymies such as the expression *the White House* when used to 'stand for' the executive staff working within it. Predicational metonymies represent entire statements in which one predication may be used to 'stand for' another; in (3) *She was able to solve the problem* metonymically stands for the statement *She solved the problem.* Panther and Thornburg's analyses suggest that there is an important interaction between Gricean pragmatics and cognitive forces, which needs a great deal more attention in future research. However, the only difference between (5) and the kind discussed by Panther and Thornburg is that in the case of (5) (and (1b)), the metonymy is one of POTENTIALITY FOR NON-ACTUALITY wherein a predication of 'ability' may trigger a counterfactual implicature.

A similar counterfactual metonymy is evidenced in the diachronic development of the modal *would*, as shown in Ziegeler (2000b); this is an example of Panther and Thornburg's (1999) VIRTUALITY FOR ACTUALITY metonymy, in which the expression of modal necessity, obligation, permission, and desire may stand for the actuality of the proposition it predicates, e.g. Panther and Thornburg's example of a 'hedged' performative: *I would like to invite you to my party* (1999: 343), in which the desire to invite the hearer to the party stands for the invitation itself. In the Helsinki Corpus, though, a number of examples appear in which there is a modal expression followed by a contrastive (*but*) clause, indicating the pathway of development to a VIRTUALITY FOR NON-ACTUALITY counterfactual metonymy, e.g.:

(11) Vnto þe kirk he wald haue gane, Bot þederward way wist he nane.
'He would have gone to the church, but he didn't know the way.'
(1350–1420) *The Northern Homily Cycle*
(Ed. Nevanlinna), p II, 204

Even with the contrastive clause removed, the modal expression in (11) alone may stand for the counterfactual inference that the subject did not go to the church; e.g. *Did he go to the church? He would have gone ...* . In such cases, the cancellation of an R-based implicature originally suggesting the actuality of the proposition predicated of the modal becomes part of the meaning of the modal itself, and the modal acquires negative inferences via a metonymic process. Such processes are similarly described for the development of sentence-final particles out of conjunctions in Japanese, by Okamoto (this volume), in which ellipsis of a subordinate clause originally introduced by a conjunction (*koto*) results in the modal meanings it conveyed becoming conventionalized as part of the semantics of the new construction; also, in the case of independent *if*-clauses in English, German and French (see Panther and Thornburg, this volume), the semantics of the ellipted main clauses are conventionalized as part of the meaning of a resulting speech act function for the stranded *if*-clause. In all such cases, the metonymy is 'part' for 'whole'.

The example in (11) might illustrate a possible diachronic route for the development of counterfactual implicatures as the result of metonymic inferencing, and indicate the role played by the Gricean maxim of Quantity (revised by Horn (1984) in terms of R- and Q-based implicatures on Quantity scales) in the development of metonymic inferences of this kind. The Quantity implicature is brought about by the quantificational evaluation of information in an utterance, and will of necessity involve the understanding of part-whole relationships, one of the types of metonymic relationships discussed by Kövecses and Radden (1998). On the Horn-scale, as discussed above, part-whole relationships are represented by weak and strong counterparts of gradable qualities, quantities, and entities. In proposing modality as a measurement on a Horn-scale, the part-whole relationships are seen as corresponding to predicational equivalents of modal versus non-modal propositions. The expression of counterfactuality, marked by only a modal predication type, involves the assertion of a part (the modality) for an implicit whole (the modality and the negated proposition it quantifies factually). The metonymic extension that creates the counterfactual implicature is of necessity grounded in the operation of the maxim of Quantity 1, or Q-based implicatures (canceled R-based implicatures), and must be considered linked to Gricean principles of conversational inferencing.

## 3. Aspect and grammatical environment

Apart from consideration of formal prolixity, there are a number of other considerations that must be accounted for in formulating a hypothesis based on a metonymical analysis. The examples given by Levinson (1987) and Horn (1984) illustrate only one possible function for the use of past ability expressions, and that is in expressing the attainment of a result. Less than adequate consideration has been given to the possibility that expressions of past ability can, and frequently do occur in describing, for example, the inherent attributes of the subject, also discussed by Panther and Thornburg as a type of POTENTIALITY FOR ACTUALITY metonym, the domain of 'character disposition'

(1999: 348). In such environments, the likelihood of a Q-based, counterfactual implicature may never arise; for example:

(12) a. John had the ability to solve problems for people.
b. John had the ability to foresee the future.
c. John had the ability to drive people crazy.

In Levinson's original example (1b), the complement of the semi-modalized expression contains an accomplishment verb in the Vendler (1967) sense – it is a goal-oriented process with a natural endpoint, and is lexically perfective in terms of the inherent qualities of the verb itself. In (12a–c), however, the complement of *had the ability* refers to what may be a generic characteristic of the subject in (12). All such situations are lexically or grammatically imperfective: (12b) contains a stative verb and (12c) a process verb, and (12a) is imperfective by virtue of its plural indefinite object, the grammatical aspect defining the situation as one of an indefinite series of events extending over an unbounded period of time. None of (12a–c) are likely to convey Q-based implicatures of counterfactuality, i.e., that the predicted event did not occur, as the events complemented of the ability expression are not single occurrences. Instead, the characterizing use conveys the presumption of repeated observations of actual occurrences, or at least an evidential basis for establishing a generic fact, and for hypothesizing about possible future occurrences; each are examples of the POTENTIALITY FOR ACTUALITY metonym (the Acquired Skills metonymy in Panther and Thornburg 1999: 349–350).

All the modal alternates mentioned so far, *could* as well as *was/were able to*, could be used with imperfective situations as in (12). However, only the modal *could* is likely to create ambiguity with meanings of hypothetical possibility in such situations (e.g. *John could drive people crazy* – hypothetical possibility or past ability). *Had the ability to* + *V* in fact may be restricted from use in some contexts in which *could* and *was/were able to* are possible:

(13) John rang to see if we could/were able to/*had the ability to meet him.

The first two forms are acceptable for the possible reason that they can both be used to express potentiality or possibility; *had the ability to* + *V* has not yet grammaticalized its modal meanings in this way. As such it may be predicted to be a recent introduction into the paradigm.

As well as aspectual changes in the environment of the past ability expression, a number of other factors may come into play, which affect the type of inferences obtainable. The first is the environment of factive clauses. A factive clause, in the present definition, is not intended to be defined in exactly the same way as Kiparsky and Kiparsky (1970) define such predicates; that is, as determined by the presupposition of truth in the *that*-clause complement or the gerund complement of a matrix clause containing a particular factive verb; e.g. *regret* (*I regret that she was ill*). In some cases, though, there is overlap with their definitions; e.g. a relative clause with a referring head noun can be classed as factive as it usually contains a presupposition. There is also factivity associated with complements of verbs of reporting or communication (*that*-clauses), which depends on the nature of the matrix verb: e.g. *prayed/wished that* introduces a non-factive or counter-factive environment, while *said that, promised that, realized that, and found that* are superordinate to clauses that are taken in the present study to be factive.[1] Examples of such clauses will appear in the diachronic texts (see Sections 5.2.3–4); however, as an illustration of the effect of such clauses on the inferences derived from modal and semi-modal expressions, the following examples may suffice:

(14) a. John found that he had the ability to solve the problem.
b. John found that he could solve the problem.

In both (14a–b) the inferences are more likely to point to the actuality of the complemented event, rather than the non-actuality. The stronger senses of positive prediction are the result of the embedding of the modal or semi-modal in a subordinate clause governed by a verb introducing a proposition of presupposed factuality.[2] Relative clauses may also contain a presupposition of factuality, as noted above:

(15) a. The students who could solve the problem were given credit points.
b. The students who had the ability to solve the problem were given credit points.

In both (15a–b) the environment of a restrictive relative clause also carries a presupposition of the factuality of its contents, suggesting that there existed students who solved the problem, and a counterfactual implicature is not likely in the case of the relative clause in (15b). Other environments may include restrictors, such as *only*:

(16) a. Of all the people, only John could solve the problem.
b. Of all the people, only John had the ability to solve the problem.

Sentence (16b) seems to imply that, in all probability, John had the ability to solve the problem, and he did. Why this should be so is unclear, but perhaps reasons attributable to sentence focus may provide a clue, the use of a restrictor shifting attention away from the modality to the subject referent instead.

A final argument against the M-inferences explanation for the contrast in (1) might be found in the negative alternatives of (1a–b). If, as Levinson (1995) suggests, M-inferences are characterized by 'marked descriptions' warning 'marked situations,' then it should not make any difference whether those marked descriptions occur in the negative or not. The relationship of markedness appears unchanged in such examples; however, in modal and semi-modal expressions, the relationship alters dramatically:

(17) a. John could not solve the problem (Q2 + > 'and he didn't')
b. John did not have the ability to solve the problem (? M + > 'but he did solve it')

The implicature in (17b) should, if M-inferences derive inferences to the complement of the unmarked alternative, contrast with the R-based (Q2) inferences obtainable from (17a), but instead, the inferences obtained are the same, that the problem was not solved in either case. This is because the implicatures obtained from the modal expression in (1b) are not M-inferences, but are primarily Q-based, and markedness is only the *means* by which they are derived. There is a compelling argument in such examples that both (17a–b) contain scalar-derived implicatures, and cannot be considered as contrasting in any other way. According to Horn (1989: 388), while the weaker element implicates the negative of the stronger element on a scale, at the same time there is a downward entailment that the negative of the weaker element is incompatible with the stronger element; therefore $\sim W$ entails $\sim S$, whether or not a Q-based or an R-based implicatum is involved. Hence the pragmatic contrast exhibited between (1a) and (1b) is neutralized in the case of negatives and the inferences in both (17a) and (17b) are entailments. This is a problem for implicature analyses not based on a scalar explanation, and differences derived from the co-occurrence with negatives cannot be accounted for in a non-scalar model. The implications of such matters for the historical development of past ability expressions will be seen in the data presented in Section 5.2.

## 4. Interim summary

In the previous sections we have examined the question of whether the counterfactual implicatures derived from the use of a semi-modal expression *had the ability to* in contrast to a modal verb *could* are the result of M-inferences of the type described by Levinson (1995) or Q-based implicatures of the type described by Horn (1984) (and are therefore accountable by metonymic processes) and it is suggested that the M-inference argument fails on a number of grounds:

i. The direction of the implicature associated with *could* is, in the first place, environmentally conditioned, as it cannot occur in a bare declarative clause referring to past ability of a single event. This is because the senses of past temporality have all but completely disappeared in its grammaticalization into a modal of hypothetical possibility. The two alternates therefore may not be considered sufficiently similar in meaning to be referred to as marked and unmarked variants of one another.
ii. Another semi-modal of similar meaning, *was/were able to*, is not referred to by Levinson, and it may also be classed as a marked alternate of *could*. However, the implicatures produced by the use of this form are R-based, and predict the actuality, not the non-actuality, of the modal complement. Furthermore, both *was/were able to* + *V* and *had the ability to* + *V* may be canceled by a contrasting clause of negation, suggesting that R-based implicatures are basic in all such modalized clauses.
iii. The direction of the implicature also varies according to aspectual environment, and complements that refer to repeated events or habitual characteristics, i.e. imperfective complements, are more conducive to an R-based inference.
iv. When the modalized expressions are negated, the inferences produced in both cases are the same, regardless of the comparative markedness of the operator. The reasons for this can only indicate that the modal is a quantifier on a scale of the type described by Horn, since on such scales negation of the weaker element always entails negation of the stronger element.
v. Finally, the relation between the older modal verb form and the newer, periphrastic modal is not unequivocally one of complementary implicatures; the more periphrastic form may instead suggest a canceled prediction. The metonymic relationship is revealed by the facility with which a contrastive or adversative clause may follow on from the modalized expression, suggesting that the modalized expression alone may stand for a diachronically earlier stage in which the canceling clause was overtly expressed in conjunction with it.

In order to verify these points, and to investigate whether such a stage existed, it is necessary to consider the function of marking past ability modality in its historical context. It is for this reason that the following survey was undertaken.

## 5. A survey of diachronic texts

### 5.1 Data and environments

Because of the surprisingly small number of tokens actually found, the survey covered all the diachronic portion of the Helsinki Corpus, from Old English (OE) to Early Modern English (EME), and including also the majority of the Middle English texts (ME).[3] The time periods referred to within these categories were as listed: Old English: 850–1150; Middle English: 1150–1500, and Early Modern English: 1500–1710. In some of the time categories, very few examples were obtained (less than 70 in total for all categories apart from occurrences of *could* in the EME data); however, the individual tokens were recorded, as the infrequency of their occurrence is nevertheless significant to the hypothesis presented.

The level of grammaticalization of the modal or semi-modalized expression was seen as dependent on environmental factors, such as the lexical aspect of the complement verb, the factive nature of a subordinate clause, and co-occurrence with negation. However, since the function in many cases could be ambiguous, with some retention present of lexical senses relating to earlier stages of development, it was decided not to attempt to differentiate the examples on the basis of categorial function, except in cases in which there was a clear lexical function as indicated by the presence of a nominal object (either a noun phrase or a noun clause). Such instances were the only ones listed as 'lexical' in the data; the remainder should be considered non-lexical, but occurring with varying degrees of grammaticalization. With verbal complements, factors such as animacy of the subject, negation, and lexical aspect of the complement verb all are likely to have an inhibiting influence on the grammaticalization of the modal or semi-modal expression, and in many cases, the function could not be objectively determined. Ultimately, the goal of the survey was to investigate whether there were any particular environments that favored the development of R-based implicatures at the expense of Q-based ones, promoting the conventionalization of the implicature, to determine whether such environments were frequently-occurring, and to assess whether Q-based, counterfactual implicatures occurred as a metonymic development of canceled R-based ones, as seems possible for the modal *would* discussed above. In order to satisfy such objectives, the data were classified into: (i) occurrences of *was/were able to* +*V* in ME, and EME texts (none appeared in OE texts); (ii) occurrences of *could* in OE, ME, and EME texts.

Within the categories listed above, the data were divided into main and subordinate clauses. Main clauses included lexical or non-lexical functions (for *could*), features such as negation, interrogativity (listed as non-factivity), and counterfactuality or hypotheticality (if non-past) marked by the presence of a canceling or suspending clause. A canceling clause could be introduced by a conjunction such as *but*, or in the case of a suspending clause, *if*, such clauses introducing a condition on the actuality of the event predicted in the main clause. Aspectual features such as a generic or characterizing predicate, expressing the skills or abilities of the subject, were listed as 'characterizing.' Subordinate clauses included lexical types (for *could*), i.e. those in which the lexical function was clearly marked by the presence of a nominal object or complement. All other types including those ambiguous between lexical and non-lexical functions were classed as non-lexical. Other features included factive or non-factive clauses, and negation. Negation was defined as not only negation of the modal form itself, but also as including cases in which the subject or object of the modal form referred to a negative entity; e.g. *none*. Generic or characterizing predicates were clearly discernible from context, and examples will be given below. Factive clauses, as discussed earlier, included not only complements of verbs of reporting and saying, and relative clauses, but also clauses introduced by *wh*-subordinators such as *what*, *how*, (but not *whatever* or *however*) and temporal subordinators such as *when*, *until*, adverbial clauses of reason introduced by *for* or *because*, adverbial clauses of degree (*so X that Y*). Non-factive clauses were those introduced by subordinators such as *if* or *whether*, or were in the form of interrogatives (in which case main clauses could also be non-factive), and also included nominal clauses functioning as objects of verbs of thinking or hoping and adverbial clauses of comparison (e.g. *as X as Y*). The results are listed below.

## 5.2 Results and discussion

*Be able to* + *past*-ENVIRONMENTS

**Table 1.** Frequency and distribution of *was/were able to* + *V* in the diachronic survey. Synonymous forms also investigated included *hable*; *abel*; *abil*; *abul*.[3]

N: 23 = 100%

| Time period | OE | ME | EME |
|---|---|---|---|
| | 0 | 1 (4.3%) | 22 (95.6%) |

## Middle English

Total = 1 (Subordinate clause, factive)

## Early Modern English

**Table 2a.** Distribution by function and environment of *be able to* + past in EME main clauses.

N = 6

| **Environments** | | **neg.** | **TOTALS** |
|---|---|---|---|
| Non-factive clauses | 1 | | 1 |
| Characterizing | 1 | 2 | 3 |
| Other | 1 | 1 | 2 |
| TOTALS | 3 | 3 | 6 |

**Table 2b.** Distribution by function and environment of *be able to* + past in EME subordinate clauses.

N = 16

| **Environments** | | **negative** | **characterizing** | **TOTALS** |
|---|---|---|---|---|
| Factive clauses | 5 = 31.25% | 7 = 43.7% | 2 = 12.5% | 14 = 87.45% |
| Non-factive clauses | 1 = 6.25% | 1 = 6.25% | | 2 = 12.50% |
| TOTALS | 6/16 = 37.5% | 8/16 = 49.95% | 2/16 = 12.5% | 16 = 99.95% |

### *could*-ENVIRONMENTS

**Table 3.** Frequency distribution of *could* forms in the diachronic survey. Forms investigated included *cuð, coud, couþ, couth, cuþ, kowth, cuth, cowd, koud, kowd, cowth, kuð, kouth, cou'd, culd, kouth.*

N: 215 = 100%

| Time period | OE | ME | EME |
|---|---|---|---|
| | 8 (3.7%) | 41 (19%) | 166 (77.2%) |

## Old English

Total = 8

**Main Clauses:** N = 1 (Lexical)

**Subordinate Clauses:** N =7

**Table 4.** Distribution by function and environment of *could* forms in OE subordinate clauses.

N = 7

| Environments | | negative | negative factive clause | TOTALS |
|---|---|---|---|---|
| Lexical uses* | | 1 | 1 | 2 |
| Factive clauses | 2 | 2 | | 4 |
| Non-factive clauses | 1 | | | 1 |
| TOTALS | 3/7 | 3/7 | 1/7 | 7 |

*These include two examples of the use of the past participle *cuð*, 'known,' a non-finite form, which is discussed as a lexical item distinct from the modal paradigm by Goossens (1992: 381). However, it is included in the present analysis because a number of non-finite forms are included in the data for *be able to*.

## Middle English

Total = 41

**Main Clauses:** N= 25/41 = 60.9%

**Table 5a.** Distribution by function and environment of *could* forms in ME main clauses.

N = 25

| Environments | | negative | TOTALS |
|---|---|---|---|
| Lexical uses | 6 = 24% | 1 = 4% | 7 = 28% |
| Characterizing | 16 = 64% | 1 = 4% | 17 = 68% |
| Other | | 1 = 4% | 1 = 4% |
| TOTALS | 22/25 = 88% | 3/25 = 12% | 25 = 100% |

**Subordinate Clauses:** N = 16/41 = 39%

**Table 5b.** Distribution by function and environment of *could* forms in ME subordinate clauses.

N = 16

| Environments | | lexical | negative | TOTALS |
|---|---|---|---|---|
| Factive clauses | 3 = 18.75% | 1 = 6.25% | 1 = 6.25% | 5 = 31.25% |
| Non-factive clauses | 9 = 56.25% | 1 = 6.25% | 1 = 6.25% | 11 = 68.75% |
| TOTALS | 12/16 = 75% | 2/16 = 12.5% | 2/16 = 12.5% | 16 = 100% |

## Early Modern English

Total = 166

**Main Clauses:** N = 44/166 = 26.5%

**Table 6a.** Distribution by function and environment of *could* forms in EME main clauses.

N = 44

| Environments | | negative | characterizing | TOTALS |
|---|---|---|---|---|
| Non-factive clauses | 7 = 15.9% | 3 = 6.8% | | 10 = 22.7% |
| Counterfactuals/ hypotheticals | 6 = 13.6% | 5 = 11.3% | 1 = 2.2% | 12 = 27.1% |
| Characterizing | 3 = 6.8% | | | 3 = 6.8% |
| Negative main clauses | 19 = 43.1% | | | 19 = 43.1% |
| TOTALS | 35/44 = 79.4% | 8/44 = 18.1% | 1/44 = 2.2% | 44 = 99.7% |

**Subordinate clauses:** N = 122/166 = 73.5%

**Table 6b.** Distribution by function and environment of *could* forms in EME subordinate clauses.

N = 122

| Environments | | negative | counterfactual | characterizing | TOTALS |
|---|---|---|---|---|---|
| Lexical uses | 1 = 0.8% | | | | 1 = 0.8% |
| Factive clauses | 27 = 22.1% | 43 = 35.2% | 4 = 3.3% | 1 = 0.8% | 75 = 61.4% |
| Non-factive clauses | 42 = 34.4% | 4 = 3.3% | | | 46 = 37.7% |
| TOTALS | 70/122 = 57.3% | 47/122 = 38.5% | 4/122 = 3.3% | 1/122 = 0.8% | 122 = 99.9% |

The data presented, as mentioned earlier, show a surprisingly low number of tokens for all forms, even for the modal *could* in its various orthographic representations. The method of presenting the data is, as noted, to display most effectively the most frequent types of environments that may be associated with the increasing grammaticalization of the modal over time. For this reason, percentages are given for overall statistics for one particular form in a given time period, and the data are separated into main clauses and subordinate clauses. At the same time, the clauses were subcategorized first into factive or non-factive, and lexical uses, negatives, or characterizing uses were distinguished either as a feature of the basic subcategories of factive/non-factive, or as a separate clausal category in themselves depending on whether the basic factive/non-factive distinctions were present initially. The only possible skewing that this method of categorization may present is in the number of scores for characterizing uses in the Middle English *could* main clauses: 12 of the 17 tokens came from a single text: Chaucer's *The General Prologue to the Canterbury Tales*. However, the tokens for the other features are all fairly evenly distributed throughout the texts. The forms will be examined in turn, and their role in the overall grammaticalization of the function of expressing past ability will be discussed.

### 5.2.1 *Was/were able to- forms*

As evident in the results of the survey, there were no appearances of *was/were able to* + *V* occurring in the Old English texts, and Visser's first example of this expression appears c.1380. This is clear evidence for the likelihood that the expression was introduced as a renewal of *could*, at a time when possibly the lexical meanings of past ability on the part of the subject were beginning to become ambiguous with more abstract meanings of possibility and potentiality (see example (25) below). The timing of the first appearances (c.1380 for Visser's example, and at the time of Chaucer (1350–1420) for the examples from the Helsinki texts) is important: it was at this time, according to Bybee (2003), that the original meanings of knowledge ('know how to') and experience, first associated with the lexical uses of the present-tense counterpart modal *can*, were developing into meanings of ability and physical skill, and such meanings are clearly evident in the examples from Chaucer (26). One would expect, then, that the past or preterite form of *can* would follow the same path of development in its early stages, to come to express past ability at around that time. Therefore, *was/were able to* would enter the paradigm as a more lexicalized alternate of *could*, replacing the weakening lexical senses of past ability in some environments. Both the ME examples appear in factive subordinate clauses, which are, as discussed above, an optimum environment for the development of R-based implicatures, since such clauses presuppose the actuality of the proposition contained in them. The examples found are from Chaucer:

(18) A monk there was …
A manly man, to been an abbot **able**

1350–1420. Chaucer. *The General Prologue to the Canterbury Tales*. p. 26 C1

The predicate of past ability is dislocated in (18) because of the metrical restrictions of the verse, without which the sentence might be read as 'there was a monk, a manly man, (who was) able to have been an abbot,' thus providing the earliest example of this form in the texts, if such a reconstructed context might serve as an adequate example. The use of the form refers to the abilities and general characteristics of the subject, the monk, and reflects no possible senses of past actuality; in fact, the non-actuality (that he was not a monk) is more apparent, though this is not the dominant meaning in (18). The use of the form has a general characterizing function. The only ME example in Visser also has a generic predicate:

(19) the hauene was not **able** to dwelle in winter
'the harbour was not suitable for winter dwelling'
c1380. Wyclif. *The Acts of the Apostles*, 27. 12
Visser (1969: 1750)

In (19) the subject is inanimate ('the harbour') and the predicate is a stative verb ('dwell'), thus illustrating again a characterizing function in the semi-modal, and describing general facts about the subject. (It should be noted that the subject of *was* is not the same as the subject of *dwelle*, suggesting that the modal sense had not by then evolved.) There are no other examples of the semi-modal appearing in either Visser or the Helsinki Corpus in the Middle English data surveyed.

The Early Modern English data showed a far higher frequency of occurrence of the form: 22 tokens overall, with 6 in main clause uses and 16 in subordinate clauses. The uneven distribution between main clauses and subordinate clauses reflected that of all the forms across all the data: with the exception of ME *could*, there was consistently a greater number of subordinate clause uses than main clause functions. The reason may be that subordinate clause functions usually reflect subjunctive moods, as noted by Bybee et al. (1994), and such environments are semantically modal in any case, making them more readily receptive to the introduction of modal and semi-modal forms. Factive clauses again ranked high in frequency (87.45% in total), and negatives were relatively frequent overall (49.95%).

Thus, by far the largest number of occurrences in the EME data for *was/were able to +V* came from factive subordinate clauses, examples of which occur in temporal subordinate clauses; e.g.:

(20) But yet wee must say plainely, That it appeareth strange vnto vs, when wee **were able to shew** it, that since the comming to our Crowne, it was never denyed vs by any of his predecessors
1570–1640. Robert Cecil, *The Edmondes Papers*
(Ed. G. G. Butler). p. 402

The basic meaning of *were able* in (20) seems to express the generic past abilities of the subject, but restricted to a specific time reference; it is not clear whether the time reference refers to a single event or a series of events ('whenever'). At the same time, the presupposition is that the proposition predicated of the expression of past ability was actually accomplished (either at one event or at many), and this is due to the factive environment of a temporal clause. In slightly later examples, factive subordinate clauses express the accomplishment of a past event as conditional upon another event:

(21) And this power of approaching the Cushion by vertue of the operation of its own steams, was so durable in our vigorous piece of Amber, that by once chafing it, I **was able to make** it follow the Cushion no less than ten or eleven times.

1675–1676. Robert Boyle, *Electricity and Magnetism*. p. 20

By the late 17th century, then, examples had started to appear in which the use of *was/were able to* coincided with a meaning of ability specific to a single event; i.e. accomplishment. In (21) the single event is still not totally independent of other conditions, but the data suggests that this is the route by which meanings of past accomplishment may have developed out of earlier, more lexical functions expressing the skills and general abilities of the subject. In negative constructions, however, the path to the development of meanings of non-actuality is much faster. By the early part of the EME period, non-accomplishment of specific events was already part of the meaning of the form in factive subordinate clauses:

(22) and some of those that came thyther with the duke, **not able to dissemble** theyr sorow, were faine at his backe to turne their face to the wall

1500–1570. Thomas More, *The History of King Richard III* (Ed. R. S. Sylvester). p. 77

In (22) there is again a deleted relative clause understood in the context ('who were not able to dissemble their sorrow'), and the clause is factive. The context indicates that the inability of the subjects was related to a specific moment; i.e. when they came with the duke, and was not an inherent characteristic or generic feature of a time-stable nature. This suggests that time-specific uses were already appearing by the early 16th century, at least in negative subordinate clauses. No negative examples appear before the EME period in the data, though, clearly, (19) appears in Visser's data as an example of a negative characterizing function. By the 17th century, examples are appearing in negative main clauses, with the meaning of negative accomplishment (non-actuality) of a specific event:

(23) Before he was twenty, he came into the house of commons, and was on the king's side, and undertook to get Wiltshire and Dorsetshire to declare for him, but he **was not able to** effect it.

1640–1710. Gilbert Burnet, *Burnet's History of My Own Time I* (Ed. O Airy). p. 1, I, 172

If the path of development of *was/were able to* appears to parallel that of *had the ability to*, it is likely that, in earlier, more lexical functions, the meanings of ability or skills of the subject were restricted to generic time-frames, or time-stable situations, and that it was only gradually, with the increase of use in factive subordinate clauses, especially those embedded in constructions of specific time reference, that meanings of ability specific to a given event began to merge. In the extension to such environments, the R-based implicatures of actuality of the past event, interpretable as a POTENTIALITY FOR ACTUALITY metonym, could easily emerge. However, the process by which time-stable, generic characterizing functions became extended to functions associated with specific event situations could not be attributed to the development of R-based implicatures or grammaticalization processes: a generic event entails, and does not imply, the actualization of an event at a specific moment in time. Once the form had spread to use in time-specific environments, only then could the implicatures of actuality start to develop. In the negative forms, the development of non-actuality meanings from earlier senses of inability could not be due to an R-based implicature, but to an entailment, as explained in Section 3, since potentiality may be considered to be in scalar relationship with actuality.

### 5.2.2 *Could-forms*

The use of the modal of past ability was much more frequent in the survey, indicating that it is an older layer in the paradigm and therefore more highly grammaticalized than the other two forms. Only eight tokens appear in the Old English data, one in main clauses and seven in subordinate clauses. Three out of the eight OE functions are unambiguously lexical, with noun phrase or nominal clauses as objects, while factive subordinate clauses also occupy more than half of the tokens, either lexical or non-lexical. Four of the eight appear in negative sentences. In (24), *could* has a lexical function also expressing negation, in which the object is a NP, illustrating the earliest uses of the modal as a verb expressing knowledge or the mental ability of the subject:

(24) ∂a he þa geornlicor me frægn be his þingum, þa sæde ic ∂æt ic his ∂inga feola ne **cu∂ e**.

'When he earnestly asked me about these things, I then said I did not know much about them.'

850–950. *Alexander's Letter.* (Ed. S. Rypins). p. 27

Lexical functions continue into Middle English uses (which number 41 in total), where they still occupy a proportion of 22% of all environments. The percentage of negatives, though, drops to around 12.1%, a much lower proportion than in the Old English data. A significant proportion (26.8%) of all environments (apart from lexical) is found in non-factive subordinate clauses, which do not carry presuppositions as do factive clauses, and therefore are likely to render the modal meanings contained in them to be hypothetical in nature. Some non-factive subordinate clause environments included comparative clauses of indefinite degree, or comparative clauses with non-referring subjects:

(25) the mair, John Norhampton, reherced as euel as he **koude** of the eleccion on the day to-forn

1384–1425. Thomas Usk, *A Book of London English* (Ed. R. W. Chambers & M. Daunt). p. 28

The subordinate clause in (25) does not contain an assertion nor does it contain a presupposition, indicating that the extent of the subject's abilities is unknown. However, at the same time, Chaucer's work is still replete with examples illustrating the unambiguous characterizing use of *could*, which he uses profusely in one text to describe the attributes of the characters in *The Canterbury Tales, e.g.:*

(26) Therto he **koude** endite and make a thyng,
Ther **koude** no wight pynche at his writyng;
And every statut **koude** he pleyn by rote.

1350–1420. Geoffrey Chaucer, *The General Prologue to the Canterbury Tales.* (Ed. L. D. Benson). p. 28

In (26) three different functions are represented simultaneously: in the first example, the use of *could* describes the capabilities of (presumably) the lawyer, in a characterizing function; in the second the function expresses inability, nonactuality and since the context does not refer to a single event, thus impossibility for the subject to *þynche at* ('find fault with') his writing; in the third, the earlier use of the modal is represented in a full lexical verb meaning 'know.' This example provides good evidence to demonstrate the co-existence of overlapping stages of grammaticalization at one synchronic time-point and is indicative of the gradualness of the developmental route from meanings of knowledge to physical ability or skills, and finally to senses of possibility (or impossibility in the case of negatives). Most of the examples from this text, though, illustrate a characterizing function for *could*, and 15 of the 17 characterizing uses listed in Table 5a are found in this one text.

The EME data is marked by an absence of lexical functions (only one example), an increase in negatives (44.6% overall) and an increase in the number of factive subordinate clauses (61.4% of all subordinate clauses; 45% of the total EME figures). Also noteworthy is the emergence of counterfactual/hypothetical meanings, created by the cancellation of R-based implicatures in main clause environments. One such example is the following:

(27) I **could** be content, but it will aske some time, and I am going to such a place vpon speciall busines.
1593. George Gifford, *A Handbook of Witches*. P. B2R

The R-based implicature in the first clause, suggesting that the subject will potentially be content, is canceled by a conjoining clause expressing contrast and therefore implying that the subject will not be content after all as he or she is asking for more time. It should also be noted that by this time in the grammaticalization of *could*, most of the temporal meanings have faded and the modal now refers to the potentiality of the predicate to be realized after, not prior to the moment of speaking. In order to restore the bleached temporal meanings, the perfect auxiliary *have* is now used, as noted earlier:

(28) I **could haue** bin well content to haue chose seuen Yeres Imprisonment, ... rather than I would this Day haue gyuen Euidence against Sir (Nicholas Throckmorton) but sithence I must needes confesse my Knowledge, I must confesse all that is there written is true.
1554. *The Trial of Sir Nicholas Throckmorton* (Ed. F. Hargrave) P 1, 67.C2

In such constructions, the R-based implicature of the past potentiality of the predicated state or event is canceled by a clause of contrast, providing evidence to suggest that such inferences are basic to the meaning of *could*, and hypothetical or counterfactual meanings are derived by the co-occurrence with clauses of contrast or adversity. The derived inference is now that the subject did not choose to have seven years of imprisonment and gave evidence in confession against Throckmorton instead. With time, the expression of potentiality may come to stand alone for the entire construction of the modal clause plus the conjoined contrastive clause together, so that the contrastive clause is no longer required, and the modal clause becomes a metonym of counterfactuality, derived from a canceled R-implicature. This metonymic shift, already observed for the development of counterfactual/hypothetical meanings in *would* and discussed in Section 2.4, can be seen in at least one EME example, in which there is no contextual support from conjoining clauses of contrast:

(29) In trueth, husbande, my stomacke did so rise against her, that I **coulde haue** found in my heart to haue flowen vpon her.

1593. George Gifford,
*A Handbook of Witches and Witchcraft*. PB2V

When the modal clause alone (*could have V-ed*) may stand to represent the former modal clause + canceling clause (*could have X but Y, therefore not-X*), the counterfactual POTENTIALITY FOR NON-ACTUALITY metonym has developed. What is important though, is that at the basis of its development is a scalar implicature, an R-based implicature that has been canceled by an appended contrastive or adversative clause. That the basis is scalar is determined by the entailment of impossibility in the negated modal (see e.g. (17)); such inferences are the result of relationships between weak and strong elements on scales of the type discussed in Horn (1972, 1984). There is no metonymic link between negative potentiality and negative actuality, as negative potentiality is simply incompatible with actuality. This development may be said to convert the implicature into a Q-based one, thus creating a counterfactual metonym: the weakened factuality contained in the modal expression now stands metonymically for the counter-factuality of what it predicates.

It is clear from the data in the survey that the use of *could* as a verb meaning past ability never generalized to attain meanings of past actuality, in the same way as *was/were able to*. If it had, it would be hardly appropriate to suggest grammaticalization as a motivation, since the generalization of generic meanings to mark specific, time-stable events is an instance of entailment, and not of the conventionalization of conversational implicatures typically associated with the processes of grammaticalization. Furthermore, there is a notional increase of agentivity that could be associated with the past actuality meanings in *able*, an adjectival predicate, though *could* grammaticalized to undergo a loss of lexical meaning instead of an increase, with its concurrent development as an auxiliary verb. The loss of lexical uses that is clearly evident in the EME period was also accompanied by a development of potentiality meanings in main clauses, which could be modified by the addition of a coordinate clause of contrast or adversity, or a subordinate clause of condition, concession or qualification of the hypothetical meanings.

### 5.2.3 *Had the ability to*

As noted earlier, this form was not recorded at all in the diachronic texts, which may indicate its relatively late introduction into the paradigm. The absence of this form in the diachronic survey means that predictions about the types of inferences associated with it must be restricted to the possibilities discussed earlier in the chapter regarding current usage. As noted in Subsections 2.2–2.4, the implicature of counterfactuality in the complement of the ability expression is hypothesized to be directly related to the Quantity implicature and not to markedness. The effect of the markedness may increase the quantification of the modal expression, but it is likely that the 'default' implicature associated with such expressions will always be future-projecting, and therefore R-based, as discussed with respect to examples (3) and (12).

The diachronic survey, therefore, reveals that the expression may be a recent renewal in the paradigm, possibly associated only with Present-Day English. Although a full survey of PDE usage would not be within the scope of the present analysis, it was possible to describe an approximate pattern of its present-day uses in a small random sample extracted from the British National Corpus of (using the restricted sampling procedure).[5] Forty-eight instances were found, and in only one was a counterfactual implicature (suggesting the presence of Q-based inferences) present as part of the meaning (28). The majority of uses were to describe the particular skills or habits of the subject, in other words, as 'characterizing' functions. The distribution of the data is presented in Table 7.

**Table 7a.** Frequency and distribution of *had the ability (to + V)* in main clauses in a small sample of the British National Corpus. Forms also included *did not have the ability (to + V), had no ability to*, and *had the ability to + V* occurring within the scope of a negative matrix clause or a negative subject NP.

Total: 48 = 100%
**Main Clauses** 27 = 58.3%

| **Environments** | | **counterfactual** | **negative** | **TOTALS** |
|---|---|---|---|---|
| Characterizing | 22/27 = 81.5% | 1 = 3.7% | 3 = 11.1% | 26 = 96.3% |
| Negative | 1 = 3.7% | | | 1 = 3.7% |
| TOTALS | 23/27 = 85.1% | 1/27 = 3.7% | 3/27 = 11.1% | 27 = 100% |

Although this small sample may not be totally representative of present-day usage, it is probably safe to suggest that the strong bias towards characterizing functions would be likely to persist in a larger body of data, even if the exact proportion is not known, since the bias is too great to be accidental (96.3% of

**Table 7b.** Frequency and distribution of *had the ability (to + V)* in subordinate clauses in a small sample of the British National Corpus.

**Subordinate Clauses** 21 = 41.6%

| Environments | | characterizing | counterfactual | TOTALS |
|---|---|---|---|---|
| Factive clauses | 4 = 19% | 15 = 71.4% | 1 = 4.7% | 20 = 95.1% |
| Non-factive clauses | | 1 = 4.7% | | 1 = 4.7% |
| TOTALS | 4/21 = 19% | 16/21 = 76.2% | 1/21 = 4.7% | 21 = 99.9% |

main clauses and 76.2% of subordinate clauses). The clearly low percentage of counterfactual implicatures is obvious, and may suggest that Levinson's (1995) example (1b) is not typically representative of current patterns of use, and that the analysis given to it suffers from the usual risks of employing constructed examples to make generalizations about language use. This can be seen in the following example, the only valid instance in the sample in which a counterfactual inference might be said to develop:

(30) The penal jurisdiction of the county courts was to apply only where the debt had been contracted under circumstances which implied an intention to defraud (which upset Wetherfield) or where the debtor **had the ability to** pay but would not. (BPH 718)

The necessity in (30) is for a canceling clause, *but would not*, denying the possibility of an R-based implicature derived from the use of the ability expression ('had the ability to pay, and did pay'). The possibility is, of course, increased by its environment, a relative clause that is factive in nature. However, even in a main clause, cancellation is possible with a *but*-clause of adversity, suggesting the likely non-actuality of the potential event:

(31) … I **had the ability to** communicate verbally but at a child's level and almost no ability to read. (CGU 719)

The hearer's expectations of the speaker's ability to communicate are modified by the presence of a clause of adversity canceling or at least suspending the development of an R-based implicature suggesting that the speaker had the ability to communicate verbally, and did actually do so. However, since these implicatures are easily defeasible, they are expected to be less conventionalized than those associated with *was/were able to*; the adversative clauses do not have to be in the form of an explicit negation of R-implicatures, as shown. Negation is still inferable from the information provided in the adversative clause alone. For the same reason, a reinforcing clause is also still possible, introduced by *and* and co-occurring with *had the ability* expressions without redundancy or contradiction:

(32) She **had the ability** and now she had the break. (BP7 2026)

(33) All through his career he's **had the ability to** lead and inspire and he's really got through to our players and conveyed that. (CBG 13033)

In (32) the predicate is not supplied, but may be implied in the previous context. The conjoining clause (and now she had the break) suggests that the subject had the opportunity to accomplish the realization of the predicate, and would be inappropriate if the first clause carried a default Q-based implicature of the non-actuality of the focus of ability. It may also be redundant if the R-based implicature was conventionalized (consider *She was able to win the race, and now she had the break, and therefore she did win* in which the conjoining clause is not required). Sentence (33) is a similar example, in which the reinforcing clause (*and he's really got through to our players and conveyed that*) provides later confirmation of the subject's characteristic skills or abilities; thus 'he's had the ability to lead and inspire, and he has done that' reinforces the R-based implicature of the actuality of the subject's abilities. In the data there were three instances of reinforcement in main clauses and one in subordinate clauses.

The majority of the examples, though, as noted, described the generic skills and abilities of the subject, with no modification, except perhaps the presence of a frequency adverb such as *always* (in five of the main clauses and in two of the subordinate clauses), e.g.:

(34) While Enzo Ferrari always had the ability to attract the best drivers in the world, … the one man he never managed to get was Britain's Stirling Moss. (EXI 438)

The counterfactual inference, though, is more likely to develop from examples in which the ability expression is contained in a (non-negative) main clause environment, and with a predicate referring to a single event, as in (1b). None of these appear in the data; instead generic situations (characterizing functions) are the most typically represented, with an average total of 86.25% of all uses.

## 6. Comparison of the three alternates

The modal verb *could*, then, which at one stage of its development expresses meanings of past ability, does not follow the same path of periphrastic modal expressions of past ability such as *was/were able to* and go on to express past actuality. The reason for this may be that as an older form of modality, it was reduced, less periphrastic, and had a more frequent use historically, which led in turn to semantic erosion and bleaching of its lexical senses of temporality and ability. In the case of *could*, there is a possibility that characterizing uses created the evidential basis for the generation of hypothetical statements about the potentiality of the subject, in both main clauses as well as subordinate clauses. The weakening of temporal meanings of pastness in the modal would contribute thus to the development of such meanings. Therefore, past actuality in main clauses was never a stage in the grammaticalization path, as the loss of temporal meanings ensured that it would never occur in such clauses. Generic meanings of ability as a past characteristic may have served to justify the predictive nature of the new developing potentiality meanings: hence the chameleon-like appearance of examples in the later part of the survey with interpretations ambiguous between past ability or potentiality and future potentiality (e.g. (25)). As the modal progressed on its way to become a marker of potential modality, the past ability meanings were then renewed by *was/were able to*, confirming the fact that the temporal meanings had been weakened. When at a later stage, the meanings of potentiality were re-extended to past contexts, the auxiliary *have* was introduced as a reinforcement, marking what appears to be back-formation in *could have* + *V-ed* types.

Thus, what appear to be predominantly generic uses of *was/were able to* in the earlier texts become extended in EME to meanings of ability relative to a specific time point. Once the function has generalized in this way, R-based implicatures producing metonymic extensions of past actuality familiar to main assertive clauses will start to develop, as illustrated in (21). *Had the ability to*, though, appears to be still at the stage at which the most frequent use is in the expression of time-stable characteristics attributable to the subject, and examples similar to Levinson's (1995) example (1b) that refer to single events are found only with modifying clauses of adversity or contrast (see e.g. (30) in the data surveyed). The presence of a modifying clause suggests that there is an underlying R-implicature of potentiality associated with such expressions, and the modifying clause acts to cancel or suspend it. No likely examples of Q-based implicatures occur in *had the ability to* + *V* forms in bare or unmodified main declarative clauses; the future conventionalization of this implicature to either an R-based direction or a Q-based one is uncertain, and will depend on the types of environments with which it most frequently occurs.

Curiously enough, no examples of *was/were able to* appeared in the texts surveyed co-occurring with such canceling or suspending elements, so it is impossible to suggest that a counterfactual metonym could have arisen in its historical development. This may be because the implicatures became conventionalized before this happened. Both *had the ability to* and *could have + V-ed* forms show examples in which modifying elements do occur in the context, suggesting that this is the means by which POTENTIALITY FOR NON-ACTUALITY (counterfactual) metonyms may develop.

## 7. Conclusions

It was concluded in the interim summary in Section 4 that M-inferences are not the source for the derivation of counterfactual implicatures in periphrastic modalities. It seems that counterfactual implicatures have developed from metonymic extensions in past modal verbs, especially with perfect auxiliaries, e.g. *could have + V-ed*, in which the modal clause may stand alone for the entire construction containing a modal clause and followed by an adversative or contrastive clause. In such cases, a POTENTIALITY FOR NON-ACTUALITY metonym has arisen where once there might formerly have been a two-clause construction. In the small amount of data available for *had the ability to*, the two-clause stage has not yet developed into the counterfactual metonym, although the possibility that it may happen is apparent in examples (30) and (31). *Was/were able to*, however, developed into a POTENTIALITY FOR ACTUALITY metonym, as described by Panther and Thornburg (1999), possibly due to its frequent occurrence in factive subordinate clauses, which carry a presupposition and hence provide the optimum conditions for the development of R-based implicatures in modal forms, but otherwise because of the fact that its use in generic situations entailed a generalization to specific events, as long as the lexical senses of past ability were retained in the expression. There is no evidence in the data that such implicatures were canceled before they conventionalized. *Could* is not found in the survey to have ever contained inferences of the actuality of its complement in unmodified main clauses, in spite of what Levinson (1995) claims (as illustrated in (1a) for the presence of Q2 (Horn's R-based) implicatures. The absence of actuality as an inference is most likely due to the bleaching of temporal meanings of pastness, which would not present a problem for the periphrastic modals.

Thus the results of the changes taking place in the development of the modals and semi-modal equivalents may be described within the terms of a metonymic analysis, but underlying the creation of the metonymic inferences are certain principles explaining the direction of the metonym: either to express the actuality of the predicated event or its non-actuality, and such principles appear to be founded in pragmatics and the notion of scalar relationships between items. With further research in the field the correlations between the pragmatic principles of Quantity scales and metonymic inferences may contribute an important cognitive dimension to the study of the Gricean co-operative principle. The prospects remain an exciting possibility for future research to reveal.

## Notes

* I would like to thank Klaus Panther and Linda Thornburg particularly for their assistance in the presentation of this paper at the "Metonymy and Pragmatic Inferencing" workshop during the 7th International Pragmatics Conference, Budapest, July 7–14, 2000. A longer, more detailed version of the paper may be found under the title "Past ability modality and the derivation of complementary inferences" in *Journal of Historical Pragmatics* 2: 273–316 (2001).

1. As pointed out by an anonymous referee, there is reason to doubt the factivity of clauses following *said that* and *promised that*. However, in the present study, they will be classed as such (with all good faith in the word of the subject referent) on the basis of the slightly higher degree of expected realization of their complement propositions than can be attributed to the members of the non-factive category.

2. The strength of the inferences may vary according to the verb in the matrix clause, as suggested by the same referee.

3. The forms investigated were spelling variants taken from the *OED*. The only variants appearing in the Helsinki Corpus (apart from *able*) were *abil* and *hable*, the earliest (and only) citation for *abil* dated at 1350–1420 (the ME period), in *The Cloud of Unknowing and the Book of Privy Counselling*, and the earliest citation for *hable* being in Roger Ascham's *The Scholemaster* (1563–1568), in the EME period.

4. Acknowledgment is due to Matti Rissanen for permitting me access to the diachronic part of the Helsinki Corpus of English Texts. Reference should be made to Kytö (1996) for details on word count totals and for additional information regarding sources. A small portion of the Middle English corpus (ME IV, as listed in the manual) was unavailable.

5. This corpus can be found online at: http//sara.natcorp.ox.ac.uk. The sample is taken from the 100 million-word corpus, but restricted to a maximum of 50 tokens.

## References


Athanasiadou, Angeliki & Dirven, René (Eds.). (1997). *On Conditionals Again*. Amsterdam and Philadelphia: Benjamins.

Atlas, Jay D. & Levinson, Stephen C. (1981). *It*-clefts, informativeness, and logical form: Radical pragmatics. In P. Cole (Ed.), *Radical Pragmatics* (pp. 1–61). New York: Academic Press.

Bybee, Joan L. (1988). Semantic substance vs. contrast in the development of grammatical meaning. *Berkeley Linguistics Society, 14*, 247–264.

Bybee, Joan L. (2003). The role of repetition in grammaticization: CAN in English. In R. Janda & B. Joseph (Eds.), *Handbook of Historical Linguistics*. Oxford: Blackwell.

Bybee, Joan L., Perkins, Revere D., & Pagliuca, William (1994). *The Evolution of Grammar: Tense, Aspect and Modality in the Languages of the World.* Chicago: The University of Chicago Press.

Denison, David (1998). Syntax. In S. Romaine (Ed.), *The Cambridge History of the English Language, Vol. IV: 1776–1997* (pp. 92–329). Cambridge: Cambridge University Press.

Fauconnier, Giles & Sweetser, Eve (Eds.). (1996). *Spaces, Worlds, and Grammar* [Cognitive Theory of Language and Culture 2]. Chicago and London: The University of Chicago Press.

Grice, H. Paul (1975). Logic and conversation. In P. Cole & J. L. Morgan (Eds.), *Speech Acts* [Syntax and Semantics 3] (pp. 41–58). New York: Academic Press.

Horn, Laurence R. (1972). *On the Semantic Properties of the Logical Operators in English.* Los Angeles: UCLA dissertation.

Horn, Laurence R. (1984). Towards a new taxonomy for pragmatic inference: Q-based and R-based implicature. In D. Schiffrin (Ed.), *Meaning, Form and Use in Context: Linguistic Applications* [GURT '84] (pp. 11–42). Washington, DC: Georgetown University Press.

Horn, Laurence R. (1989). *A Natural History of Negation.* Chicago: The University of Chicago Press.

Horn, Laurence R. (1991). Given as new: when redundant information isn't. *Journal of Pragmatics, 15*, 313–336.

Horn, Laurence R. (2000). From *if* to *iff*: Conditional perfection as pragmatic strengthening. *Journal of Pragmatics, 32*, 289–326.

Kiparsky, Paul & Kiparsky, Carol (1970). Fact. In M. Bierwisch & K. E. Heidolph (Eds.), *Progress in Linguistics: A Collection of Papers* (pp. 143–173). The Hague: Mouton de Gruyter.

Kövecses, Zoltán & Radden, Günter (1998). Metonymy: developing a cognitive linguistic view. *Cognitive Linguistics, 9*, 37–77.

Kuteva, Tania (1998). On identifying an evasive gram: Action narrowly averted. *Studies in Language, 22*(1), 113–160.

Kytö, Merja (compiler). (1996). *Manual to the Diachronic Part of the Helsinki Corpus of English Texts: Coding Conventions and Lists of Source Texts* (3rd ed.). Helsinki: University of Helsinki, Department of English.

Levinson, Stephen C. (1987). Pragmatics and the grammar of anaphora: a partial pragmatic reduction of binding and control phenomena. *Journal of Linguistics, 23*, 379–434.

Levinson, Stephen C. (1995). Three levels of meaning. In F. R. Palmer (Ed.), *Grammar and Meaning: Essays in Honor of Sir John Lyons* (pp. 90–115). Cambridge: Cambridge University Press.

Palmer, Frank R. (1986). *Mood and Modality*. Cambridge: Cambridge University Press.

Panther, Klaus-Uwe & Thornburg, Linda (1998). A cognitive approach to inferencing in conversation. *Journal of Pragmatics, 30*, 755–769.

Panther, Klaus-Uwe & Thornburg, Linda (1999). The POTENTIALITY FOR ACTUALITY metonymy in English and Hungarian. In K.-U. Panther & G. Radden (Eds.), *Metonymy in Language and Thought* [Human Cognitive Processing 4] (pp. 333–357). Amsterdam and Philadelphia: Benjamins.

Van der Auwera, Johan (1997). Conditional perfection. In A. Athanasiadou & R. Dirven (Eds.), *On Conditionals Again* (pp. 169–190). Amsterdam and Philadelphia: Benjamins.

Vendler, Zeno (1967). *Linguistics in Philosophy*. Ithaca: Cornell University Press.

Visser, F. Th. (1969–1973). *An Historical Syntax of the English Language. Part III*. Leiden: E. J. Brill.

Ziegeler, Debra P. (2000a). *Hypothetical Modality: Grammaticalisation in an L2 Dialect*. Amsterdam and Philadelphia: Benjamins.

Ziegeler, Debra P. (2000b). The role of quantity implicatures in the grammaticalisation of *would*. *Language Sciences, 22*, 27–61.

Ziegeler, Debra P. (2001). Past ability modality and the derivation of complementary inferences. *Journal of Historical Pragmatics, 2*, 273–316.

## Primary sources

### Old English

Rypins, S. (Ed.). (1971). (1924). *Alexander's Letter* (Early English Text Society 161). New York: Kraus Reprint Co.

### Middle English

Benson, L. D. (Ed.). (1987). *The Riverside Chaucer*. Boston: Houghton Mifflin.

Chambers, R. W. & Daunt, M. (Eds.). (1967, 1931). Thomas Usk *Appeals: A Book of London English 1324–1425*. Oxford: Clarendon.

### Early Modern English

Airy, O. (Ed.). (1897, 1900). Gilbert Burnet, *Burnet's History of My Own Time*. Oxford: Clarendon Press.

Butler, G. G. (Ed.). (1913). Robert Cecil, *The Edmondes Papers*. London: J. B. Nichols and Sons.

Gifford, George (1593). *A Handbook of Witches and Witchcraftes* [Shakespeare Association Facsimiles 1]. London: Humphrey Milford and Oxford University Press, 1931.

Gunther, R. W. T. (Ed.) (1927). Robert Boyle *Electricity and Magnetism* [Old Ashmolean Reprints 7]. Oxford: Oxford University Press.

Hargrave, F. (Ed.) (1730). *The Trial of Sir Nicholas Throckmorton, Vols. I and IV*, 2nd ed. London: J. Walthoe Sen.
Sylvester, R. S. (Ed.). (1963). Thomas More, *The History of King Richard III* [The Complete Works of St. Thomas More, Vol. II]. New Haven and London: Yale University Press.

# Metonymy and pragmatic inference in the functional reanalysis of grammatical morphemes in Japanese*

Shigeko Okamoto

## 1. Introduction

It has been recognized that metaphor and metonymy are two major processes at work in grammaticalization (e.g. Hopper & Traugott 1993). In this chapter I consider the role of metonymy in instances of grammaticalization in Japanese that involve reanalyses of complementizers as sentence-final particles – reanalyses of grammatical morphemes that are quite common in Japanese and that provide interesting examples of functional shifts in linguistic forms.

In Japanese, a verb-final language, there are many grammatical morphemes used as markers of subordinate clauses – i.e. conjunctive particles (e.g. *ba* 'if', *noni* 'although', *node* 'because') and complementizers (see below for examples). These morphemes may also be used as sentence/utterance-final particles, expressing various pragmatic meanings. As discussed in a number of recent studies (e.g. Ohori 1995; Okamoto 1995; Suzuki 1999), the latter usage (i.e. sentence-final particles) can be considered as resulting from the functional reanalyses of the former (i.e. markers of subordinate clauses) that involve a shift of subordinate clauses to main clauses, constituting independent grammatical constructions in the sense of Fillmore et al. (1988), Kay and Fillmore (1999), etc. The question is how and why these reanalyses may take place. The present study addresses this question, focusing on the reanalysis of complementizers (COMPS) as sentence-final particles (SFPS). It considers what motivates and enables such a reanalysis, paying special attention to the nature of pragmatic inference involved in the process of reanalysis, in particular, the role of metonymy.

The chapter is organized as follows: It first presents example morphemes that can function either as COMPS or as SFPS (Section 2). Using the morpheme *koto* as an illustration, it then offers arguments for treating the SFP usage as distinct from the COMP usage (Section 3) and analyzes the process of the reanalysis of *koto* from a COMP to an SFP, focusing on the pragmatic inference involved (Sections 4). Finally, it discusses the role of metonymy in the reanalysis of COMPS as SFPS, as illustrated by the morpheme *koto* (Section 5).

## 2. Morphemes used as COMPS and as SFPS

There are a number of morphemes in Japanese that can be used either as complementizers or as sentence-final particles – e.g. *no, koto, to, tte,* and *ka.* As COMPS, these morphemes have two functions: to mark a clause boundary by nominalizing a complement clause and to indicate the epistemic status of the proposition in the complement clause. For example, *no* is typically used for a concrete or directly perceived event/state (e.g. (1));[1] *koto* for an abstract or indirectly perceived event/state (e.g. (2)); and *to/tte* for a quotative remark (e.g. (3)) (cf. Kuno 1973; Josephs 1976).[2,3]

(1) *Boku wa Yoshio ga Masao o butsu* ***no*** *o (*koto o/*to)*
I TM SM OM hit COMP OM
*mi-ta.*
see-PST
'I saw Yoshio hitting Masao.'

(2) *John wa nihongo ga muzukashii* ***koto*** *o (*no o/*to) manan-da.*
TM Japanese SM difficult COMP OM learn-PST
'John learned that Japanese is difficult.' (Kuno 1973)

(3) *Yoshio wa Masao ga shin-da* ***to/tte*** *(*no o/*koto o) it-ta.*
TM SM die-PST COMP say-PST
'Yoshio said that Masao died.'

These morphemes as SFPS do not have a nominalizing function; rather they highlight the "original" complement clauses as main clauses and function primarily as modality markers, indicating the speech act types involved and/or the speaker's attitudes toward the proposition in question: for example, *no* is used for giving or requesting an explanatory or clarifying comment with regard to a certain situation in the discourse context (e.g. (4)) (cf. Kuno 1973; Teramura 1984; Cook 1990; Maynard 1992); *koto* for expressing exclamation (e.g. (5)) or for giving an order or direction (e.g. (6)); *to* for expressing defiance (e.g.

(7)) or for self-affirmation (e.g. (8)); and *tte* for reporting a proposition expressed by someone else (e.g. (9)) or for expressing the speaker's insistence on the proposition (e.g. (10)).[4]

(4) <from natural conversation>
A: *Nee, kono zukini wa tada chiizu o mabush-ita dake na* ***no.***
hey this zucchini TM only cheese OM coat-PST only COP SFP
'Hey, did you coat this zucchini only with cheese?'
B: *Aa, are, panko to hanhan na* ***no.***
oh that breadcrumbs with half-half COP SFP
'Oh, that is half bread crumbs and half cheese.'

(5) *Ii o- tenki da* ***koto.***
nice PPX weather COP SFP
'What nice weather!'

(6) <from *Asahi Shinbun*, a daily newspaper>
*Toku ni ta no habatsu ni tsuite wa issai hure-nai* ***koto.***
especially other factions about TM at all discuss-NEG SFP
*Miyazawa-ha no jimusyo ni konna ohuregaki ga haridas-are-ta.*
faction-GEN office in such order notice SM post-PASS-PST
'In particular, you must not discuss other factions at any time. Such a notice of orders was posted in the office of the Miyazawa faction.'

(7) *Nan da* ***to.*** *Tsumaranai da* ***to.***
What COP SFP boring COP SFP
'What?! Boring?!'

(8) *Moo kippu wa kat-ta* ***to.***
already ticket TM buy-PST SFP
'I've already bought the ticket.'

(9) <from a TV drama>
*Yama tte abunai n desu* ***tte.***
mountain TM dangerous AUX SFP
'Mountains are dangerous, I hear.'

(10) <from a TV drama>
*Hontoo da* ***tte.*** *Ore puropoozu nan ka shite-nai* ***tte.***
true COP SFP I proposal such a thing do-NEG SFP
'It's true, really. I didn't propose marriage to her, really.'

## 3. *Koto* as an SFP in the [S *koto*] construction

One might argue that utterances such as (4)–(10) above are elliptical expressions, or the result of main clause deletion, and hence that these morphemes in question are not truly SFPS at all, but rather are COMPS. For example, the morpheme *koto* for exclamation (e.g. (11a)) might be analyzed as a COMP, that is, as an abbreviation of an expression such as S *koto ni odoroita* '(I) was amazed that S' (e.g. (11b)) or S *koto to ittara nai* 'it is indescribable that S' (e.g. (12b)):

(11) a. *O- niwa ga kiree da* ***koto.***
PPX garden SM pretty COP SFP
'How pretty the garden is!'
b. *O- niwa ga kiree na/*da* ***koto*** *ni odoro-ita.*
PPX garden SM pretty COP COMP be amazed-PST
'I was amazed that the garden is so pretty.'

However, such an argument cannot be supported, if one examines closely the morphosyntactic and semantic-pragmatic properties associated with these SFPS and the corresponding COMPS. That is, I will demonstrate below that the morphemes in question in utterances like (4)–(10) are best regarded as SFPS, and that these utterances are not elliptical, but rather instances of independent main-clause grammatical constructions, which may be called *subordinate-clause-as-main-clause constructions* (SCMCCS). I demonstrate this point using the morpheme *koto* as an example, since space does not permit me to discuss all the relevant morphemes.[5] I will first discuss the exclamatory *koto* (e.g. (11a)) and then the directive *koto* (e.g. (6)).

Morphosyntactically, the exclamatory *koto* differs from the COMP *koto* as follows: *Koto* as a COMP must take the prenominal form, not the final form, of a predicative adjective, or so-called adjectival noun phrase, (e.g. *kiree na/*da* in (11b)), whereas the exclamatory *koto* takes the final form (e.g. *kiree da* in (11a)). Furthermore, the final *koto* can be preceded by the polite honorific *desu* (or *masu* in the case of a verb), as in (12a), whereas *koto* as a COMP cannot, as in (12b):

(12) a. *Maa, suteki desu koto.*
oh nice COP SFP
'Oh, how nice!'
b. *Suteki na /*desu koto to ittara nai.*
nice COP COMP indescribable
'It is indescribable how nice it is.'

The honorific *desu*, for the addressee of an utterance, is normally used sentence-finally; it cannot occur in a complement clause. These morphosyntactic constraints indicate that *koto* in sentences like (5) and (11a) is not a COMP, but an SFP.

Semantic and pragmatic evidence also supports the treatment of the exclamatory *koto* as a true SFP. As mentioned above, one might 'paraphrase' *koto* in (11a) as *koto ni odoroita, koto to ittara nai*, etc. However, all these "paraphrases" are more descriptive and explanatory, and lack the spontaneity of real exclamations. Accordingly, an interjection such as *maa* 'oh' co-occurs more naturally with the exclamatory *koto* (e.g. (12a)) than with a descriptive phrase (e.g. (12b)). Moreover, stylistically, utterances ending with *koto* are considered definitely feminine, but the corresponding descriptive expressions are neutral. Thus, the exclamatory *koto* and its expansions cannot be considered paraphrases.

Another piece of evidence concerns the inferability of unexpressed meanings. As is well known, elliptical utterances are pervasive in Japanese. They are used when the meaning is assumed to be inferable from the context without an explicit mention. For example, the subject noun phrase in (12a) is not mentioned because its referent is considered inferable. However, the "predicate" of the utterance with the exclamatory *koto* seems opaque unless the interpreter knows the conventional meaning associated with *koto* in this usage (see below for further discussion). In other words, utterances such as (11a) and (12a) cannot be regarded as elliptical expressions (of [S1 *koto* S2]).

In the second usage – *koto* for giving an order or direction – *koto* has the following syntactic-semantic constraints. First, the action denoted by the verb in [S *koto*] must be controllable by the addressee, or the subject-referent, as shown in examples (13) and (14):

(13) *Saku no naka ni hair-anai* ***koto.***
fence GEN inside in enter-NEG SFP
'You must not go inside the fence.'

(14) **Hana ga hayaku saku* ***koto.***
flower SM quickly bloom SFP
'The flowers must bloom quickly.'
(* indicates that the utterance is unacceptable as an order.)

Furthermore, the verb cannot be in the so-called potential form (-(*rar*)*e*). For example, (13a) does not have a directive force:

(13) a. **Saku* *no* *naka* *ni* *hair-e-nai* **koto.**
fence GEN inside in enter-can-NEG SFP
'You cannot go inside the fence *koto*.'

Similarly, (15), in which the verb is followed by the auxiliary *nakereba naranai* 'must,' is unacceptable as a directive utterance:

(15) **Oya* *o* *daiji* *ni* *shinakereba* *naranai* **koto.**
parent OM take good care of must SFP
'You must take good care of your parents *koto*.'

These examples indicate that a sense of duty is associated with *koto*, and that *koto* imparts to the utterance a directive sense.

One might argue that (13), for example, could be paraphrased as (13b):

(13) b. *Saku no naka ni hairanai* **koto** *o* **meejiru.**
COMP OM order
'I order you not to go inside the fence.'

However, (13b) is an explicit performative utterance; it is authoritative, hence stronger as an order than (13). In addition, (13) can convey the point in a more concise manner. The problem of inferability of the "implied" meaning discussed above is also applicable in this usage of *koto*. Thus, the directive [S *koto*] and its expansions cannot be considered paraphrases, suggesting that the directive sense is associated with *koto* in the [S *koto*] construction.

From the foregoing discussion, we can conclude that *koto* in utterances such as (11a) and (13) is not a COMP, but an SFP used to express exclamation in a feminine manner or to give an order or direction in a more indirect, but concise manner than an explicit performative expression. In other words, [S *koto*] in both usages is not an elliptical expression. Rather, it is best regarded as an independent grammatical construction used as a main clause (i.e., an SCMCC), in which *koto* functions as a modality marker. In fact, the definitions of the morpheme *koto* in Japanese dictionaries include the two meanings of the SFP *koto* as directive and exclamatory.

## 4. Pragmatic inference in the reanalysis of *koto*

The conclusion that the exclamatory or directive *koto* in [S *koto*] is not a COMP raises the question of how *koto* has come to be used as an SFP, or a modality marker. Is this usage simply arbitrary or is it motivated?

Although it was said in Section 3 that *koto* as an SFP should be distinguished from *koto* as a COMP, that does not mean that the two usages are unrelated. Rather, it seems most reasonable to assume that the former has evolved from the latter by means of functional reanalysis. As we saw earlier, there exist clear semantic-pragmatic similarities between the [S *koto*] construction and its corresponding "full" expression ([S1 *koto* S2]), suggesting that *koto* as an SFP originates in the conversational implicature of an abbreviated expression in the sense that [S *koto*] does not mean only [Proposition *koto*], but stands for [[Proposition *koto*] Modality]. The form [S *koto*] thus may be regarded as a kind of metonymic expression in a broader sense in that the whole is represented by its part. That is, the reanalysis of *koto* from a COMP to an SFP presumably involves a shift of conversational implicatures to conventional implicatures (Grice 1975; Traugott & König 1991) – i.e. an instance of conventionalization of conversationally implied modalities for the propositions in question. At the initial stage of reanalysis, the two specific modalities in question, namely, exclamation and directive, are conveyed as conversational implicatures assumed to be inferable from the context. When this pattern of use is repeated in certain contexts, these modalities come to be generally associated with [S *koto*] as conventionalized implicatures, and eventually semanticized, or pragmaticized, as part of the meanings of *koto* in the [S *koto*] construction (see also Panther & Thornburg, Stefanowitsch, and Ziegeler in this volume for discussions of conventionalized implicatures).

Let us consider how the form [S *koto*] might be used (at the initial stage of reanalysis) as an abbreviated expression to convey a particular modality as a conversational implicature. On the surface, the use of [S *koto*] to convey [[Proposition *koto*] Modality] violates Gricean Maxims, but the addressee is assumed to be able to infer the conversationally implied modality. What allows the speaker to assume that the addressee is able to infer the implied modality? The Gricean approach itself does not offer an adequate answer. I argue that there are two kinds of knowledge required for appropriately inferring the implied modality: (1) knowledge of certain frames (i.e. the frames for clause linkage and the frames for certain modalities, or expressions of speaker's stances with regard to propositions in question), and (2) knowledge of the specific context of utterance. The former can be regarded as part of the general knowledge of the world, including the world of things and events, the world of word forms and their meanings, and the world of concepts (Radden & Kövecses 1999). This encyclopedic knowledge has been termed variously as *frames* (Fillmore 1982), *Idealized Cognitive Models* (Lakoff 1987), *scenarios* (Panther & Thornburg 1998, 1999), etc. In what follows I will explain, with examples, how the two kinds of knowledge may be used in establishing the link between [S *koto*] and [[Proposition *koto*] Modality].

Suppose, for example, (16) is used as an abbreviated expression:

(16) *Mainichi ha o migaku* **koto.**
every day teeth OM brush
'You brush your teeth every day-*koto*.'

To interpret (16) as a directive, one must among others know the frame for directives. Modifying the scenario for requests given by Panther and Thornburg (1998), I present a simplified frame for directives in (17):

(17) Simplified frame for directives

| | |
|---|---|
| The BEFORE: | H can do A (the action in question). |
| | Doing A is desirable. |
| | Sp wants H to do A. |
| | Sp has the authority to put H under obligation. |
| The CORE: | Sp puts H under strong obligation to do A. |
| The RESULT: | H must/should do A. |
| The AFTER: | H will do A. |

As we can see, S in [S *koto*] refers to the AFTER component in this frame.

In addition, the role played by *koto* in [S *koto*] cannot be ignored. As mentioned in Section 2, *koto* as a COMP is typically used to indicate the epistemic status of the proposition in the complement as being abstract or indirectly perceived state of affairs. Further, it indicates that [S *koto*] is a constituent of the main clause that may express the result of some kind of mental or perceptual activity, including one's attitude toward the proposition expressed by S. This attitude, or stance, may be epistemic (e.g., *Yamada-kun ga Amerika ni itta* ***koto*** *wa tashika da* 'It's certain that Yamada went to Amerika'), evaluative or emotional (e.g., *Ryooshin ga rikon-suru* ***koto*** *ni sansei da* 'I agree that my parents will get divorced'), or deontic (e.g., *Saku no naka ni hairanai* ***koto*** *o meejiru* 'I order you not to go inside the fence'). This is a simplified frame for *koto* as a COMP, which highlights the part relevant to the interpretation of [S *koto*] as an abbreviated expression. This is summarized in (18):

(18) Simplified frame for *koto* as a COMP in [S1 *koto* S2]
- S1 represents an abstract or indirectly perceived state of affairs (P),
- S2, the main clause, may express one's stance toward P in S1, a stance that may be epistemic, evaluative/emotional, or deontic.

An utterance in the form of [S *koto*] (e.g. (16)) then serves as a kind of hint for the implied meaning. On hearing such an utterance, the frame for *koto* as a COMP may be activated, which suggests that some kind of speaker's stance toward the proposition expressed in S is not explicitly mentioned (cf. Ohori 1997).[6] Considering the proposition in S and the extralinguistic context, one may then interpret the implied speaker's stance as being deontic, in particular, directive. That is, the frame for *koto* ((18)) is coupled with the frame for directives ((17)) by regarding the proposition in S as the AFTER component of the frame for directives and metonymically linking it to the CORE in the same frame (see also Radden and Seto, this volume, for discussion of speech act metonymy). At the initial stage of reanalysis, one's knowledge of the specific context seems indispensable in that the implied meaning (i.e. the CORE in the frame for directives in (17)) is inferable, only if there are sufficient contextual clues for relating the utterance to the frame for an appropriate speech act. For example, in the case of (16), the proposition in S can be considered the AFTER component of the frame for directives, only if the context fits the frame, for example, if the context satisfies (some of) the conditions stipulated in the BEFORE components in the frame for directives: if the speaker is the addressee's parent or teacher and is considered to have the authority of giving orders to the addressee, if the action in question, brushing teeth every day, is considered desirable, and if the addressee is assumed to be able to perform this action.

The points in (19) summarize the process of interpretation of [S *koto*] as an abbreviated expression, conversationally implying the speaker's directive stance:

(19) Summary of interpretive process:
- [S *koto*] as an abbreviated expression may be interpreted as a directive on the basis of (a) knowledge of the frame for *koto* as a COMP, (b) knowledge of the frame for directives, and (c) knowledge of the specific context.
- [S *koto*] activates the frame for *koto* as a COMP, suggesting that the speaker's stance for the proposition expressed by S is implicit. Given the context, the frame for directives may then be activated. That is, the implicit speaker's stance may be regarded as deontic, in particular, as directive, because S in [S *koto*] corresponds to the AFTER component of the frame for directives, and because its context satisfies the conditions in the BEFORE component of the same frame.

As we can see in (19), knowledge of frames is indispensable in the interpretation of [S *koto*] as an abbreviated expression. It prompts the search for the implicit meaning so that one can make sense of a given "incomplete" utterance, or situation, making reference to previously known, or familiar, situations. Metonymic reasoning – as a cognitive process in which one conceptual entity provides access to another within the same frame, or ICM (Radden & Kövecses 1999) – also plays an important role in this search process in that it helps find, or construct, the whole (i.e. the frame for directives, or the CORE in this frame) from its part (i.e. the AFTER and BEFORE components) based on the conceptual contiguity within the frame in question.

The interpretation of the implicature of [S *koto*] as exclamatory can be explained in a similar manner.

(20) *Maa oishii koto.*
oh delicious
'Oh, it is delicious-*koto*.'

Suppose (20) is used as an abbreviated expression intended to convey exclamation as a conversational implicature. In this case, the addressee is assumed to be able to construe the intended meaning on the basis of his/her knowledge of the frames for exclamations and the COMP *koto* and specific contextual knowledge. A simplified frame for exclamations is presented in (21):

(21) Simplified frame for exclamations

| | |
|---|---|
| The BEFORE: | P (or the state of affairs in question) is true.<br>Sp thinks that P is not a normal state of affairs, that P is surprising.<br>P is (un)desirable. |
| The CORE: | Sp conveys to H that Sp thinks that P is not a normal state of affairs, that P is surprising. |
| The RESULT: | H realizes Sp's evaluation of P. |
| The AFTER: | H is (dis)pleased with Sp's evaluation. |

According to this frame, S in [S *koto*] for exclamation states only the first condition in the BEFORE component, that is, the truthfulness of the proposition in question. The frame for *koto* as a COMP (i.e. (18)) indicates that the speaker is taking some stance for this proposition, or state of affairs. From the context, one knows that this state of affairs (the fact that the food is delicious) is true, desirable, and surprising, which satisfies the BEFORE component in the frame for exclamations ((21) above), and that it is worth mentioning. Here, again, the interpretation of the elliptical utterance requires sufficient contextual clues (e.g. the speaker is in a position to praise the food, the speaker's tone of voice and facial expression). Under these circumstances, the implied meaning may then be construed as the speaker's evaluative or exclamatory attitude toward this state of affairs.

As mentioned, when the form [S *koto*] is used repeatedly for indirectly giving an order or for expressing exclamation, the implied meaning comes to be generally associated with [S *koto*] as an independent construction. In other words, conventionalization of conversational implicatures takes place and gives rise to a functional reanalysis; and the originally implied meaning is semanticized and may no longer be inferable from the context. To put it differently, the interpretation of the [S *koto*] construction no longer requires a complex inferential process, as illustrated above (although some inference may be necessary to identify which one of the two usages of *koto* as an SFP is applicable to the given utterance). At the same time, the morpheme *koto* as an SFP, or the [S *koto*] construction, further develops its own special morphosyntactic and semantic-pragmatic properties, as discussed in Section 3.

## 5. The role of metonymy in the reanalysis of grammatical morphemes

The reanalysis of the morpheme *koto* in Japanese discussed in this study illustrates the important role metonymy may play in grammaticalization at both linguistic/rhetorical and cognitive levels. I have suggested that the reanalysis of *koto* from a COMP to an SFP is based on the use of [S *koto*] as a kind of metonymic expression in that the whole is represented by its part. The motivations for the reanalysis, or the use of such a metonymic expression, seem to be rhetorical and social concerns: (1) to foreground the information in the "original" complement as the most important part of the message, (2) to bring about certain expressiveness, that is, to perform a given speech act with particular stylistic nuances – i.e. spontaneity for the exclamatory *koto* rather than a descriptive expression and conciseness for the directive *koto*, and (3) to use a socially appropriate expression in a given situation – i.e. an indirect, less imposing expression of directive and a less imposing and "feminine" expression of exclamation. Thus, the reanalysis of *koto* utilizes metonymy as an effective linguistic device, or trope, that can satisfy these rhetorical and social needs (see also Radden & Kövecses 1999).

Further, the process of reanalysis discussed above indicates that metonymy is not simply a way of speaking, or a matter of trope. Rather, it illustrates another important aspect of metonymy, namely, its role in thought processes (Croft 1993; Panther & Thornburg 1998; Gibbs 1999; Radden & Kövecses 1999). I have argued that in the reanalysis of *koto*, conversational implicatures have presumably been conventionalized and semanticized, as part of the meanings of *koto*. In this process, the involvement of metonymy can be considered twofold. At the initial stage of reanalysis, in using [S *koto*] to conversationally implicate a particular modality, the addressee is assumed to be able to infer the implicature on the basis of his/her knowledge of certain frames and understanding of the specific context. As discussed above, in this inferential process, metonymic reasoning based on the conceptual contiguity within frames in knowledge representations plays an important role in linking [S *koto*] to [[P *koto*] Modality]; it facilitates the search for the "answer" (or the "whole") by means of a "hint" (or a "part").

Metonymy is also at work at the next stage of reanalysis, that is, when conversational implicatures are conventionalized for *koto* as an SFP. That is, meanings are metonymically transferred through contiguity in linguistic and pragmatic contexts. Repeated uses of the same linguistic form in like circumstances bring about the semanticization of the implied meaning as part of that form. This semantic transfer can be regarded as an instance of pragmatic strengthening in grammaticalization in that the semantic change involves an increase in the speaker's subjectivity (Traugott 1988, 1989; Traugott & König 1991; Hopper & Traugott 1993). The reanalysis of COMPS in Japanese offers an interesting example of grammaticalization, since it is not a prototypical example of grammaticalization in which a lexical item develops into a grammatical item (Hopper & Traugott 1993).

Metonymy thus plays important roles in the reanalysis of *koto*. Note, however, that because the meanings of *koto* as an SFP are now conventionalized, or semanticized, the interpretation of utterances like (16) and (20) may not involve a complex inferential process based on metonymic reasoning. As cautioned by Gibbs (1999: 74), a direct link between metonymy in language and metonymy in thought must not always be assumed, particularly when an expression is conventionalized, as in the case of the [S *koto*] construction (see also Stefanowitsch, this volume, for discussion of the conventionalized implicatures in grammatical constructions for indirect speech acts). The [S *koto*] construction may originate in an abbreviated expression, as discussed above, but it differs from "regular" elliptical expressions. As mentioned earlier, elliptical utterances are widely used in Japanese when the meanings are considered inferable from the context. For example, it is common not to mention the subject of a sentence, as in (22):

(22) *Kinoo eiga o mi-ta*
yesterday movie OM see-PST
'(I) saw a movie yesterday'

In (22) the subject referent is assumed to be inferable based on the knowledge of the frame for *miru* 'seeing' and that of the specific context (see Okamoto 1985 for further discussion).[7] As explained above, the interpretations of an utterance in the form [S *koto*] as an abbreviated expression follows the same kind of inferential process. However, once [S *koto*] is reanalyzed as a main clause grammatical construction, the "original" implicature is semanticized, whereas in "regular" elliptical utterances the implied meanings are not conventionalized and vary depending on the context.

As mentioned at the beginning of this chapter, the reanalyses of subordinate-clause markers (i.e. conjunctive particles and complementizers) as SFPS seem to be quite common in Japanese, suggesting that the clause-final position is an important locus of grammaticalization (see Ohori 1997). That is, the structure of Japanese may be conducive to the development of SFPS from COMPS in that the complement clause is followed by the main clause and that the verb is placed in the clause-final position, followed by an auxiliary verb or a particle to express a modality. The reanalysis of COMPS as SFPS in Japanese may also be related to the Japanese preference for avoiding explicit expressions under certain social situations, because, as discussed by Martin (1975), a final particle "imparts some additional hint of the speaker's attitude toward what he is saying" (*ibid.*: 914) without explicitly articulating it.

The present study has mainly discussed the morpheme *koto*, but there are many other subordinate clause markers (conjunctive particles and complementizers) that need to be examined with regard to the process of their reanalysis as SFPS.[8] Needless to say, such research must be accompanied by investigation of historical data (see Suzuki (1999) for discussion of historical evidence for grammaticalization of certain particles in Japanese; see also Ziegeler, this volume, for discussion of historical evidence for the development of counterfactual implicatures in English). Furthermore, the use of subordinate clauses as main clause grammatical constructions is not restricted to Japanese, as demonstrated by Panther and Thornburg (this volume) (see also Ziegeler, this volume, which discusses the development of a single-clause construction for a counterfactual implicature from two-clause phenomena). More cross-linguistic studies are called for to investigate the process of pragmatic inferences involved in the use of these clauses as independent main clause constructions.

## Notes

* I would like to thank Klaus-Uwe Panther and Linda Thornburg for their valuable comments and discussions.

1. Note that the characterizations given here for *no* and *koto* have many "exceptions" the discussion of which is beyond the scope of this study.

2. *Tte* is a colloquial form of *to*.

3. The following abbreviations are used in this paper: A = action, AUX = auxiliary verb; COMP = complementizer; COP = copula; GEN = genitive case marker; H = hearer; NEG = negative auxiliary; OM = object marker; P = proposition; PASS = passive voice; PPX = polite prefix; PST = past tense marker; S = sentence; SFP = sentence-final particle; SM = subject marker; SP = speaker; and TM = topic marker.

4. Although not discussed here, the form *tto* is another variant of *to* and is used as an SFP for making a declaration in a casual manner.

5. See Okamoto (1995) for discussion of the morphemes *no* and *to/tte*.

6. Ohori (1997) discusses what he calls suspended clause constructions in Japanese that involve conjunctive particles (e.g. *kara* 'because,' *noni* 'although'). Treating them as grammatical constructions, he accounts for their interpretation in terms of "framing effects," in which "the possible range of interpretation of the clause-linking form is constrained by the constructional frame" (p. 476).

7. Okamoto (1986) discusses the inferential process in the interpretation of "regular" elliptical utterances in Japanese, which makes use of one's knowledge of frames and that of the specific context.

8. The degree of reanalysis seems to differ depending on the morpheme; that is, some (previously) subordinate clauses (e.g. those with *koto*), but not others (e.g. those with *node* 'because'), seem to have been fully established as main clause grammatical constructions with "genuine" SFPS. Further study on this issue will certainly enhance the understanding of the process of reanlaysis concerning these grammatical morphemes.

## References

Cook, Haruko M. (1990). An indexical account of the Japanese sentence-final particle *no*. *Discourse Processes, 13*, 401–439.

Croft, William (1993). The role of domains in the interpretation of metaphors and metonymies. *Cognitive Linguistics, 4*, 335–370.

Fillmore, Charles J. (1982). Frame semantics. In Linguistics Society of Korea (Ed.), *Linguistics in the Morning Calm* (pp. 1–138). Seoul: Hanshin.

Fillmore, Charles J., Kay, Paul, & O'Connor, Mary C. (1988). Regularity and idiomaticity in grammatical constructions: the case of *let alone*. *Language, 64*, 501–538.

Gibbs, Raymond W., Jr. (1999). Speaking and thinking with metonymy. In K.-U. Panther & G. Radden (Eds.), *Metonymy in Language and Thought* (pp. 61–75). Amsterdam and Philadelphia: John Benjamins.

Grice, H. Paul (1975). Logic and conversation. In P. Cole & J. L. Morgan (Eds.), *Speech Acts* [Syntax and Semantics 3] (pp. 41–58). New York: Academic Press.

Heine, Bernd, Claudi, Ulrike, & Hünnemeyer, Friederike (1991). *Grammaticalization: A Conceptual Framework*. Chicago: The University of Chicago Press.

Hopper, Paul & Traugott, Elizabeth C. (1993). *Grammaticalization*. Cambridge: Cambridge University Press.

Josephs, Lewis S. (1976). Complementation. In M. Shibatani (Ed.), *Japanese Generative Grammar* [Syntax and Semantics 5] (pp. 307–369). New York: Academic Press.

Kay, Paul & Fillmore, Charles J. (1999). Grammatical constructions and linguistic generalizations: The *What's X doing Y?* construction. *Language, 75*, 1–33.

Kuno, Susumu (1973). *The Structure of the Japanese Language*. Cambridge, MA: The MIT Press.

Lakoff, George (1987). *Women, Fire, and Dangerous Things: What Categories Reveal About the Mind*. Chicago and London: The University of Chicago Press.

Martin, Samuel E. (1975). *A Reference Grammar of Japanese*. New Haven: Yale University Press.

Maynard, Senko K. (1992). Cognitive and pragmatic messages of a syntactic choice: The case of the Japanese commentary predicate *n(o) da*. *Text, 12*, 563–613.

Ohori, Toshio (1995). Remarks on suspended clauses: A contribution to Japanese phraseology. In M. Shibatani & S. Thompson (Eds.), *Essays in Semantics and Pragmatics: In Honor of Charles J. Fillmore* (pp. 201–218). Amsterdam and Philadelphia: John Benjamins.

Ohori, Toshio (1997). Framing effects in Japanese non-final clauses: Toward an optimal grammar-pragmatic interface. *Berkeley Linguistics Society, 23*, 471–480.

Okamoto, Shigeko (1985). Ellipsis in Japanese Discourse. Ph.D. dissertation. University of California, Berkeley.

Okamoto, Shigeko (1995). Pragmaticization of meaning in some sentence-final particles in Japanese. In M. Shibatani & S. Thompson (Eds.), *Essays in Semantics and Pragmatics: In Honor of Charles J. Fillmore* (pp. 219–246). Amsterdam and Philadelphia: John Benjamins.

Panther, Klaus-Uwe & Thornburg, Linda (1998). A cognitive approach to inferencing in conversation. *Journal of Pragmatics, 30*, 755–769.

Panther, Klaus-Uwe & Thornburg, Linda (1999). The POTENTIALITY FOR ACTUALITY metonymy in English and Hungarian. In K.-U. Panther & G. Radden (Eds.), *Metonymy in Language and Thought* (pp. 333–357). Amsterdam and Philadelphia: John Benjamins.

Radden, Günter & Kövecses, Zoltán (1999). Towards a theory of metonymy. In K.-U. Panther & G. Radden (Eds.), *Metonymy in Language and Thought* (pp. 17–59). Amsterdam and Philadelphia: John Benjamins.

Suzuki, Ryoko (1999). Grammaticalization in Japanese: A study of Pragmatic Particle-ization. Ph.D. dissertation. University of California, Santa Barbara.

Teramura, Hideo (1984). *Nihongo no Shintakusu to Imi II.* (Japanese Syntax and Semantics II). Tokyo: Kuroshio Shuppan.

Traugott, Elizabeth C. (1988). Pragmatic strengthening and grammaticalization. *Berkeley Linguistics Society, 14*, 406–416.

Traugott, Elizabeth C. (1989). On the rise of epistemic meanings in English: An example of subjectification in semantic change. *Language, 65*, 31–55.

Traugott, Elizabeth C. & König, Ekkehard (1991). The semantics-pragmatics of grammaticalization revisited. In E. Traugott & B. Heine (Eds.), *Approaches to Grammaticalization (I)* (pp. 189–218). Amsterdam and Philadelphia: John Benjamins.

Part IV

# Metonymic inferencing across languages

# Metonymic construals of shopping requests in HAVE- and BE-languages

Günter Radden and Ken-ichi Seto

## 1. Introduction

Requests are intrinsically face-threatening acts. In normal, polite interaction requests are, therefore, typically alleviated. The way a face threat of a request is mitigated in a particular language may, amongst others, be determined by typological properties as well as the cultural background of the particular language. This paper looks at typological differences pertaining to the coding of 'possession' and 'transfer of possession' and the impact this typological property and the culture have on conventionally construing requests.

In his crosslinguistic study of 'possession,' Heine (1997: 83–108) distinguishes eight event schemata used to express the notion of possession. This paper will be concerned with two such schemata: the Possession Schema,[1] which is used by "HAVE-languages" such as English, and the Location Schema, which is used by "BE-languages" such as Japanese.[2] HAVE-languages express possession by means of a transitive construction with 'have' as in *John has two children*, BE-languages express possession by means of 'be' and a locational expression as in Japanese, where this sentence is rendered as 'At/To John are two children' (see (9b) below). English and Japanese will be the two languages mainly considered in this paper as prototypical instances of a HAVE- and a BE-language. A scenario in which possession and its transfer as well as the form of requests are highly relevant is that of the shopping situation, which has been chosen as the object of this study.

In English, requests are typically expressed indirectly. The relationship between an indirect speech act and its intended meaning has been analyzed as involving metonymic reasoning: the hearer has to infer the speech act meaning as a whole from the part explicitly mentioned, such as one of its preconditions (see Gibbs 1986, 1994: 351–357; Thornburg & Panther 1997; Panther & Thornburg 1999). Since HAVE- and BE-languages construe the notion of 'possession' differently, the metonymies linking the indirect wording to the intended speech act meaning will also be different, i.e. different speech communities make use of different metonymic reasoning in coding and understanding a request.

This paper investigates the successive stages of the shopping scenario in which the notion of possession is relevant and compares the ways a speaker of a HAVE-language metonymically asks for goods in a shop as opposed to a speaker of a BE-language. We will first present contrastive data of HAVE- and BE-languages on the metonymic construal of requests in a prototypical shopping scenario and then discuss these findings.

## 2. Metonymic construal of shopping requests in HAVE- and BE-languages

A shopping event is a complex scenario that involves, amongst other things, a precondition, namely the article's availability, and the commercial transaction, or the proper act of buying. The customer initiates both these phases: he or she first finds out whether the article is available and then requests its transaction. The requested transaction itself typically involves several successive subevents: the salesperson hands the article over to the customer, the customer receives the article, the article changes ownership, the customer accepts the sale and pays the price. Commercial events of course involve many more subevents such as choosing the right article, providing information about the article, settling on conditions of payment, etc. which, however, do not directly relate to the issue of possession and will therefore be disregarded in this paper. The stages of the shopping scenario that bear on the issue of metonymic construal of shopping requests are the following:

i. precondition: the article is available;
ii. transaction:
   a. transfer: the salesperson transfers the article to the customer;
   b. reception: the customer receives the article;
   c. result: the article passes into the customer's possession.

Typically, only the precondition and one of the transaction stages are expressed in communicating a shopping request. We will first look at the ways the precondition of a shopping request, i.e. the article's availability, is conceptualized and will find that HAVE- and BE-languages make use of different metonymies in construing the concept of 'availability' (Section 2.1). We will then examine the ways in which one of the three successive subevents of a commercial transaction may be metonymically utilized in HAVE- and BE-languages to stand for the commercial transaction as a whole (Sections 2.2-2.4)

## 2.1 Precondition: the article's availability

The availability of an article represents the most important precondition for asking for it. In terms of obstacle theory (Francik & Clark 1985; Gibbs 1986), it is the first potential obstacle to be overcome. If a customer is not sure whether a store carries the type of article s/he is looking for, s/he will, as a first step, ask about its availability. For example, s/he may be looking for a 40-watt light bulb in the electrical appliance section of a department store. S/he knows that such light bulbs are produced but may not be sure if the store carries them. In an English-speaking country, the customer will ask a question such as (1a), while a Japanese customer will express his or her question as in (1b):

(1) a. *Do you have 40-watt light bulbs?*
b. *40 watto no denkyuu (wa) ari- masu ka.*
40 watt POSS light bulb THEME be- HON Q?
Lit.: 'Are 40-watt light bulbs?'
'Are there 40-watt light bulbs [available at this store]?'

Both types of languages typically construe the notion of availability by means of metonymy. In asking whether the salesperson "has" a certain article for sale, the speaker of a HAVE-language like English literally asks a question about the article as a possession. An object which one possesses exists, is accessible and is under one's control and thus can be manipulated and given to other people – in short, possessions can be made "available" by the possessor. The metonymy POSSESSION FOR AVAILABILITY is, therefore, well motivated in the shopping scenario, in which the store is in control of the goods it offers for sale. BE-languages like Japanese, by contrast, form a question about an article's availability by literally asking about its existence as in (1b).[3] An object's existence establishes an essential precondition for its availability and accounts for the motivation of the metonymy EXISTENCE FOR AVAILABILITY.

In order to ask about an article's availability, an English speaker cannot use the EXISTENCE FOR AVAILABILITY metonymy. A customer's question *Are there 40-watt light bulbs?* can only be interpreted by the salesperson in the non-metonymic sense of existence ('Do 40-watt light bulbs exist?') and not in the sense of availability ('Are there 40-watt light bulbs available at this shop?'). Conversely, a Japanese speaker cannot use the POSSESSION FOR AVAILABILITY metonymy in the shopping scenario: the question *40 watto no denkyuu mottemasu ka* ('Do you have 40-watt light bulbs?') can only be understood in the sense of personal possession ('Do you personally have 40-watt light bulbs?'), not in the sense availability.

A question about an article's availability invites the conversational implicature that it is wanted by the customer. Thus, in both English and Japanese the salesperson may answer the question about the article's availability in (1) by replying 'How many do you want?' In this case, a possession or existence question is understood as a request for its transaction, i.e. as POSSESSION FOR TRANSACTION in HAVE-languages and EXISTENCE FOR TRANSACTION in BE-languages. The sense of availability is, however, still prevalent. Thus, an availability question may not be used to stand for the shopping request if the article's availability is taken for granted in a given scenario. For example, people "know" that McDonald's sells hamburgers and post offices sell stamps so that, unless special circumstances apply, asking for their availability as in (2) is felt to be a "stupid question" rather than a metonymic request.

(2) a. #*Do you have a Big Mac?*
b. #*Big Mac hitotsu ari- masu ka.*
'Big Mac one be- HON Q?'
Lit.: 'Is there a Big Mac?'

Asking such a question only makes sense in a situation in which the customer may reasonably suspect that the item is no longer available. In sentence (2), such a situation might arise at the moment the fast-food joint is closing.

The article's availability is an essential precondition for its purchase. It either needs to be explicitly asked about by the customer or is taken for granted. The customer cannot, as a rule, jump into the buying phase of a commercial event unless s/he feels sure that the article is available. Thus, if 40-watt light bulbs are usually only sold at electrical appliance stores, the customer will not directly ask for one at a gas station without first inquiring whether they are available. In this situation, a request such as *Can I have a 40-watt light bulb?* or *40 watto no denkyuu o kudasai* (lit.: 'Give me a 40-watt light bulb') is pragmatically inappropriate.

## 2.2 Transfer of the article to the customer

The transfer of the article by the salesperson establishes the central subevent of the commercial transaction requested by the customer. In terms of obstacle theory, this phase represents the second potential obstacle to be overcome. The obstacle consists in having another person perform an accomplishment (in the sense of Vendler 1967). Like requests in general, directly asking for an article in a shop is a potential face threat and avoided in many cultures. For example, in buying a paper at a news-stand, an English-speaking customer will hardly choose a direct request such as (3a) and might not even use a more indirect wording such as (3b):[4]

(3) a. #*Give me "The Times"!*
b. ?*Could you give me "The Times"?*

In other HAVE-languages, directly requesting the salesperson to "give" the article may be quite appropriate as in Lithuanian (4a) and Croatian (4b):

(4) a. *(Duokit) "Lietuvos Rytą"!*
(Give-2.PL) Lithuanian.GEN Morning.ACC
'Can I have the "Lithuanian Morning"?'
b. *Dajte mi 3 marke za Austriju!*
Give.IMP me 3 stamps.ACC to Austria!
'Can I have three stamps to Austria?'

In the East-Asian BE-languages Japanese, Chinese and Korean, asking the salesperson to "give" the customer an article is not considered offensive – it is, in fact, the most neutral way of expressing a shopping request as illustrated in the Japanese sentence (5):[5]

(5) *Asahi shinbun (o) kudasai.*
Asahi newspaper OBJ give.HON
Lit.: 'Give the Asashi paper!'
'Can I have the Asashi, please?'

In other BE-languages, requesting the salesperson to "give" the article may sound rather inappropriate, as for instance in Hungarian #*Adjon nekem egy "Magyar Hírlapot"* ('give.IMP me a "Magyar Hírlap.ACC"!'). Using this direct form of request is only justified after the salesperson has ignored several polite attempts at being given the sales item.

As a variant form of request to be given the article the Hausa shopper uses the word for 'bring.' A shopping dialogue in Hausa proceeds as follows:[6]

(6) Buyer: *Àkwai tùmaatìr̃?*
there.are tomatoes?
Seller: *Ii, àkwai.*
yes, there.are
Buyer: *Tôo, kàawoo kilòo biyu.*
good, bring kilo two
Lit.: 'Good, bring two kilos'

The verbs used to refer to the article's transfer in the shopping scenario, 'give' and 'bring,' imply that the object bought will be received by the customer and pass into his or her possession. These expressions thus conceptually conflate the three stages of a transaction. But even these central subevents are metonymic in the sense that they do not include all of the relevant aspects of a commercial transaction: thus, giving and bringing do not, as a rule, imply payment. The metonymy involved is CENTRAL SUBEVENT FOR THE WHOLE EVENT of the shopping scenario, or, more specifically with reference to the transfer stage, TRANSFER FOR TRANSACTION.

## 2.3 Reception of the article by the customer

The transaction of an article is only successful if the customer receives the article bought. This final stage of the transaction represents an achievement in Vendler's (1967) typology of situation types: it describes the non-volitional termination of an event. An achievement verb may often be used metonymically to stand for an action leading to its achievement as in *I am catching fish*, where the punctual achievement verb *to catch* is used in the dynamic sense of 'trying to catch.' In the shopping scenario, the achievement of the buyer's reception of the article may be used to stand for its transaction by the salesperson, i.e. the buyer expresses his wish to be given an article by means of the metonymy RECEPTION FOR TRANSACTION. This metonymy is conventionally used in some HAVE-languages like German (7a) as well as in many BE-languages like Japanese (7b), Polish (7c), Chinese, Hungarian and Finnish and, in special situations, also in Korean.[7]

(7) a. *Ich bekomme zwei Kilo Tomaten.*
I receive two kilo tomato-PL
'Can I have two kilos of tomatoes?'
b. *Tomato o ni kilo itadaki-masu/moraimasu.*
tomato OBJ two kilo receive-HON
Lit.: 'I'll receive two kilos of tomatoes.'

c. *Czy mogę dostać dwa kilo pomidorów?*
Q may receive two kilo tomato.GEN.PL
Lit.: 'May I get two kilos of tomatoes?'

The RECEPTION FOR TRANSACTION metonymy has the effect of mitigating the face threat of the request, which may, amongst other things, be further alleviated by the use of a modal verb and the question form as in (7c). The indirectness conveyed by this metonymy accounts for its widespread use in the shopping situation. In Japanese, *itadakimasu* or *moraimasu* as in (7b) are the conventional forms used by a customer to express his or her shopping request. In other languages, the use of the reception phase for the article's transaction is pragmatically inappropriate. This applies to the HAVE-languages English (cf. #*I'll get/receive two kilos of tomatoes*), Croatian and Lithuanian.

## 2.4 Result of the article's transaction

As a result of a commercial transaction, the article bought passes into the customer's possession. This future state of an article's possession may, at least in some languages, metonymically stand for its requested transaction. A HAVE-language that conventionally uses the metonymy POSSESSION FOR TRANSACTION is English. It applies to situations that are mainly restricted to the ordering of food or drinks in a restaurant such as (8a), i.e. to non-permanent possessions. Of the BE-languages considered, only Hungarian allows the speaker to order food or drinks by metonymically referring to the resulting state as illustrated in sentence (8b), which might be said in the situation in which each member of a group places their order to a waiter. In accordance with its status as a BE-language, Hungarian construes such a request by means of the metonymy EXISTENCE FOR TRANSACTION.

(8) a. *I'll have a beer.*
b. *Nekem egy sör lesz.*
'me a beer become'

Most of the HAVE- and BE-languages studied do not permit either of these metonymies. This may be because, in the chain of stages in the shopping scenario, the resulting state is one step further removed from the central subevent of transfer than the before-mentioned reception stage.

## 2.5 Summary

The metonymic construals of shopping requests used in the eleven HAVE- and BE-languages selected for this study are listed in Table 1.

Table 1. Metonymic construal of shopping requests in HAVE- and BE-languages

| stages | HAVE-languages | BE-languages |
|---|---|---|
| i. availability | POSSESSION FOR AVAILABILITY (English, German, Lithuanian, Croatian) | EXISTENCE FOR AVAILABILITY (Japanese, Chinese, Korean, Finnish, Hungarian, Polish, Hausa) |
| ii. transaction | | |
| a. transfer | TRANSFER FOR TRANSACTION (Lithuanian, Croatian) | (Japanese, Chinese, Korean, Hausa) |
| b. reception | RECEPTION FOR TRANSACTION (German) | (Japanese, Chinese, Korean, Polish, Hungarian, Finnish) |
| c. result | POSSESSION FOR TRANSACTION (English) | EXISTENCE FOR TRANSACTION (Hungarian) |

Even if the number of languages analyzed is too small to claim any typological generalizations, the comparative results allow us to discern certain cross-linguistic tendencies of metonymic construal. We can note the following observations, which will be discussed in Section 3.

First, as should be expected from their typological status, HAVE- and BE-languages use their own metonymic construals to express (i) availability and, to a lesser extent, (ii.c) the result of a requested transaction as 'possession' and 'existence,' respectively.

Secondly, the metonymic construal of the transfer stage (ii.a), i.e. the possibility of directly asking the salesperson to "give" the article wanted, is avoided in most European languages but commonly used in the East-Asian BE-languages Japanese and Chinese and, to a lesser extent, in Korean.

Thirdly, the metonymic construal of the reception stage (ii.b) is rare in most European languages but commonly found in the three East-Asian BE-languages as well as some European languages.

## 3. Discussion

The ensuing discussion will attempt to find cognitive and cultural explanations for the three phenomena observed. It is claimed that at least some of the structural differences discovered are not just arbitrary phenomena of language but reflect conceptual and possibly cultural differences.

We will first look at the notions of 'possession' and 'existence,' which, amongst other things, account for the different construals of availability. We will next consider two forms of politeness, indirectness and deference, which account for the absence and use of direct forms of request. Lastly, we will look at the notions of action vs. process, which might account for the differences found with respect to the metonymization of the reception stage.

### 3.1 Possession vs. existence

We will investigate the conceptual impact of the notions of 'possession' and 'existence' by looking at interlingual and intralingual differences. As shown in the two different types of metonymy for availability, HAVE-languages make use of the Possession Schema while BE-languages use the Location Schema. An insightful conceptual analysis of these two schemata as in English (9a) and Japanese (9b) has been provided by Ikegami (1991: 299):

(9) a. *John has two children.*
b. *John ni wa kodomo ga futari iru.*
John at/to TOPIC child SUBJ two be
Lit.: 'At/To John are two children'
'John has two children.'

HAVE-languages like English pick out the possessor both as the theme and the subject of the sentence and, thus, give prominence to the human. This is in conformity with many other areas in which HAVE-languages, unlike BE-languages, focus on the human.[8] BE-languages such as Japanese may topicalize the possessor as in (9b), but do not subjectize it. BE-languages thus downplay the human element and present the relationship between the two entities as a contiguity relation, where the subject (the children) describes something that exists and the complement (John) describes something in relation to which the subject's existence is predicated. The Location Schema prototypically applies to the spatial location of things, but it also applies to the existence of things in the sense of availability.

In light of these observations we may now reanalyze the questions used in asking about an article's availability. In asking a question such as (1a) *Do you have 40-watt light bulbs?*, the English speaker presents the issue of availability in terms of one's personal possession,[9] while a Japanese speaker asks a question about an article's existence as in (1b) *40 watto no denkyuu (wa) arimasu ka* ('Are there 40-watt light bulbs?'). The metonymy EXISTENCE FOR AVAILABILITY is in accordance with a strong tendency in Japanese to avoid direct reference to persons, particularly in addressing the interlocutor. Especially in conversation, personal subjects tend to be avoided and deleted in 'have'-constructions and other transitive constructions. This tendency may be reinforced by the great number of personal pronouns, each of which has its own stylistic value. The most natural solution to the difficulty of choosing the appropriate personal pronoun among more than a dozen pronouns referring to 'you' is to make no reference to the interlocutor at all, which can be achieved in Japanese by using the existence construction.

The distinction between HAVE- and BE-languages tacitly assumes that the concomitant distinction between 'possession' and 'existence' is a matter of a clear-cut division. This is, however, not the case if the schemata are looked at intralingually. In the same way that HAVE-languages have forms meaning 'be' to express the notion of existence, BE-languages have forms meaning 'have' to express notions of possession. The question is where, in a given language, the notion of possession passes over into that of existence.

We will once again illustrate this issue by focusing on Japanese. The Japanese word that comes closest to the English meaning of 'have' is *motsu*. *Motsu* typically applies to personal possessions as in *watashi-wa ie-wo motteiru* 'I have a house.' A question with *motsu* such as (10) will, therefore, not be understood as a question about an article's availability as in (1b) but as a question about someone's personal belongings:

(10) *kashimiya no seetaa o motte- masu ka.*
cashmere POSS sweater OBJ have- HON Q?
'Do you have a cashmere sweater?'
(= 'Do you personally possess a cashmere sweater?')

This poses the question of what counts as personal possession in Japanese. For example, stamps do, so that I may use *motsu* in asking a friend to help me out with stamps as in *50 yen kitte 10 mai motte-masu ka* ('Do you have ten 50-yen stamps?'). However, due to their temporary nature, hamburgers are not considered personal possessions and, therefore, do not go well with *motsu*: **Big Mac motte-masu ka* ('Do you have a Big Mac?'). Possessions may also be abstract things such as interest or expenses, which may be 'had': *kyoomi-o motsu* 'have interest' and *hiyo-o motsu* 'cover the expenses.' Also money may be possessed but is more likely to be seen as existing: for example, 'Do you have some money?' is rendered as *ikuraka okane aru* (Lit. 'Some money be/exist?'). Things that cannot be possessed are humans: thus, it is impossible to say 'I have two children' instead of (9b), i.e. children are not regarded as personal possessions in Japanese.

The notions of 'possession' and 'existence' are to be seen as forming a conceptual continuum, which different languages may cut up differently. In Japanese, only prototypical physical objects and abstract things can be possessed – these are things that can be controlled. Humans, transitory objects including money, objects that are available but exist independently of us, and objects in space cannot be possessed – they are only seen in a contiguity relation to us.

Other languages may make different distinctions. The BE-language Polish, for example, uses the Existence Schema in questions about an article's availability but the Possession Schema in negated replies, i.e. something that is available "exists" as in (11a), whereas something that is not available is "had" as in (11b):

(11) a. *Czy jest duńskie masło?*
Q is Danish butter
Lit.: 'Is (there) Danish butter?'
'Do you have Danish butter?'
b. *Nie ma.*
not have
'We don't have any.'

The Possession Schema also takes over in shopping situations in which a customer regularly buys a certain product at a certain shop. For example, the customer may ask for his regular brand of beer such as EB by using a 'have'-question: *Pani ma EB?* (Lit.: Mrs. have EB?, 'Do you have EB?'). The relationship between the customer and the shop owner has become a personal one, and the commercial event appears like an exchange of possessions.[10]

The reverse situation holds in HAVE-languages, such as Lithuanian.[11] A customer asking a salesperson whether a specific item is available in the shop will ask a 'have'-question as in (12a), but a third person asking the shopper if the item is available in the shop will use a 'be'-question as in (12b):

(12) a. *Ar turite 40 vatų lempučių?*
Q have-2P.PL 40 watt lamp-GEN.DIMIN
'Do you have 40-watt bulbs?'

b. *Ar yra (ten) 40 vatų lempučių?*
Q be-3P.SG (there) 40 watt lamp-GEN.DIMIN
'Are there 40-watt bulbs?'

In asking question (12b), the third person takes a distanced view of the shopping scenario: the speaker's attention is directed towards the existence of the article in the shop, and the possessive relationship between the shop and the article is out of focus.

## 3.2 Indirectness vs. Deference

A major difference between western and eastern cultures pertains to the ways a person is attended to. Speakers of western languages tend to mitigate face-threatening acts by using strategies of indirectness. A direct request such as (3a) *#Give me "The Times"!* is felt to be rude in English and is therefore avoided in polite interaction. The Japanese equivalent (5) *Asahi shinbun (o) kudasai* and those of Chinese and Korean show, however, that direct requests are the normal forms used in speaking to salespersons. However, it would be misleading to consider Japanese and English forms of request from a structural point of view only.

As convincingly argued by Matsumoto (1988), the notion of 'politeness' and the linguistic strategies of politeness employed by a speaker are culture-specific and fundamentally different in Western and Japanese cultures. The Western notion of 'politeness' is based on the individual's public self-image, and impositions on an individual's face are minimized by means of redressive strategies such as conventional forms of indirectness. The Japanese notion of 'politeness' is based on a person's position in society, and forms of politeness are used to show the speaker's deference to the supposedly higher-ranking addressee. The most important "relation-acknowledging devices" are honorifics, i.e. conventional lexical or morphological forms by means of which the speaker exalts the addressee and humbles himself or herself. Interestingly, salespersons, who are of a much lower social rank than customers, are also spoken to in Japanese, Chinese and Korean by using honorific forms.

The deferential aspect of honorifics can be seen in the etymology of some Japanese honorific words. *Kudasai* in sentence (5) *Asahi shinbun (o) kudasai* has as its bare form the honorific word *kudasaru*, which is etymologically related to *kudaru* 'go down' and suggests passing a favor down to an inferior person. Thus, in using the exalting form *kudasai*, the Japanese speaker used to express respect to a higher-ranking person. The same applies to the word *itadaki-masu* in (7b) *Tomato o ni kilo itadaki-masu* ('I'll receive two kilos of tomatoes'). Etymologically, *itadaku*, the bare form of *itadaki masu*, means 'to put something up above one's head, to be crowned,' which one might do when one receives something important from a person higher up in status. In using this honorific verb the speaker used to demonstrate his lower status.

Most Japanese speakers are, of course, no longer aware of the original honorific meanings of *kudasai* and *itadaku*. Hence, they do not feel any contradiction between their use and present-day society, in which it is salespersons who show deep respect to their customers rather than the other way around. Politeness in a shopping situation shows up in another guise: for example, an elderly Japanese woman may be vague in expressing her shopping request and ask the clerk at the post office to be given "about two 50-yen stamps" as in (13a) or "two or three 50-yen stamps" as in (13b):

(13) a. *Gojuen kitte o ni mai hodo kudasai.*
50 yen stamps OBJ two pieces about give
'Please give me about two 50 yen stamps.'
b. *Gojuen kitte o ni san mai kudasai.*
50 yen stamps OBJ two three pieces give
'Please give me two or three 50 yen stamps.'

Vagueness is listed among Brown and Levinson's (1987) strategies of politeness. As a quantity hedge, an expression of vagueness provides not as much or less information as might be expected (Brown & Levinson 1987: 166). Its effect of politeness derives from appearing less intrusive: the final decision about a quantity is left to the other person. However, in a shopping request like the one under (13), the clerk of course needs to know the exact number so that the ensuing dialogue is about settling the number of stamps wanted. The use of vague and, hence, unintrusive and polite language appears to be so natural that the shopper is not necessarily aware of saying something puzzling.[12]

### 3.3 Action vs. process

Section 2.3 showed that some languages, in particular the three East-Asian languages, allow the speaker to refer to the requested transaction by metonymically highlighting the reception stage of the shopping scenario. We will look again at Japanese, where shopping requests are typically expressed as in (7b) *Tomato o ni kilo itadaki-masu* ('I'll receive 2 kilos of tomatoes'). The metonymy has the effect of focusing away from the agent's action and viewing the event as a process. This may be seen as a manifestation of more general typological properties of Western as opposed to Eastern languages.

The distinction made by Ikegami (1991) between 'DO-languages' and 'BECOME-languages' seems to be relevant here. DO-languages such as English tend to emphasize the agent and his result-oriented actions while BECOME-languages such as Japanese tend to weaken the notion of agentivity and present things as happening. These different views are illustrated in the contrast between the ungrammatical English sentence **I burned it but it didn't burn* and the grammatical Japanese equivalent *moyashita keredo moenakatta*. The English sentence involves a contradiction between an agent's accomplishment of burning a thing, which results in its being burned, and the statement that it did not burn. The Japanese counterpart, however, is acceptable because *moyasu* describes the process of burning but does not necessarily imply a final result. *Moyasu*, like many other Japanese transitive verbs, is less telic in meaning and more process-oriented. The different types of metonymy used in English and Japanese shopping requests are thus in line with general tendencies observed in these two languages. English as a DO-language focuses on the result, while Japanese as a BECOME-language focuses on the process.

## 4. Conclusions

This study investigated the ways requests in an everyday situation, the shopping scenario, are coded in different languages. Such requests are typically construed metonymically, where the different stages of a commercial scenario may serve as metonymic vehicles. These are, in particular, the availability of the article, the transfer of the article by the salesperson, the reception of the article by the customer, and the resulting possession of the article by the customer. The choice of metonymies was shown to depend, amongst other things, on typological properties of the given language. The two types of languages distinguished for this purpose are HAVE- and BE-languages, the former being typically represented by English, the latter by Japanese. HAVE-languages metonymically express the notions of availability and, to a lesser extent, that of requested transaction, as possession, BE-languages construe these notions as existence. It has been argued that the notions of possession and existence form a conceptual continuum, which is cut up differently by different languages and thus also accounts for different metonymic usages.

HAVE- and BE-languages also tend to display different metonymic usages with respect to the transfer and reception stage of the commercial transaction.

The use of a direct request is felt to be impolite in Western cultures but represents, in conjunction with honorifics as expressions of deference, the normal form of shopping requests in East-Asian languages. The different cultural systems of politeness – indirectness vs. deference – account for the absence or presence of the TRANSFER FOR TRANSACTION metonymy. The metonymic use of the reception stage for a requested transaction in East-Asian languages may be relatable to culture-specific ways of viewing events: DO-languages such as English focus on actions and their results, BECOME-languages such as Japanese focus on processes as happening.

## Notes

1. In Heine's typology, possessive *have* is subsumed under the Action Schema *X takes Y*, since possessive verbs of 'having' derive from earlier meanings of 'seize,' 'hold' and the like.

2. The terms 'HAVE-language' and 'BE-language' are used by Ikegami (1991) in his analysis of representational differences between English and Japanese.

3. A selection of BE-languages that render sentence (1a) in a fashion similar to Japanese in (1b) is listed below. We would like to express our thanks to Changhong Sui, Koo Izen, Jae Jung Song, Jeong-Hwa Lee, Aila Radden, Karol Janicki, Elżbieta Tabakowska, Vitalija Liutvinskiene, Joe McIntyre, Rita Brdar-Szabó and Mario Brdar for providing data on their native languages.

| | | | | | | |
|---|---|---|---|---|---|---|
| Chinese: | *You* | *40 wa* | *de* | *dengpao* | *ma?* | |
| | be.HON | 40 watt | of | light bulb | Q | |
| Korean: | *40-wattu* | *cenkwu* | *iss-upnikka?* | | | |
| | 40-watt | light bulb | be-HON? | | | |
| Finnish: | *Onko* | *teillä* | *40 watin* | *lamppuja?* | | |
| | be.3SG.Q | PRON.2PL.ADESS | 40 watt-GEN.SG | lamp.PART.PL | | |
| Hungarian: | *Van/Lenne* | *40-wattos* | *villanykörtéjük?* | | | |
| | is/would be | 40-watt.ADJ.SUFFIX | light bulb.POSS | | | |
| Polish: | *Czy* | *są* | *czterdziesto* | *watowe* | *żarówki?* | |
| | Q | are | 40 | watt | light bulb.GEN.PL | |
| Hausa: | *Àkwai* | *ƙwan* | *fitilàa* | *mài* | *Watt* | *àr̃bà'in?* |
| | there.is | egg.of | lamp | owner.of | watt | 40 |

4. A customer will only express a request that the item be transferred to him or her in special situations; for example, when the customer has decided on one item from a choice of similar things displayed before him or her as in *Could you please give me the green one* or when a specific kind of transfer is involved as in *Could you deliver it to my home.*

5. Cf. the comparable forms in Chinese and Korean:

Chinese: *Qing gei wo yi fen renmin ribao!*
please give me one copy people daily
Lit.: 'Please give me a copy of People's Daily'
'Can I have the People's Daily?'

Korean: *Tonga-ilpo(-lul) cwu-si-psiyo*
Tonga-daily(-ACC) give-HON.VERBAL SUFFIX-HON. IMP.
Lit.: 'Please give [me] the Tonga-daily.'
'Can I have the Tonga Daily?'

6. The Hausa examples have kindly been provided by Joe McIntyre.

7. Cf. Without a contrastive context the following Korean sentence is barely acceptable:

?*thomatho i khilo-lul pat-keyss-upnita.*
tomato two kilo-ACC receive-FUT-HON.IND.
Lit.: 'I will receive two kilos of tomatoes.'

Contrastive situations that might render the sentence acceptable are, for example, those of a customer who wants twó kilos of tomatoes, not thrée, or two kilos of tomátoes, not potátoes, or of a customer who, after resisting buying tomatoes, finally accepts. The buyer will then introduce the sentence with the discourse response marker *kulem* 'so, then,' which is set off by a pause, indicated here by a comma:

[...] *kulem, thomatho i khilo-lul pat-keyss-upnita.*
[...] then tomato two kilo-ACC receive-FUT-HON.IND.
Lit.: 'So (*or* Then), I will receive two kilos of tomatoes.'

8. Some of Ikegami's pairs of examples in which English emphasizes the human where Japanese presents the situation as thing-like or event-like include the following: English *I have a temperature* corresponds to Japanese 'temperature is,' English *John ran out of money* is rendered in Japanese as '(As for John), money became null,' English *I don't understand you* is expressed in Japanese as 'I *don't* understand what you say,' etc.

9. Wordings such as (1a) in fact involve a further metonymy: it is not the salesperson who possesses the items but the store, i.e. the person is used to stand for the institution. The metonymy PERSON FOR INSTITUTION is motivated by a general principle of cognitive salience (see Radden & Kövecses 1999): humans are in general more salient than institutions, and entities we interact with, i.e. salespersons, are more salient than entities we do not interact with, i.e. the shop. This does not, however, apply to the Japanese view of the world: Japanese does not extend humans to institutions. Ikegami (1991:301) nicely observed that the notice *We are closed today* on the door of a shop would strike a Japanese speaker as odd. Hence, the goods that are for sale at a store are neither seen as possessions of the store nor metonymically as possessions of the salesperson but simply as existing in contiguity to the store.

10. We are indebted to Elżbieta Tabakowska for the Polish data. The situation is, in fact, more complex. The Existence Schema is associated with the standardized shopping scenario and expectations derived from it, while the Possession Schema tends to be associated with negative expectations. Thus, a Polish customer may no longer expect to get rolls at a bakery

near closing time and ask 'Do you still have bread?' rather than 'Is there still bread?,' or he may not expect to find a specific book in a bookstore and, therefore, form the Polish question as 'Do you have books by Shakespeare?' and not 'Are there books by Shakespeare?' If the Possession Schema is used in situations that normally require the Location Schema as in 'Do you have beer?' asked at a supermarket, the resulting meaning of counter-expectation is that of the beer being sold illegally.

11. We owe this interesting observation to Vitalija Liutvinskiene.

12. We thank Yoshihiko Ikegami for providing this delightful example of Japanese politeness.

## References


Brown, Penelope & Levinson, Stephen (1987). *Politeness: Some Universals in Language Usage.* Cambridge: Cambridge University Press.

Francik, Ellen P. & Clark, Herbert H. (1985). How to make requests that overcome obstacles to compliance. *Journal of Memory and Language, 24*, 560–468.

Gibbs, Raymond W., Jr. (1986). What makes some indirect speech acts conventional? *Journal of Memory and Language, 25*, 181–196.

Gibbs, Raymond W., Jr. (1994). *The Poetics of Mind: Figurative Thought, Language and Understanding.* Cambridge: Cambridge University Press.

Heine, Bernd (1997). *Cognitive Foundations of Grammar.* New York, Oxford: Oxford University Press.

Ikegami, Yoshihiko (1991). 'DO-language' and 'BECOME-language': Two contrasting types of linguistic representation. In Y. Ikegami (Ed.), *The Empire of Signs: Semiotic Essays on Japanese Culture* (pp. 285–326). Amsterdam and Philadelphia: Benjamins.

Matsumoto, Yoshiko (1988). Reexamination of the universality of face: Politeness phenomena in Japanese. *Journal of Pragmatics, 12*, 403–426.

Panther, Klaus-Uwe & Thornburg, Linda (1999). The POTENTIALITY FOR ACTUALITY metonymy in English and Hungarian. In K.-U. Panther & G. Radden (Eds.), *Metonymy in Language and Thought* (pp. 333–357). Amsterdam and Philadelphia: Benjamins.

Radden, Günter & Kövecses, Zoltán (1999). Towards a theory of metonymy. In K.-U. Panther & G. Radden (Eds.), *Metonymy in Language and Thought* (pp. 17–59). Amsterdam and Philadelphia: Benjamins.

Thornburg, Linda & Panther, Klaus-Uwe (1997). Speech act metonymies. In W. A. Liebert et al. (Eds.), *Discourse and Perspectives in Cognitive Linguistics* (pp. 205–219). Amsterdam and Philadelphia: Benjamins.

Vendler, Zeno (1967). *Linguistics in Philosophy.* Ithaca, NY: Cornell University Press.

# Metonymic coding of linguistic action in English, Croatian and Hungarian

Mario Brdar and Rita Brdar-Szabó

## 1. Introduction

There are numerous means of coding linguistic action in different languages. In addition to a number of structures that English has at its disposal primarily or exclusively for this purpose (e.g. reporting verbs taking complement clauses in indirect speech), English also employs certain constructions with predicative adjectives to report linguistic actions, such as those illustrated in (1):

(1) a. I must be *open* with her, whatever the cost.
b. Dear colleagues, I'll be *brief*.
c. Arthur was *brief* about his other teachers in his recollections.
d. The President was *clear* on the matter.
e. The buyers were *emphatic* in declaring that they were right.
f. Livingstone, even when being *humorous* about a very distressing period, could not disguise the discomfort.

In this paper we shall be concerned with this type of construction in English and its counterparts in Croatian and Hungarian. We shall first briefly show the metonymic nature of these English predicative structures in Section 2, and then give an overview of contrasts that obtain between English, on the one hand, and Croatian and Hungarian, on the other, in Section 3. A closer look at the type of English constructions illustrated in (1), as well as some related ascriptive constructions and other types of metonymy, will reveal in Section 4 a cluster of cognitive and pragmatic phenomena working in unison to make possible this particular way of reporting linguistic action. Finally, in a second round of contrasting in Section 5 we shall offer a tentative account of why Croatian and Hungarian fail to make any extensive use of predication metonymy in coding linguistic action, as well as place our findings in a more general perspective.

## 2. Reporting linguistic action and metonymy

The constructions listed in (1) apparently deviate from what we expect to find under the rubric of reporting linguistic action. According to Goossens (1990: 326), reporting linguistic action, i.e. talking about linguistic interaction, involves secondary speakers and secondary hearers. The former produce utterances in which they report to the latter what was said by primary speakers to primary hearers. Our constructions in (1) above do not at first blush really look like reports of linguistic action on this definition. They are unusual in that there is no reporting verb in the traditional sense. There is often no mention of the primary hearer (but cf. in (1a) the prepositional phrase *with her*). Even less conforming to the definition is the fact that frequently there is actually barely any trace of reported words apart from the indication of the subject matter. Rather, these are reports of the fact that some linguistic action took or will take place as well as comments on the style and contents of this linguistic action. These constructions may, therefore, be considered to be, in a sense, a way of effecting secondary reports or meta-reports. These are the reasons why we shall henceforth be using the term *coding* of linguistic action, as indicated in the title, and not the term *reporting*.

A number of excellent studies have concerned themselves with general problems of speech acts and the garden variety of reports of linguistic action, e.g. Leech (1980), Verschueren (1980, 1984, 1985), Rudzka (1982), and Goossens (1985, 1987). A series of more specialized discussions have analyzed in great detail the role of metaphors in extending the set of reporting predicates, e.g. Dirven et al. (1982) and Rudzka-Ostyn (1988). The issue of metonymy in reporting linguistic action has only recently received more attention, as shown by studies by Goossens (1990, 1995) and Rudzka-Ostyn (1995).

Before we try to substantiate our claim that these constructions, exhibiting a number of subtypes, are crucially based on a MANNER FOR (LINGUISTIC) ACTION metonymy, it appears necessary to review some basic traditional insights into metonymy as well as compare them with some more recent suggestions. Some further, more specific points of interest concerning metonymic models will be introduced in Sections 4 and 5.

A fairly frequent way of defining metonymy has been to contrast it with metaphor (and occasionally with synecdoche) and focus on two central points of difference. One of the crucial points of contrast that most authors point out is that metonymy is based on contiguity, whereas metaphor is based on similarity (cf. Ullmann 1962: 212; Taylor 1989: 122). Contiguity is taken in its broader sense to cover all associative relations except similarity. The other important point of contrast, due to observations by cognitive linguists, concerns the number of conceptual domains involved. Metonymic mapping occurs within a single domain, while metaphoric mapping takes place across two discrete domains. However, in the case of metonymy, it is important to bear in mind that the single conceptual domain involved is structured by an *Idealized Cognitive Model* (ICM) in the sense of Lakoff (1987: 288) and may exhibit some internal complexity. It is thus possible for metonymic mapping to occur within a single domain matrix that contains a number of subdomains (cf. Croft 1993: 348). In other words, metonymic mapping across different domains within a single domain matrix, involving the conceptual effect of domain highlighting, is also possible.

We are now in a position to determine the type of mapping taking place in the above set of examples. Adopting the typology of pragmatic metonymies proposed in Panther and Thornburg (1999: 335f.), we can assume that the constructions in (1) above, along with most of the other examples in our corpus are cases of propositional metonymy.[1] We may occasionally come across examples like (1b), which can also be interpreted as a type of illocutionary metonymy, since the statement *I'll be brief* in fact functions as a commissive speech act. However, the illocutionary metonymy appears to be superimposed here on a more basic and conceptually prior propositional metonymy.

Propositional metonymies come in two subtypes (cf. Panther & Thornburg 1999). In referential metonymy one referring expression, chiefly a noun phrase, is the vehicle for an implied target that is also a referring expression normally realized as a noun phrase.

(2) More than customary aggravation was generated by the discovery that *the conference* would be sleeping in one building, eating in another, and meeting for lectures and discussions on the main campus, thus ensuring for all concerned a great deal of tiresome walking to and fro on paths and pavements made dangerous and unpleasant by the snow.

In (2) the noun phrase *conference* is used to refer to only one essential ingredient of a conference, viz. its participants.

In predicational metonymy one propositional content stands for another propositional content. Assuming that the locus of metonymic mappings in the examples listed in (1) above is indeed the predicatively used adjective, we may classify them as predicational metonymies. It need not, however, be self-evident that these are predicational metonymies, particularly in view of the widely held traditional view that metonymy resides in the realm of nominals (which is the reason why referential metonymies can perhaps also be called nominal metonymies).

We shall reexamine our examples in light of the possibility that some can perhaps be interpreted as referential or nominal metonymies, but let us now review some evidence pointing in the direction of the conclusion that we are dealing with predicational metonymies in the set of examples in (1) above.

The constructions we focus on here are not a spectacular type of metonymy, and, just like many other types, are quite easy to overlook. However, a closer look will reveal a number of relevant features. All the adjectives in the above examples seem to specify one aspect of the linguistic action involved, viz. the way in which it was performed, carrying more or less strong expectations as to the effectiveness and ultimate result of the linguistic action, or the lack thereof. That they denote the manner in which an implicit linguistic action is carried out becomes obvious from paraphrases such as:

(3) a. I must *speak openly* with her, whatever the cost.
b. The President *spoke clearly* on the matter.
c. Livingstone, even when *speaking humorously* about a very distressing period, could not disguise the discomfort.

Of course, it must be admitted that not all examples readily allow this type of paraphrase. In some cases it is stylistically clumsy, while in other cases the context also supports a paraphrase in which a mental predicate (verb or a complex verbo-nominal expression, e.g. *think, have an opinion,* etc.) is used.

Notice that (1e), repeated here as (4a), actually has an explicit verb denoting linguistic action in the prepositional complement following the predicative adjective:

(4) a. The buyers were *emphatic* in declaring that they were right.

A prepositional complement introduced by *about*, without a clause, would make it identical to (1c) and (1f):

(4) b. The buyers were *emphatic about* their rights.

The phenomenon of so-called "conceptual anaphors" (Gernsbacher 1991) has been frequently observed with referential metonymies: anaphoric pronouns are not coreferential with expressions functioning as vehicles but as targets:

(5) a. Cruse (1986), *which* is one of the best course books on lexical semantics, ...

b. I need to call the garage (where my car is being serviced). *They* said they'd have it ready by five o'clock.

In the case of predicational metonymy, it is possible for the target expression to appear explicitly somewhere in the broader cotext. Cf. the following passage:

(6) Camaioni *says* little about motives but contrasts what she sees as the social function of proto-communication with the tool use hypothesis. Bloom (1993) similarly *argues* for an expressive rather than instrumental function for the development of language, but is interestingly more *explicit* and *coherent* about the driving motive.

Just like paraphrases, this also seems to indicate that the type of constructions we are interested in here indeed involve predicational metonymies.

The set of predicative adjectives that appear in this construction includes the following:

(7) accurate, articulate, baroque, bitter, blunt, boring, brief, bullish, clear, coherent, cynical, definite, direct, dramatic, earnest, emphatic, explicit, harsh, entertaining, factual, firm, forthright, frank, lukewarm, lyrical, mum, poetic, open, pompous, precise, sarcastic, serious, short, silent, specific, vague …

Most of these take prepositional complements introduced by *about*, occasionally by *on*, *with* or *in*. The most frequent preposition *about*, as well as *on*, may be taken as a further piece of evidence that we are dealing here with predicational metonymies targeting verbs of linguistic action, since they also introduce prepositional complements of verbs of linguistic action such as *speak* or *talk*.

Although the typology of metonymy-producing relationships provided by Radden and Kövecses (1999) does not explicitly provide for the metonymy in question, it may provisionally be characterized as a configuration relating whole ICMs and conceptual entities that function as their parts. More precisely, a part of an event stands for the whole event. In Seto's system, they would be closest to temporal metonymies of the whole event-subevent type, where the notion of subevent is extended in the case of reporting verbs in such a way that "the sounds, manners, gestures, etc. that accompany events can all be good candidates for the metonymy of this type" (Seto 1999: 107).

## 3. A preliminary crosslinguistic comparison

One might expect that a similar array of metonymically motivated constructions used to report linguistic action will be found to be fairly frequent in crosslinguistic terms. Although metonymy is a universally attested cognitive process, it does not follow, however, that various languages must make use of it in the same way, and in the same contexts. Indeed, Lakoff (1987:78), in discussing metonymy, warns: "[...] general principles are not the same in all languages, one cannot simply say that anything can stand for anything else in the right context. One needs to distinguish which principles work for which languages." Such crosslinguistic comparisons could help tease out some new and interesting facts leading to a better understanding of the phenomenon. A similar position is implicitly entertained by Langacker (1991:538), too, when he outlines the range of phenomena that have been handled within the cognitive framework. Regrettably, comparisons of languages with a view to specifically investigating metonymy have been few. The insights that these few examples, however, offer us, make it clear that it is a worthwhile enterprise, to say the least, as borne out, for example, by Kalisz (1983) and more recently by Panther and Thornburg (1999) and Radden and Seto (this volume).

The phenomenon of metonymy used to code linguistic action, the central concern of this paper, promises to be a real contrastive hunting ground because even a superficial juxtaposition of English data with those from languages such as Croatian and Hungarian will suffice to reveal that the latter languages exhibit only some of the subtypes found in English, with considerable differences concerning the distribution of individual subtypes. Compare the acceptability of the Croatian and Hungarian sentences in the following sets that are counterparts of the English sentences (1a–f) above:

*Croatian*

(8) a.′ Moram *biti otvoren* s njom, po svaku cijenu.
must-1SG be open with her at any price
'I must be open with her, whatever the cost'

a.″ Moram *otvoreno porazgovarati* s njom, po svaku cijenu
must-1SG openly speak with her at any price.
'I must speak openly with her, whatever the cost'

b.′ Dragi kolege, bit ću *kratak*.
dear colleagues be will-1SG brief
'Dear colleagues, I'll be brief'

c.′ *Arthur je u svojim prisjećanjima bio *sažet/kratak* o
Arthur AUX in his recollections been brief/short about
ostalim učiteljima.
other teachers
'Arthur was brief about his other teachers in his recollections'

c.″ Arthur je u svojim prisjećanjima *sažeto govorio* o…
Arthur AUX in his recollections briefly spoken about…
'Arthur spoke briefly in his recollections …'

d.′ Predsjednik je bio *jasan* po tom pitanju.
President AUX been clear about that matter
'The President was clear on the matter'

d.″ Predsjednik je *jasno govorio* o tom pitanju.
President AUX clearly spoken about that matter
'The President spoke clearly about that matter'

d.‴ Predsjednik je bio *jasan* kada je govorio o tom
President AUX been clear when AUX spoken about that
pitanju.
matter
'The President was clear when he spoke on the matter'

e.′ Kupci *su odlučno izjavili* da imaju pravo.
Customers AUX emphatically declared that have-3PL right
'The buyers declared emphatically that they were right'

e.″ ?Kupci su bili *odlučni izjavljujući* da imaju pravo.
Customers AUX been emphatic declaring…
'The buyers were emphatic in declaring that they were right'

f.′ *Livingstone, čak i kad je bio *duhovit* o vrlo teškom
Livingstone, even when AUX been witty about very difficult
periodu…
period
'Livingstone, even when he was humorous about a very distressing period, …'

f.″ Livingstone, čak i kad je *duhovito* govorio o vrlo
Livingstone, even when AUX wittily spoke about very
teškom periodu…
difficult period
'Livingstone, even when he spoke humorously about a very distressing period, …'

f.‴ Livingstone, čak i kada se *šalio* o vrlo teškom
Livingstone, even when REFL joked about very difficult
periodu...
period
'Livingstone, even when he joked about a very distressing period,...'

*Hungarian*

(9) a.′ *Nyíltan* kell vele *beszélnem*, kerüljön, amibe kerül.
open must with-her speak...
'I must speak openly with her, whatever the cost'

a.″ **Nyíltnak* kell vele lennem.
open must with-her be
'I must be open with her, whatever the cost'

b.′ Kedves kollégák, *rövid* leszek.
Dear colleagues, brief be-FUT-1SG
'Dear colleagues, I'll be brief'

b.″ ..., ígérem, *rövid* leszek.
promise brief be-FUT-1SG
'I promise to be brief'

c.′ Arthur visszaemlékezéseiben *röviden említette* a többi tanárt.
Arthur recollections-POSS-in briefly mentioned DEF other teacher
'Arthur mentioned briefly in his recollections other teachers'

c.″ *?Arthur *rövid* volt a többi tanárral kapcsolatban.
Arthur brief was DEF other teacher concerning
'Concerning other teachers, Arthur was brief'

c.‴ *?Arthur *rövid* volt.
Arthur brief was
'Arthur was brief'

d.′ Az elnök *világosan nyilatkozott* / *szólt* ezzel az üggyel kapcsolatban.
DEF president clearly spoke spoke this-with DEF matter concerning
'The President spoke clearly on that matter'

d.″ *Az elnök *világos* volt.
DEF President clear was
'The President was clear'

d.‴ *Az elnök *világos* volt ezzel az üggyel kapcsolatban.
DEF President clear was this-with DEF matter concerning
'Concerning that matter, the President was clear'

e.′ A vevők *hangsúlyozták*, hogy igazuk volt/van.
Customers emphasized that ...
'The customers emphasized that they were right'

e.″ *A vevők *hangsúlyosak* voltak annak kijelentésében
DEF customers emphatic were in declaring....
hogy igazuk volt/van.
that right were/are
'The buyers were emphatic in declaring that they were right'

f.′ Livingstone még akkor sem tudta elrejteni
Livingstone even then not could hide
kellemetlenségérzetét, mikor *viccelődött* egy mozgalmas
discomfort when joked one difficult
időszakkal kapcsolatban.
period concerning
'Livingstone, even when he joked about a very distressing period, could not hide ...'

f.″ *... *vicces* volt egy mozgalmas időszakkal kapcsolatban
witty was one difficult period concerning
'... he was humorous about a very distressing period, ...'

f.‴ *... *humoros* volt egy mozgalmas időszakkal kapcsolatban
witty was one difficult period concerning
'... he was humorous about a very distressing period, ...'

A number of interesting contrastive facts emerge from these data. First of all, we see that Croatian and Hungarian appear reluctant to make use of this type of predication metonymy. This ties in nicely with the findings by Panther and Thornburg, who report that another predication metonymy that seems to be subject to restrictions of typological nature, POTENTIALITY FOR ACTUALITY, is systematically blocked or only weakly exploited in Hungarian. We see that in our Croatian and Hungarian examples, constructions with predicative adjectives can be used very rarely, and they seem to be licensed only if the adjective takes no further complement. Finally, Croatian and Hungarian favor the explicit mention of the linguistic action in the verbal part of the predicate, the counterparts of English predicative adjectives are rendered in both languages as adverbials of manner, phrasal or clausal. We also note the explicit mention of the verb of linguistic action in temporal adverbial clauses in Croatian (cf. (8d‴ and f″). The fact that Croatian and Hungarian tend to explicitly mention the linguistic actions and the tendency to render English adjectives as adverbs of manner, lends further indirect support to the view that we are dealing here with a predicational metonymy of the MANNER FOR (LINGUISTIC) ACTION TYPE.

It is significant that referential metonymy, however, does not seem to be constrained in either Croatian or Hungarian in such a systematic way. Some examples, or concrete metonymies in Blank's terms (1999: 183), may be culture-specific and therefore lack metonymic counterparts in other languages, but, generally, at the level of types of contiguity, i.e. in terms of image schemas, there is a fairly close correspondence between English on the one hand, and Croatian and Hungarian on the other. Compare some examples:

(10) a. *Beijing's* difficulties in Tibet boil down to the Chinese leadership's relations with one man ...

*Croatian*

b. teškoće *Pekinga* u Tibetu svode se na odnose
difficulties Beijing-GEN in Tibet boil-down REFL on relations
kineskog vodstva s jednom osobom ...
Chinese-GEN leadership-GEN with one person
'Beijing's difficulties in Tibet boil down to the Chinese leadership's relations with one man ...'

*Hungarian*

c. ... *Peking* Tibettel kapcsolatos nehézségei a kínai
Beijing Tibet-with concerning difficulties DEF Chinese
vezetésnek egy személlyel való viszonyára
leadership-POSS one person-with concerning relations-to
vezethetők vissza ...
relatable back
'... Beijing's difficulties in Tibet boil down to the Chinese leadership's relations with one man ...'

(11) a. Not even the great *brains* of Cambridge could solve his problem.

*Croatian*

b. Niti veliki *mozgovi* iz Cambridgea nisu mogli
Not-even great brains from Cambridge NEG-AUX could
riješiti njegov problem.
solve his problem

*Hungarian*

c. Még a nagy cambridgei *koponyák* sem tudták az ő
even DEF great Cambridge skulls NEG could DEF his
problémáját megoldani.
problem-POSS-ACC solve

(12) a. Let's have *another glass.*

*Croatian*

b. Popijmo još *jednu čašu.*
drink-IMP yet one glass

*Hungarian*

c. Igyunk még *egy pohárral.*
Drink-IMP yet one glass

(13) a. Dad used *Scotch tape* to piece together the torn-up photograph.

*Croatian*

b. Tata je koristio *selotejp* da sastavi poderanu sliku.
Daddy AUX used tape-ACC that fix torn-up photo

*Hungarian*

c. Papa *cellux-szal* ragasztotta meg az eltépett képet.
Daddy tape-with fixed PREF DEF torn-up photo

These interesting crosslinguistic regularities seem to indicate that the distinction between referential, predicational and illocutionary metonymies may be an important parameter in establishing a typology of metonymies. The differences in the distribution of referential and predicational metonymies in the three languages investigated here could lead us as far as to suppose that there may perhaps obtain a sort of implicational relationship between the referential and the predication type of metonymy, predicting that a language that makes extensive use of the latter will also make heavy use of the former, while there will be languages that will restrict themselves to referential metonymic models only. This suggestion is a far cry from postulating an implicational universal, it is rather to be understood as an invitation to a systematic study of the relationship between various types of metonymies in as many languages as possible. The evidence available at present seems to indicate (i) that the pattern we present here is found repeatedly, across languages and across domains, and (ii) that the kind of constraints on the two types of metonymies are very different in nature (cf. Brdar-Szabó & Brdar 2001; Brdar-Szabó & Brdar 2002; Brdar-Szabó 2002; and Brdar, Brdar-Szabó, Gradečak-Erdeljić, & Buljan, in press, where metonymies involving three cognitive domains are studied in eight languages).

However, regardless of whether the observed crosslinguistic differences can be shown to be more universal or not, the fact remains that Croatian and Hungarian behave very differently from English, and that some explanation has to be offered. In the remainder of our paper, we shall try, making use of both synchronic and diachronic data, to show that these differences are the result of an intricate interplay of cognitive and pragmatic, lexical and morphosyntactic factors.

## 4. Referential vs. predicational metonymy, polysemy of adjectives and the role of grammatical constructions in English

The few examples in Croatian and Hungarian in (1) where we apparently have acceptable metonymic counterparts, can in fact be interpreted as referential and not as predicational metonymies, i.e. they lend themselves to an analysis in which the subject, which in our examples always denotes a person, i.e. the speaker, stands for his/her utterance:

(14) I'll be brief. ('My speech/words, etc. will be brief')

This SPEAKER FOR UTTERANCE metonymy can be seen as a special case of the more ubiquitous AGENT FOR ACTION metonymy. The same applies to the English example with *brief*. Corresponding Croatian and Hungarian adjectives take no complements, and the same is true of *brief* when it allows the interpretation as a referential metonymy; otherwise, as a predicational metonymy it takes a complement introduced by *about*. This means that an apparent counterexample to our crosslinguistic generalization disappears: it is precisely those English adjectives that can be interpreted as nominal/referential metonymies that have closest correspondents in Croatian and Hungarian, presumably because they are in fact nominal/referential metonymies in the latter languages as well.

A diachronic survey of the English adjectives listed in (7) above may be very rewarding. It may show that many of these cases of today's predicational metonymies apparently started as yesterday's referential metonymies. See Figure 1 with *blunt* and *coherent*, for which some data could be found in the second edition of the Oxford English Dictionary on CD-ROM (OED). The

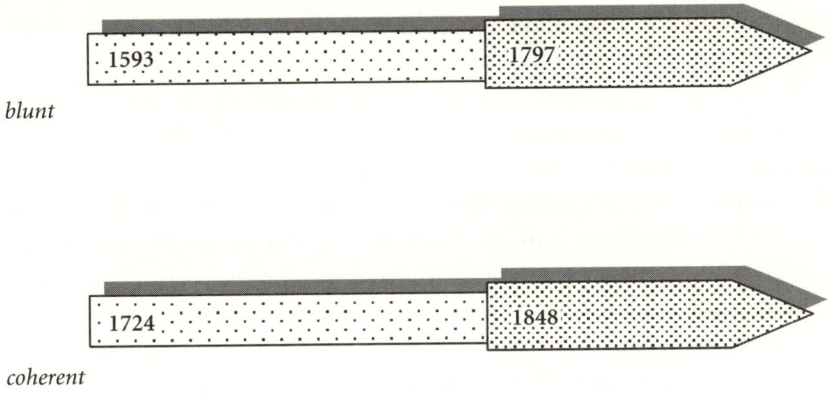


**Figure 1.** Shifts from referential to predicational metonymy with *blunt* and *coherent*

numbers refer to the year in which a given use is first recorded in the OED; the lighter shaded area denotes the time period in which adjectives collocated with subject NPs that could be interpreted as referential metonymies, while the darker shaded area denotes the period in which the adjective is used metonymically to code linguistic action. The two periods may overlap a great deal, so that the referential metonymy continues in parallel with the predicational one, or may perhaps sometimes be discrete, but as our main point is to demonstrate that the referential metonymy temporally precedes the predicational one, the issue of their overlap is of secondary importance here.

(15) a. 1593 Shakes. 3 Henry VI, v. i. 86 Trowest thou that Clarence is so harsh, blunt, unnatural.
b. 1797 Mrs. Radcliffe Italian xiii. (1824) 606 Be pretty blunt with them if they want to come in here.
c. Trollope Belton Est. iii. 27 He was blunt in his bearing, saying things which her father would have called indelicate and heartless.

(16) a. 1724 Watts Logic iii. iv. 1 A coherent thinker, and a strict reasoner, is not to be made at once by a set of rules.
b. 1848 Dickens Dombey 51 Be plain and coherent, if you please.

The data are sparse and not easy to come by, but it is significant that, while we can, as yet, admittedly adduce only a few clear-cut cases, we have not been able to find adjectives whose development would contradict our stipulations.

A similar proposal is put forward by Waltereit (1998:63ff., 119ff.; 1999: 235f.), who, discussing verbal valency on French material, distinguishes between so-called insertional and role-level contiguities. He claims that the latter type, involving polysemy and lexicalization, developed diachronically from the former type, which largely corresponds to referential metonymies.

The intriguing question is what factors brought about this switch from nominal to predicational metonymy in English, but are absent in Croatian and Hungarian, as they do not seem to have progressed in these languages from the referential/nominal metonymy. The answer is bound to be a complex one, and we can only probe a couple of directions in which we believe the search should proceed. In this section we shall concentrate on the issue of polysemy of the English adjectives under investigation and the role of the specific constructions in which they appear.

We believe that the difference in the type of metonymy, i.e. referential vs. predicational, may correlate with the differences in the mode of their interpretation, the difference in the degree of their conventionalization, and consequently with the differences in the degree of their lexicalization. We are reluctant to extend these to referential and predicational metonymies in general, but they seem to manifest themselves clearly in the case of our specific metonymies.

If we adopt a position similar to Dirven's (1993), who recognizes gradations and distinguishes several types of referential metonymies as points on a continuum, with non-figurativeness at one end and complex figurativeness on the other, the referential metonymies of the SPEAKER FOR UTTERANCE type, as a special case of the more ubiquitous AGENT FOR ACTION metonymies, appear to be low-level metonymies involving hardly any semantic change in the lexical items that express them. They can be productively formed and interpreted on an ad hoc inferential basis. They are not lexicalized and do not result in polysemy of the nouns functioning as heads of subject NPs. As sentences containing such referential metonymies can be ambiguous between literal and metonymic readings, it is no wonder that we find all kinds of cotextual and contextual props steering the interpretation onto the metonymic road (cf. Ziegeler, this volume, on the role of the environment).

We shall disregard for a moment the role of prepositional complements and concentrate only on devices such as the choice of tense, the matrix verb under which the clause containing the adjective is embedded, vocatives, and the specific position within discourse at which these are found. The presence of some of these devices makes the literal interpretation less likely or even impossible, and, the speaker, following the maxim of relevance and searching for sense, switches to a metonymic interpretation, which other devices (i.e. the choice of tense, the particular matrix verb under which the clause containing the adjective is embedded, etc.) readily invite. Let us exemplify this with a pair of Croatian and Hungarian sentences in (8b′ and 9b′), respectively. In (8b′), the adjective *kratak* 'short/brief', as well as its Hungarian counterpart *rövid*, are semantically compatible with subjects denoting body parts, and in Croatian, to a degree, compatible with subjects denoting humans, but the use of the future tense (or the past tense) rules out the literal interpretation because being short is not a quality that can be brought under the subject's control and thus does not obtain for a period of time at will.

On the other hand, in predicational metonymies of the MANNER FOR LINGUISTIC ACTION type we frequently find lexicalization and polysemy of adjectival predicates. A selection of sense descriptions for a few adjectives in some pedagogical monolingual dictionaries of English is given below:

(17) a. *articulate*

| | |
|---|---|
| CCELD: | 'if you are *articulate*, you are able to express yourself easily and well, especially when you are dealing with difficult ideas' |
| LDoCE: | 'expressing or able to express thoughts and feelings clearly, esp. in words' |
| OALDoCE: | '(of a person) able to put thoughts and feelings into clear speech' |
| CIDE: | 'able to express, or expressing thoughts and feelings easily and clearly' |

b. *blunt*

| | |
|---|---|
| CCELD: | 'when someone is being blunt, they are speaking directly and simply without making any effort to be polite or to avoid upsetting people' |
| LDoCE: | '(of a person) speaking roughly and plainly, without trying to be polite or kind' |
| OALDoCE: | '(of a person, what he says) plain, not troubling to be polite' |
| CIDE: | 'saying what you think without trying to be polite or caring for other people's feelings' |

c. *brief*

| | |
|---|---|
| CCELD: | 'a piece of writing or speech that is brief, does not contain to many words or details; used of persons'; 'someone who is brief when talking to another person does not say much because they do not really want to speak to that person or discuss that subject' |
| LDoCE: | 'to speak shortly' |
| OALDoCE: | 'lasting only for a short time or containing few words' |
| CIDE: | 'lasting only a short time or containing few words' |

The formulations listed above allow us to safely conclude that the idea of linguistic action is now conventionalized to such a degree that it is incorporated into one (or more) of their sense(s). Consequently, a productive ad hoc metonymic reasoning based on an inferential model is now rendered superfluous as the targeted meaning is now part of linguistic knowledge.

We do not want to claim that all the adjectives used in predicational metonymies have to be polysemous in the way just exemplified above. Some can still be open to metonymic inferencing, and some can be used in contexts supporting both the interpretation of the sentence as a referential metonymy and as a predicational one. In (6) above we have such an example where the predicative adjectives *explicit* and *coherent* can be interpreted as predicational metonymies, but simultaneously the NP *Bloom (1993)* is interpreted as a referential metonymy.

Such co-existence of the two types of metonymies may be supposed to have provided a bridge for the gradual development and spread of predicational metonymies, and concomitant polysemy. We would like to hypothesize, however, that this polysemy and the switch from referential to predicational metonymy were facilitated by some structural (and semantic) facts about the grammatical constructions in which they occurred. Consider the effect of the presence viz. absence of the complement of the adjective in the following set of examples:

(18) a. Our boss was *vague*.
b. Our boss was *vague about* when the pay rise was due.

(19) a. I was quite *frank about* it.
b. You're not being *frank with* me, Mademoiselle.
c. I'll be quite *frank* …

It transpires that if a NP + COPULA + ADJECTIVE PHRASE construction allows both a referential metonymy in the subject and the predicational metonymy, the addition of a complement (mostly a PP) to the adjective tends to effect a switch to the latter type of metonymy, as in (18b). If the coding of linguistic action is already a conventionalized element of the meaning of the adjective, the presence or the absence of the complement will usually play no role, as in (19). This leads us to assume that the extended ascriptive construction may have played a decisive role in effecting the switch from referential to predicational metonymy and therefore in bringing about the polysemy (cf. Ziegeler, this volume, for a discussion of the extension of time-stable, generic characterizing functions to functions associated with specific event situations, as well as Brdar-Szabó & Brdar 2002; Brdar-Szabó 2002; and Brdar, Brdar-Szabó, Gradečak-Erdeljić, & Buljan, in press). While we do not have enough diachronic data showing how the rise of specific types of adjective complementation ties in with the development of metonymic models and polysemy in English, we can nevertheless synchronically compare English in this respect with Croatian and Hungarian, which will be shown in the last section to be different enough.

## 5. More contrastive data on ascriptive constructions and polysemy in predication formation

There are profound differences between English and the other two languages concerning both the basic ascriptive construction and the extended one that includes the complementation patterns of adjectives. It appears that the copular complementation pattern is less pervasive in Croatian and Hungarian than in English, and particularly so in the case of the extended construction with a PP as a complement of an adjective.

A number of contrastive studies (Ivir 1983; Brdar 1994) report that many English predicative adjectives taking various complements (but also without complements) do not find their Croatian and Hungarian counterparts in adjectives but rather in verbal predicates (which is also in keeping with the less analytic, i.e. more dynamic, typological preferences of the latter languages).

(20) a. Jack was *silent*.
b. Jack je *šutio*.
Jack AUX silent-VERB-PAST:3SG
'Jack was silent'
c. Jack *hallgatott*.
Jack silent-VERB-PAST:3SG
'Jack was silent'

(21) a. … he was greatly *afraid of* Livia and at first wholly *dependent on* her …
b. … jako *se* *bojao* Livije te *je* isprva potpuno
very REFL afraid-VERB … AUX at-first wholly
*ovisio* *o* *njoj/bio* *o* njoj *ovisan* …
depended on her AUX on her dependent
'He was greatly afraid of Livia and at first wholly dependent on her'

c. ... nagyon *félt* Liviától és az elején teljesen
greatly afraid-VERB-PAST Livia-from and at.first wholly
tőle függött ...
from-her depended
'He was greatly afraid of Livia and at first wholly dependent on her'

It is in our opinion possible to view some of these English copular constructions where adjectives are morphologically derived from or related to verbal predicates as arising through metonymic extensions: PROPENSITY FOR EVENT metonymy as a more specific case of STATE FOR EVENT metonymy. It holds here between verbal and adjectival predicates, and is clearly a predicational metonymy. This predication-forming strategy, typical of Germanic languages, creates a system that is partly parallel to the verb predication system, and partly complements it. It is well known that the resources of the English tense, aspect, and mood system allow speakers to refer to actual, more generalized or only potential events, i.e. situations, but there are certain limits. One can thus refer to a potential event using a present simple tense, but it would be difficult to express reference to a potential event in the past. Ascriptive constructions with adjectival predicates related to verbs, on the other hand, are a useful device to refer to more generic states of affairs regardless of the time reference.

However, the attachment of a complement to the adjective particularizes the situation, and makes the predicate again refer to a more specific and immediate situation while still retaining some degree of generality, as in (22b). This is why we say that this system complements the system of verbal predicates. It is a conveniently vague way of referring to both the event and the propensity at the same time.

(22) a. Other ladies were *critical.*
b. Other ladies were *critical of her.*
c. Other ladies *criticized her.*

Note that Croatian and Hungarian in such cases almost regularly fall back on verbal predicates, or at least have them as alternative renderings of (22b).

Basically the same situation obtains in extended ascriptive constructions with adjectives that are not derived from verbs. The extended ascriptive construction itself coerces an event interpretation for which a suitable verb is supplied (cf. Panther & Thornburg 1999a). Its gradual conventionalization resulted in polysemy.

This more basic and general predication metonymy and the resultant grammatical construction may have thus played a crucial role in the lexicalization/conventionalization of certain metonymies. Some referential/nominal metonymies got a free ride on the back of this construction, which resulted in the polysemy of certain adjectives so that nowadays one of their meanings, as seen in the several dictionary entries above, closely corresponds to the one predicted by our MANNER FOR LINGUISTIC ACTION metonymy. In such cases there is, concomitantly, no longer any need for pragmatic inferencing. Eventually, once the linguistic action element is incorporated into their semantics, the complements themselves can be dispensed with.

There are, of course, intermediate cases as well, where the complement steers the inferencing away from the more general ascriptive interpretation towards a more specific situation, viz. an actual event, but cannot necessarily coerce the linguistic action interpretation. This is the case with adjectives like *clear*, compatible both with linguistic and mental action interpretation:

(23) a. Peter was *clear* about it.
b. 'Peter thought clearly about it'
c. 'Peter stated it clearly'

It would be illuminating to consider briefly how various types of constructions containing adjectives from (7) fare with respect to standard Gricean properties of implicatures. Notice also that examples like (1e), which contains an overt verb of linguistic action in the complement, might be taken to exhibit Sadock's (1978) reinforceability property of implicatures.

Returning to Grice's set of properties, we may recall that one of the most conspicuous feature of conversational implicatures is their defeasibility or cancelability. Now, it turns out on closer inspection that in some cases inferences about linguistic action are cancelable. Thus, since *clear* in (23) is ambiguous between linguistic and mental action the former inference can be easily cancelled:

(23) d. Peter was *clear* about it but didn't say anything.

We intuitively expect that linguistic actions are ontologically dependent on, i.e. secondary, to mental ones, but with some effort, even the inference pointing towards mental action could be perhaps cancelled.

Some adjectives in non-extended ascriptive constructions will also allow an interpretation on which the expression was non-linguistic. Hence, the linguistic action inference is again easily cancelable:

(24) He was *emphatic* but didn't say anything.

On the other hand, we have cases of extended constructions in which the complement simply coerces the linguistic action interpretation, and the inference is non-defeasible.

(25) a. *Arthur was *brief* about his other teachers in his recollections but he didn't say anything.
b. *The buyers were *emphatic* in declaring that they were right, but they didn't say anything.

The above facts, we think, clearly show the role of structural factors, viz. grammatical constructions, in guiding this type of metonymic inferences in English, from conversational implicatures towards conventional ones.

It is quite common for English predicative adjectives taking prepositional phrases as complements to have Croatian and Hungarian counterparts that are predicative adjectives but do not take PPs as complements but rather NPs in various cases. In other words, PPs are not extensively used as complements of predicative adjectives in general in these two languages. More specifically, English adjectival predicates taking PPs as complements will regularly exhibit verbal counterparts in Croatian and Hungarian, at least as one of the possibilities, if not the only possibility. This of course also applies to our set of English adjectives exhibiting the MANNER FOR LINGUISTIC ACTION metonymy and their counterparts in Croatian and Hungarian. We further find, as shown in (8) and (9), that many of the PPs that can perhaps follow adjectives in Croatian (occasionally in Hungarian) are rather peripheral elements, adjunct-like (clauses or adverbials) rather than complements (*glede*). It appears that there are significant differences between English, on the one hand, and Croatian and Hungarian, on the other, concerning the form that the specification of the active zone of the metonymy (cf. Langacker 1995) assumes. The specification of the active zone in English is far more schematic, e.g. a prepositional phrase as a complement of the adjective. If Croatian and Hungarian allow a predicative adjective, then the referential type of metonymy (SUBJECT NP FOR UTTERANCE) is more likely, but even this usually requires more transparent coding of these events, where active zones are made quite explicit (including even the explicit mention of the verb of speaking) (cf. Brdar-Szabó & Brdar 1999).

The conclusion that we may draw from this is that Croatian and Hungarian seem to lack the structural prerequisites that would bring about the switch from referential to predicational metonymy, and lead eventually to the polysemy of adjectival predicates. Indeed, Croatian and Hungarian adjectives that correspond to the English ones listed in (7) do not exhibit a comparable kind and amount of polysemy. This may also explain why corresponding adjectives can be used in Croatian and Hungarian predicatively only if the inferencing path is secured by peripheral elements (adverbials or adverbial clauses).

The crosslinguistic pattern of variation here, viz. the fact that Hungarian and Croatian exhibit a high degree of similarity, while being markedly different from English, points toward different preferences in the formation of derived predicates. Indeed, we may ask: How extensive is the use of metonymy as a general predicate-formation strategy in the three languages we are concerned with?

It seems that Croatian and Hungarian do not tolerate extensive polysemy of predicates, but rather make use of certain morphosyntactic devices to keep predicates formally apart as much as possible, which is facilitated by their richer morphosyntactic inventories (esp. concatenative derivational devices, chiefly suffixation and prefixation, as well as the use of clitics, e.g. to express the mediopassive meaning). This is in keeping with their overall preference for the mapping of form and meaning in this area to be rather transparent and as close as possible to 1:1 (cf. Brdar 1994, 1995). Note that Dirven (1990), who contrasted the basic English and German verbs of speaking, found that German exploits to the full its morphological potential to create new forms for its meanings in this area, whereas English, possibly due to its greater syntactic flexibility, makes more extensive use a variety of syntactic devices and metaphors.

In addition to this we note that Hungarian is similar to Slavic languages in exhibiting a higher degree of communicative dynamism (in the sense of Mathesius 1961) than English, i.e. predicates in these languages tend to exhibit syntactic constructions with semantically full verbs rather than analytic constructions with delexicalized functional verbs followed by non-verbal elements.

It is as if the predicate formation in these two languages through metonymic extension were pre-emptied by adherence to a combination of two pragmatic submaxims, where the second is clearly subordinated to the first: do not be formally obscure by being functionally prolix, i.e. avoid coining and using functionally novel expressions that would cram new meanings onto existing ones if the linguistic system provides for more transparent ways of expressing these meanings.

This is all in marked contrast to English, which generally avoids being formally prolix even at the price of being functionally obscure, and is quite fond of polysemy of predicates, makes more extensive use of covert, nonconcatenative derivation in the formation of new predicative expressions (e.g. by means of full and partial conversion), and which favors the functional principle in the mapping of form and meaning (cf. Plank 1983). At the same time, as noted by Mathesius (1961) and Vachek (1961) and exemplified on structures such as (20–22), English predicates, when the language yields to formal prolixity, tend to exhibit lower degree of communicative dynamism and assume the form of analytic constructions. That the use or non-use i.e. choice of metonymies may depend on typological properties of the given language is also shown by Radden and Seto (this volume).

## 6. Conclusions

The crosslinguistic patterns of contrast that we have observed above seem to indicate that the distinction between referential, predicational and illocutionary metonymies is an important parameter in establishing a typology of metonymies. Given the distribution of referential and predicational metonymies in the three languages investigated here, one may even be tempted to try to link different types of metonymy, or at least the referential and the predicational, on an implicational scale, predicting that a language that makes extensive use of the latter, will also make heavier use of the former, while there will be languages that will restrict themselves primarily to more basic referential metonymic models. Since we would need much more data, on many more languages and many more subtypes of both referential and predication metonymies, this can, at present, be put forth as a mere suggestion for further research. At present it is also unclear whether illocutionary metonymy can be accommodated as well by such an implicational scale. However, regardless of whether the observed crosslinguistic differences can be shown to be more universal or not, the fact remains that Croatian and Hungarian behave very differently from English. In Sections 4 and 5, we suggested, making use of both synchronic and some diachronic data, that these differences are the result of an intricate interplay of cognitive and pragmatic, lexical and morphosyntactic factors.

## Note

1. Our corpus is part of a larger collection containing around 2,500 predicatively used adjectives taking various types of complements, as attested in some 10,000 sentences excerpted mostly from written sources.

## References


Barcelona Sánchez, Antonio (1998). The state of the art in the cognitive theory of metaphor and metonymy and its application to English studies. *The European English Messenger, 7*(2), 45–50.

Blank, Andreas (1999). Co-presence and succession: A cognitive typology of metonymy. In K.-U. Panther & G. Radden (Eds.), *Metonymy in Language and Thought* [Human Cognitive Processing 4] (pp. 169–191). Amsterdam and Philadelphia: Benjamins.

Brdar, Mario (1994). Infinitival Complement Clauses and Core Grammatical Relations Subject and Object in English, German, Croatian and Hungarian. PhD dissertation, University of Zagreb.

Brdar, Mario (1995). Kontrastivno-tipološki pristup proučavanju polisemije i sustava komplementacije. [A contrastive-typological approach to the study of polysemy and complementation systems]. *Filologija, 24–25*, 69–74.

Brdar, Mario, Brdar-Szabó, Rita, Gradečak-Erdeljić, Tanja, & Buljan, Gabrijela (in press). Predicative adjectives in some Germanic and Slavic languages: On the role of metonymy in extending grammatical constructions. Suvremena lingvistika (Zagreb).

Brdar-Szabó, Rita (2002). Referentielle Metonymie im Sprachvergleich. In M. Baróta, P. Szatmári, J. Tóth, & A. Zsigmond (Eds.), *Sprache(n) und Literatur(en) im Kontakt*, [Acta Germanistica Savariensia 7] (pp. 53–66). Szombathely: Maedinfo.

Brdar-Szabó, Rita & Brdar, Mario (1999). Predicative adjectives and grammatical-relational polysemy: The role of metonymic processes in motivating crosslinguistic differences. Paper presented at the *International Workshop on Motivation in Grammar*, Hamburg, July 7–9.

Brdar-Szabó, Rita & Brdar, Mario (2001). Manner-for-activity metonymy across domains and languages. Paper read at the 7th International Cognitive Linguistics Conference, Santa Barbara, July 22–27.

Brdar-Szabó, Rita & Brdar, Mario (2002). Manner-for-activity metonymy in cross-linguistic perspective. In B. Lewandowska-Tomaszczyk & K. Turewicz (Eds.), *Cognitive Linguistics Today* (pp. 235–257). Frankfurt am Main: Peter Lang.

CCELDE (1987). *Collins COBUILD English Language Dictionary*. London and Glasgow: Collins.

CIDE (1995). *Cambridge International Dictionary of English*. Cambridge: Cambridge University Press.

Croft, William (1993). The role of domains in the interpretation of metaphors and metonymies. *Cognitive Linguistics, 4*, 335–370.

Dirven, René (1990). Prototypical uses of grammatical resources in the expression of linguistic action. In S. L. Tsohatzidis (Ed.), *Meanings and Prototypes. Studies in Linguistic Categorization*. (pp. 267–284). London – New York: Routledge.

Dirven, René (1993). Metonymy and metaphor: Different mental strategies of conceptualisation. *Leuvense Bijdragen, 82*(1), 1–28.

Dirven, René, Goossens, Louis, Putseys, Yvan, & Vorlat, Emma (1982). *The Scene of Linguistic Action and Its Perspectivization by SPEAK, TALK, SAY and TELL*. Amsterdam and Philadelphia: Benjamins.

Gernsbacher, Morton Ann (1991). Comprehending conceptual anaphors. *Language and Cognitive Processes, 6*, 81–105.

Goossens, Louis (1985). Framing the linguistic action scene in Old and Present-Day English: OE *cweflan, secgan, sp(r)ecan*, and Present-Day English *speak, talk, say* and *tell* compared. In J. Fisiak (Ed.), *Papers from the 6th International Conference on Historical Linguistics* (pp. 149–170). Amsterdam and Poznań: Benjamins and Adam Mickiewicz University Press.

Goossens, Louis (1987). Dealing with linguistic action verbs in depth. In J. Verschueren (Ed.), *Linguistic Action: Some Empirical-Conceptual Studies* (pp. 95–106). Norwood, NJ: Ablex.

Goossens, Louis (1990). Metaphtonymy: The interaction of metaphor and metonymy in expressions for linguistic action. *Cognitive Linguistics, 1*, 323–340.

Goossens, Louis (1995). From three respectable horses' mouths. Metonymy and conventionalization in a diachronically differentiated data base. In L. Goossens, P. Pauwels, B. Rudzka-Ostyn, A.-M. Simon-Vanderbergen, & J. Vanparys (Eds.), *By Word of Mouth: Metaphor, Metonymy and Linguistic Action in a Cognitive Perspective* (pp. 175–204). Amsterdam and Philadelphia: Benjamins.

Grice, H. Paul (1975). Logic and conversation. In P. Cole & J. L. Morgan (Eds.), *Speech Acts* [Syntax and Semantics 3] (pp. 41–58). New York: Academic Press.

Ivir, Vladimir (1983). *A Contrastive Analysis of English Adjectives and Their Serbo-Croatian Correspondents*. Zagreb: Institute of Linguistics, University of Zagreb.

Kalisz, Roman (1983). On so called 'beheaded noun phrases' in English and Polish. *Papers and Studies in Contrastive Linguistics, 16*, 43–51.

Kövecses, Zoltán & Radden, Günter (1998). Metonymy: Developing a cognitive linguistic view. *Cognitive Linguistics, 9*, 37–77.

Lakoff, George (1987). *Women, Fire, and Dangerous Things: What Categories Reveal about the Mind*. Chicago and London: The University of Chicago Press.

Langacker, Ronald W. (1987). *Foundations of Cognitive Grammar, Volume 1: Theoretical Prerequisites*. Stanford: Stanford University Press.

Langacker, Ronald W. (1991). *Foundations of Cognitive Grammar, Volume 2: Descriptive Application*. Stanford: Stanford University Press.

Langacker, Ronald W. (1993). Reference-point constructions. *Cognitive Linguistics, 4*, 1–38.

Langacker, Ronald W. (1995). Raising and transparency. *Language, 71*, 1–62.

LDoCE (1978). *Longman Dictionary of Contemporary English*. Harlow: Longman.

Leech, Geoffrey (1980). Language and tact. In *Explorations in Semantics and Pragmatics* [Pragmatics & Beyond] (pp. 79–117). Amsterdam: Benjamins.

Mathesius, Vilém (1961). *Obsahový rozbor současné angličtiny na základě obecně lingvistickém* [A Functional Analysis of Contemporary English on a General Linguistic Basis]. Prague.

OALDoCE (1985). *Oxford Advanced Learner's Dictionary of Current English*. Oxford: Oxford University Press.

OED (1992). *Oxford English Dictionary on CD-ROM, 2nd Edition*. Oxford: Oxford University Press.

Panther, Klaus-Uwe & Radden, Günter (1999). Introduction. In K.-U. Panther & G. Radden (Eds.), *Metonymy in Language and Thought* [Human Cognitive Processing 4] (pp. 1–14). Amsterdam and Philadelphia: Benjamins.

Panther, Klaus-Uwe & Radden, Günter (Eds.). (1999). *Metonymy in Language and Thought* [Human Cognitive Processing 4]. Amsterdam and Philadelphia: Benjamins.

Panther, Klaus-Uwe & Thornburg, Linda (1999a). Coercion and metonymy: The interaction of constructional and lexical meaning. In B. Lewandowska-Tomaszczyk (Ed.), *Cognitive Perspectives on Language* [Polish Studies in English Language and Literature 1] (pp. 37–51). Frankfurt am Main et al.: Peter Lang.

Panther, Klaus-Uwe & Thornburg, Linda (1999b). The POTENTIALITY FOR ACTUALITY metonymy in English and Hungarian. In K.-U. Panther & G. Radden (Eds.), *Metonymy in Language and Thought* [Human Cognitive Processing 4] (pp. 333–357). Amsterdam and Philadelphia: Benjamins.

Plank, Frans (1983). Transparent versus functional encoding of grammatical relations: A parameter for syntactic change and typology. *Linguistische Berichte, 86*, 1–13.

Radden, Günter & Kövecses, Zoltán (1999). Towards a theory of metonymy. In K.-U. Panther & G. Radden (Eds.), *Metonymy in Language and Thought* [Human Cognitive Processing 4] (pp. 17–59). Amsterdam and Philadelphia: Benjamins.

Radden, Günter & Seto, Ken-ichi (this volume). Metonymic construals of shopping requests in HAVE- and BE-languages.

Rudzka, Brygida (1982). The verb ASK and the scene of linguistic communication. Unpublished paper. Catholic University of Leuven.

Rudzka-Ostyn, Brygida (1988). Semantic extensions into the domain of verbal communication. In B. Rudzka-Ostyn (Ed.), *Topics in Cognitive Linguistics* (pp. 507–553). Amsterdam and Philadelphia: Benjamins.

Rudzka-Ostyn, Brygida (1995). Metaphor, schema, invariance: The case of verbs of answering. In L. Goossens, P. Pauwels, B. Rudzka-Ostyn, A.-M. Simon-Vanderbergen, & J. Vanparys (Eds.), *By Word of Mouth: Metaphor, Metonymy and Linguistic Action in a Cognitive Perspective* (pp. 205–243). Amsterdam and Philadelphia: Benjamins.

Sadock, Jerrold M. (1978). On testing for conversational implicature. In P. Cole (Ed.), *Pragmatics* [Syntax and Semantics 9] (pp. 281–298). New York: Academic Press.

Searle, John R. (1975). Indirect speech acts. In P. Cole & J. L. Morgan (Eds.), *Speech Acts* [Syntax and Semantics 3] (pp. 59–82). New York: Academic Press.

Seto, Ken-ichi (1999). Distinguishing metonymy from synecdoche. In K.-U. Panther & G. Radden (Eds.), *Metonymy in Language and Thought* [Human Cognitive Processing 4] (pp. 91–120). Amsterdam and Philadelphia: Benjamins.

Taylor, John R. (1989). *Linguistic Categorization: Prototypes in Linguistic Theory*. Oxford: Clarendon Press.

Ullmann, Stephen (1962). *Semantics: An Introduction to the Science of Meaning*. Oxford: Blackwell.

Vachek, Josef (1961). Some less familiar aspects of the analytical trend in English. *Brno Studies in English, 3*, 31–44.

Verschueren, Jef (1980). *On Speech Act Verbs*. Amsterdam: Benjamins.

Verschueren, Jef (1984). *Basic Linguistic Action Verbs: A Questionnaire* [Antwerp Papers in Linguistics 37]. Antwerp: Universitaire Instelling Antwerpen.

Verschueren, Jef (1985). *What People Say They Do with Words: Prolegomena to an Empirical-Conceptual Approach to Linguistic Action*. Norwood, NJ: Ablex.

Verschueren, Jef (Ed.). (1987). *Linguistic Action: Some Empirical-Conceptual Studies*. Norwood, NJ: Ablex.

Waltereit, Richard (1998). *Metonymie und Grammatik. Kontiguitätsphänomene in der französischen Satzsemantik* [Linguistische Arbeiten 385]. Tübingen: Max Niemeyer.

Waltereit, Richard (1999). Grammatical constraints on metonymy: On the role of the direct object. In K.-U. Panther & G. Radden (Eds.), *Metonymy in Language and Thought* [Human Cognitive Processing 4] (pp. 233–253). Amsterdam and Philadelphia: Benjamins.

# Name index

# Metonymy and metaphor index

*Note:* In this index we follow the widespread convention of notating metonymies as SOURCE FOR TARGET and metaphors as TARGET IS SOURCE. In those cases in which authors have not followed this convention we have converted them into the conventional citation format.

*Metonymies*

A



B



C



D



E

*Metaphors*

# Subject index

In the PRAGMATICS AND BEYOND NEW SERIES the following titles have been published thus far or are scheduled for publication:

1. WALTER, Bettyruth: *The Jury Summation as Speech Genre: An Ethnographic Study of What it Means to Those who Use it.* Amsterdam/Philadelphia, 1988.
2. BARTON, Ellen: *Nonsentential Constituents: A Theory of Grammatical Structure and Pragmatic Interpretation.* Amsterdam/Philadelphia, 1990.
3. OLEKSY, Wieslaw (ed.): *Contrastive Pragmatics.* Amsterdam/Philadelphia, 1989.
4. RAFFLER-ENGEL, Walburga von (ed.): *Doctor-Patient Interaction.* Amsterdam/Philadelphia, 1989.
5. THELIN, Nils B. (ed.): *Verbal Aspect in Discourse.* Amsterdam/Philadelphia, 1990.
6. VERSCHUEREN, Jef (ed.): *Selected Papers from the 1987 International Pragmatics Conference. Vol. I: Pragmatics at Issue. Vol. II: Levels of Linguistic Adaptation. Vol. III: The Pragmatics of Intercultural and International Communication* (ed. with Jan Blommaert). Amsterdam/Philadelphia, 1991.
7. LINDENFELD, Jacqueline: *Speech and Sociability at French Urban Market Places.* Amsterdam/Philadelphia, 1990.
8. YOUNG, Lynne: *Language as Behaviour, Language as Code: A Study of Academic English.* Amsterdam/Philadelphia, 1990.
9. LUKE, Kang-Kwong: *Utterance Particles in Cantonese Conversation.* Amsterdam/Philadelphia, 1990.
10. MURRAY, Denise E.: *Conversation for Action. The computer terminal as medium of communication.* Amsterdam/Philadelphia, 1991.
11. LUONG, Hy V.: *Discursive Practices and Linguistic Meanings. The Vietnamese system of person reference.* Amsterdam/Philadelphia, 1990.
12. ABRAHAM, Werner (ed.): *Discourse Particles. Descriptive and theoretical investigations on the logical, syntactic and pragmatic properties of discourse particles in German.* Amsterdam/Philadelphia, 1991.
13. NUYTS, Jan, A. Machtelt BOLKESTEIN and Co VET (eds): *Layers and Levels of Representation in Language Theory: A functional view.* Amsterdam/Philadelphia, 1990.
14. SCHWARTZ, Ursula: *Young Children's Dyadic Pretend Play.* Amsterdam/Philadelphia, 1991.
15. KOMTER, Martha: *Conflict and Cooperation in Job Interviews.* Amsterdam/Philadelphia, 1991.
16. MANN, William C. and Sandra A. THOMPSON (eds): *Discourse Description: Diverse Linguistic Analyses of a Fund-Raising Text.* Amsterdam/Philadelphia, 1992.
17. PIÉRAUT-LE BONNIEC, Gilberte and Marlene DOLITSKY (eds): *Language Bases ... Discourse Bases.* Amsterdam/Philadelphia, 1991.
18. JOHNSTONE, Barbara: *Repetition in Arabic Discourse. Paradigms, syntagms and the ecology of language.* Amsterdam/Philadelphia, 1991.
19. BAKER, Carolyn D. and Allan LUKE (eds): *Towards a Critical Sociology of Reading Pedagogy. Papers of the XII World Congress on Reading.* Amsterdam/Philadelphia, 1991.
20. NUYTS, Jan: *Aspects of a Cognitive-Pragmatic Theory of Language. On cognition, functionalism, and grammar.* Amsterdam/Philadelphia, 1992.
21. SEARLE, John R. et al.: *(On) Searle on Conversation.* Compiled and introduced by Herman Parret and Jef Verschueren. Amsterdam/Philadelphia, 1992.

22. AUER, Peter and Aldo Di LUZIO (eds): *The Contextualization of Language.* Amsterdam/Philadelphia, 1992.
23. FORTESCUE, Michael, Peter HARDER and Lars KRISTOFFERSEN (eds): *Layered Structure and Reference in a Functional Perspective. Papers from the Functional Grammar Conference, Copenhagen, 1990.* Amsterdam/Philadelphia, 1992.
24. MAYNARD, Senko K.: *Discourse Modality: Subjectivity, Emotion and Voice in the Japanese Language.* Amsterdam/Philadelphia, 1993.
25. COUPER-KUHLEN, Elizabeth: *English Speech Rhythm. Form and function in everyday verbal interaction.* Amsterdam/Philadelphia, 1993.
26. STYGALL, Gail: *Trial Language. A study in differential discourse processing.* Amsterdam/Philadelphia, 1994.
27. SUTER, Hans Jürg: *The Wedding Report: A Prototypical Approach to the Study of Traditional Text Types.* Amsterdam/Philadelphia, 1993.
28. VAN DE WALLE, Lieve: *Pragmatics and Classical Sanskrit.* Amsterdam/Philadelphia, 1993.
29. BARSKY, Robert F.: *Constructing a Productive Other: Discourse theory and the convention refugee hearing.* Amsterdam/Philadelphia, 1994.
30. WORTHAM, Stanton E.F.: *Acting Out Participant Examples in the Classroom.* Amsterdam/Philadelphia, 1994.
31. WILDGEN, Wolfgang: *Process, Image and Meaning. A realistic model of the meanings of sentences and narrative texts.* Amsterdam/Philadelphia, 1994.
32. SHIBATANI, Masayoshi and Sandra A. THOMPSON (eds): *Essays in Semantics and Pragmatics.* Amsterdam/Philadelphia, 1995.
33. GOOSSENS, Louis, Paul PAUWELS, Brygida RUDZKA-OSTYN, Anne-Marie SIMON-VANDENBERGEN and Johan VANPARYS: *By Word of Mouth. Metaphor, metonymy and linguistic action in a cognitive perspective.* Amsterdam/Philadelphia, 1995.
34. BARBE, Katharina: Irony in Context. Amsterdam/Philadelphia, 1995.
35. JUCKER, Andreas H. (ed.): *Historical Pragmatics. Pragmatic developments in the history of English.* Amsterdam/Philadelphia, 1995.
36. CHILTON, Paul, Mikhail V. ILYIN and Jacob MEY: *Political Discourse in Transition in Eastern and Western Europe (1989-1991).* Amsterdam/Philadelphia, 1998.
37. CARSTON, Robyn and Seiji UCHIDA (eds): *Relevance Theory. Applications and implications.* Amsterdam/Philadelphia, 1998.
38. FRETHEIM, Thorstein and Jeanette K. GUNDEL (eds): *Reference and Referent Accessibility.* Amsterdam/Philadelphia, 1996.
39. HERRING, Susan (ed.): *Computer-Mediated Communication. Linguistic, social, and cross-cultural perspectives.* Amsterdam/Philadelphia, 1996.
40. DIAMOND, Julie: *Status and Power in Verbal Interaction. A study of discourse in a close-knit social network.* Amsterdam/Philadelphia, 1996.
41. VENTOLA, Eija and Anna MAURANEN, (eds): *Academic Writing. Intercultural and textual issues.* Amsterdam/Philadelphia, 1996.
42. WODAK, Ruth and Helga KOTTHOFF (eds): *Communicating Gender in Context.* Amsterdam/Philadelphia, 1997.
43. JANSSEN, Theo A.J.M. and Wim van der WURFF (eds): *Reported Speech. Forms and functions of the verb.* Amsterdam/Philadelphia, 1996.

44. BARGIELA-CHIAPPINI, Francesca and Sandra J. HARRIS: *Managing Language. The discourse of corporate meetings.* Amsterdam/Philadelphia, 1997.
45. PALTRIDGE, Brian: *Genre, Frames and Writing in Research Settings.* Amsterdam/Philadelphia, 1997.
46. GEORGAKOPOULOU, Alexandra: *Narrative Performances. A study of Modern Greek storytelling.* Amsterdam/Philadelphia, 1997.
47. CHESTERMAN, Andrew: *Contrastive Functional Analysis.* Amsterdam/Philadelphia, 1998.
48. KAMIO, Akio: *Territory of Information.* Amsterdam/Philadelphia, 1997.
49. KURZON, Dennis: *Discourse of Silence.* Amsterdam/Philadelphia, 1998.
50. GRENOBLE, Lenore: *Deixis and Information Packaging in Russian Discourse.* Amsterdam/Philadelphia, 1998.
51. BOULIMA, Jamila: *Negotiated Interaction in Target Language Classroom Discourse.* Amsterdam/Philadelphia, 1999.
52. GILLIS, Steven and Annick DE HOUWER (eds): *The Acquisition of Dutch.* Amsterdam/Philadelphia, 1998.
53. MOSEGAARD HANSEN, Maj-Britt: *The Function of Discourse Particles. A study with special reference to spoken standard French.* Amsterdam/Philadelphia, 1998.
54. HYLAND, Ken: *Hedging in Scientific Research Articles.* Amsterdam/Philadelphia, 1998.
55. ALLWOOD, Jens and Peter Gärdenfors (eds): *Cognitive Semantics. Meaning and cognition.* Amsterdam/Philadelphia, 1999.
56. TANAKA, Hiroko: *Language, Culture and Social Interaction. Turn-taking in Japanese and Anglo-American English.* Amsterdam/Philadelphia, 1999.
57 JUCKER, Andreas H. and Yael ZIV (eds): *Discourse Markers. Descriptions and theory.* Amsterdam/Philadelphia, 1998.
58. ROUCHOTA, Villy and Andreas H. JUCKER (eds): *Current Issues in Relevance Theory.* Amsterdam/Philadelphia, 1998.
59. KAMIO, Akio and Ken-ichi TAKAMI (eds): *Function and Structure. In honor of Susumu Kuno.* 1999.
60. JACOBS, Geert: *Preformulating the News. An analysis of the metapragmatics of press releases.* 1999.
61. MILLS, Margaret H. (ed.): *Slavic Gender Linguistics.* 1999.
62. TZANNE, Angeliki: *Talking at Cross-Purposes. The dynamics of miscommunication.* 2000.
63. BUBLITZ, Wolfram, Uta LENK and Eija VENTOLA (eds.): *Coherence in Spoken and Written Discourse. How to create it and how to describe it.Selected papers from the International Workshop on Coherence, Augsburg, 24-27 April 1997.* 1999.
64. SVENNEVIG, Jan: *Getting Acquainted in Conversation. A study of initial interactions.* 1999.
65. COOREN, François: *The Organizing Dimension of Communication.* 2000.
66. JUCKER, Andreas H., Gerd FRITZ and Franz LEBSANFT (eds.): *Historical Dialogue Analysis.* 1999.
67. TAAVITSAINEN, Irma, Gunnel MELCHERS and Päivi PAHTA (eds.): *Dimensions of Writing in Nonstandard English.* 1999.
68. ARNOVICK, Leslie: *Diachronic Pragmatics. Seven case studies in English illocutionary development.* 1999.

69. NOH, Eun-Ju: *The Semantics and Pragmatics of Metarepresentation in English. A relevance-theoretic account.* 2000.
70. SORJONEN, Marja-Leena: *Responding in Conversation. A study of response particles in Finnish.* 2001.
71. GÓMEZ-GONZÁLEZ, María Ángeles: *The Theme-Topic Interface. Evidence from English.* 2001.
72. MARMARIDOU, Sophia S.A.: *Pragmatic Meaning and Cognition.* 2000.
73. HESTER, Stephen and David FRANCIS (eds.): *Local Educational Order. Ethnomethodological studies of knowledge in action.* 2000.
74. TROSBORG, Anna (ed.): *Analysing Professional Genres.* 2000.
75. PILKINGTON, Adrian: *Poetic Effects. A relevance theory perspective.* 2000.
76. MATSUI, Tomoko: *Bridging and Relevance.* 2000.
77. VANDERVEKEN, Daniel and Susumu KUBO (eds.): *Essays in Speech Act Theory.* 2002.
78. SELL, Roger D. : *Literature as Communication. The foundations of mediating criticism.* 2000.
79. ANDERSEN, Gisle and Thorstein FRETHEIM (eds.): *Pragmatic Markers and Propositional Attitude.* 2000.
80. UNGERER, Friedrich (ed.): *English Media Texts – Past and Present. Language and textual structure.* 2000.
81. DI LUZIO, Aldo, Susanne GÜNTHNER and Franca ORLETTI (eds.): *Culture in Communication. Analyses of intercultural situations.* 2001.
82. KHALIL, Esam N.: *Grounding in English and Arabic News Discourse.* 2000.
83. MÁRQUEZ REITER, Rosina: *Linguistic Politeness in Britain and Uruguay. A contrastive study of requests and apologies.* 2000.
84. ANDERSEN, Gisle: *Pragmatic Markers and Sociolinguistic Variation. A relevance-theoretic approach to the language of adolescents.* 2001.
85. COLLINS, Daniel E.: *Reanimated Voices. Speech reporting in a historical-pragmatic perspective.* 2001.
86. IFANTIDOU, Elly: *Evidentials and Relevance.* 2001.
87. MUSHIN, Ilana: *Evidentiality and Epistemological Stance. Narrative retelling.* 2001.
88. BAYRAKTAROĞLU, Arın and Maria SIFIANOU (eds.): *Linguistic Politeness Across Boundaries. The case of Greek and Turkish.* 2001.
89. ITAKURA, Hiroko: *Conversational Dominance and Gender. A study of Japanese speakers in first and second language contexts.* 2001.
90. KENESEI, István and Robert M. HARNISH (eds.): *Perspectives on Semantics, Pragmatics, and Discourse. A Festschrift for Ferenc Kiefer.* 2001.
91. GROSS, Joan: *Speaking in Other Voices. An ethnography of Walloon puppet theaters.* 2001.
92. GARDNER, Rod: *When Listeners Talk. Response tokens and listener stance.* 2001.
93. BARON, Bettina and Helga KOTTHOFF (eds.): *Gender in Interaction. Perspectives on femininity and masculinity in ethnography and discourse.* 2002
94. McILVENNY, Paul (ed.): *Talking Gender and Sexuality.* 2002.
95. FITZMAURICE, Susan M.: *The Familiar Letter in Early Modern English. A pragmatic approach.* 2002.
96. HAVERKATE, Henk: *The Syntax, Semantics and Pragmatics of Spanish Mood.* 2002.

97. MAYNARD, Senko K.: *Linguistic Emotivity. Centrality of place, the topic-comment dynamic, and an ideology of* pathos *in Japanese discourse.* 2002.
98. DUSZAK, Anna (ed.): *Us and Others. Social identities across languages, discourses and cultures.* 2002.
99. JASZCZOLT, K.M. and Ken TURNER (eds.): *Meaning Through Language Contrast. Volume 1.* 2003.
100. JASZCZOLT, K.M. and Ken TURNER (eds.): *Meaning Through Language Contrast. Volume 2.* 2003.
101. LUKE, Kang Kwong and Theodossia-Soula PAVLIDOU (eds.): *Telephone Calls. Unity and diversity in conversational structure across languages and cultures.* 2002.
102. LEAFGREN, John: *Degrees of Explicitness. Information structure and the packaging of Bulgarian subjects and objects.* 2002.
103. FETZER, Anita and Christiane MEIERKORD (eds.): *Rethinking Sequentiality. Linguistics meets conversational interaction.* 2002.
104. BEECHING, Kate: *Gender, Politeness and Pragmatic Particles in French.* 2002.
105. BLACKWELL, Sarah E.: *Implicatures in Discourse. The case of Spanish NP anaphora.* 2003.
106. BUSSE, Ulrich: *Linguistic Variation in the Shakespeare Corpus. Morpho-syntactic variability of second person pronouns.* 2002.
107. TAAVITSAINEN, Irma and Andreas H. JUCKER (eds.): *Diachronic Perspectives on Address Term Systems.* 2003.
108. BARRON, Anne: *Acquisition in Interlanguage Pragmatics. Learning how to do things with words in a study abroad context.* 2003.
109. MAYES, Patricia: *Language, Social Structure, and Culture. A genre analysis of cooking classes in Japan and America.* 2003.
110. ANDROUTSOPOULOS, Jannis K. and Alexandra GEORGAKOPOULOU (eds.): *Discourse Constructions of Youth Identities.* 2003.
111. ENSINK, Titus and Christoph SAUER (eds.): *Framing and Perspectivising in Discourse.* 2003.
112. LENZ, Friedrich (ed.): *Deictic Conceptualisation of Space, Time and Person.* 2003.
113. PANTHER, Klaus-Uwe and Linda L. THORNBURG (eds.): *Metonymy and Pragmatic Inferencing.* 2003.
114. KÜHNLEIN, Peter, Hannes RIESER and Henk ZEEVAT (eds.): *Perspectives on Dialogue in the New Millennium.* n.y.p.
115. KÄRKKÄINEN, Elise: *Epistemic Stance in English Conversation. A description of its interactional functions, with a focus on* I think. n.y.p.